THE LOVING FRIENDS

THE
LOVING FRIENDS

A PORTRAIT OF BLOOMSBURY

———◆———

DAVID GADD

READERS UNION
Group of Book Clubs
Newton Abbot 1976

FOR MARGARET

who always understood

CONTENTS

ILLUSTRATIONS

Between pages 82 and 83

PLATE

1 Vanessa Bell
    (*by courtesy of Mrs. Barbara Bagenal*)
  Roger Fry
    (*by courtesy of Mrs. Pamela Diamand*)

2 Lytton Strachey and Ralph Partridge
    (*by courtesy of Mr. Noel Carrington*)
  Carrington
    (*by courtesy of Mrs. Ralph Partridge*)

3 Carrington, Lytton Strachey, Vanessa Bell and
    Duncan Grant
    (*by courtesy of Mrs. Ralph Partridge*)
  Clive Bell and Francis Birrell
    (*by courtesy of Mrs. Ralph Partridge*)

4 Virginia Woolf
    (*by courtesy of Mrs. Ian Parsons*)
  Leonard Woolf
    (*by courtesy of Mrs. Ian Parsons*)

5 John Maynard Keynes
    (*by courtesy of Sir Geoffrey Keynes*)
  Duncan Grant
    (*by courtesy of Mrs. Barbara Bagenal*)

6 Ottoline Morrell by Duncan Grant
    (*by courtesy of Mr. Duncan Grant*)
  Frances Partridge
    (*by courtesy of Mrs. Ralph Partridge*)

7 The Sitting Room at Charleston
    (*by courtesy of Mrs. Barbara Bagenal*)

Acknowledgements

THE bibliography on page 201 lists the works which have been of most value in the preparation of this book. Among them Michael Holroyd's biography is a rich mine of hitherto unpublished information, while Quentin Bell's life of Virginia Woolf is, in my opinion, one of the great biographies. I express my gratitude to both authors. David Garnett's selection of Carrington's letters gives a vivid picture of one of the most complex and charming members of the Bloomsbury circle, and I am grateful to Frances Partridge for permission to quote from them.

All sources of quotations have, I trust, been given, and I acknowledge my debt to the owners of the copyrights.

Mr. Noel Carrington has assisted me greatly in my portrayal of his sister, both by his accurate memory of events and by his interpretation of character. He also helped in the search for illustrations. I am much in his debt. Lord David Cecil enabled me, with his first-hand knowledge, to make a juster assessment of Ralph Partridge's role in the Bloomsbury story than would otherwise have been possible. Susan Condon, of the Christ Church library, went to great trouble to find and photostat college records of much interest. I am most grateful for their help.

I have above all been fortunate enough to have had criticism and help from Frances Partridge, who read much of my typescript and commented generously, in writing and in discussion, upon it. As a younger member of Bloomsbury she was able to correct misconceptions and to confirm tentative conclusions. She also allowed me to see her fascinating photograph albums and spent much time with me looking for prints suitable as illustrations. I could not be more grateful for her kindness and help.

Norah Smallwood of the Hogarth Press made available to me those of its early records still in the possession of the Press, and took a large share in the finding of illustrations. What was even more valuable was her careful criticism, based on her knowledge of Bloomsbury, and her unfailing kindness and encouragement. Our association has always been a pleasure as well as a great aid to me as a writer.

My thanks are also due to Mrs. Pamela Diamand, Mrs. Barbara Bagenal, Mrs. Ian Parsons and Sir Geoffrey Keynes for permission to use certain photographs; and to Mr. Duncan Grant for allowing me to reproduce his portrait of Lady Ottoline Morrell.

My daughter Jenny, who can read my handwriting, typed the whole manuscript with admirable speed and accuracy and I am very grateful to her.

Introduction

THIS is a portrait of the group of writers, artists and intellectuals who have given a new meaning to what was, before their time, simply an address. For many thousands of people who will never set foot in west central London, Bloomsbury has a significance independent of its location. It represents an attitude to life, natural to those who form the subject of this book, but novel and even shocking in their day. It was essentially a brave attitude, rejecting conventions which seemed senseless or irrelevant and accepting, without pomposity, the implications of a sharply rational examination of life and art. Those who made up what we now know as 'Bloomsbury' lived according to the conclusions to which this examination forced them. They meant, in fact, what they said: and they said a great deal.

The literature of Bloomsbury is already large and there is no doubt that it will continue to grow. Not only were its members themselves immensely articulate, but in recent years a rising tide of biography, memoir and commentary has flowed into print. It is this fact which provides one of the reasons for this book. So much exists to read that it is difficult to find a starting-point. Should it perhaps be the five volumes of Leonard Woolf's autobiography, or Michael Holroyd's thousand-page biography of Lytton Strachey, or Quentin Bell's two volumes on Virginia Woolf, or one of the many volumes of literary recollection? The choice is daunting and some will perhaps not wish to make it.

The Loving Friends, in a single volume, seeks to present Bloomsbury as it essentially was and thus to point the way for further reading. It is in this sense a reconnaissance, identifying landmarks and indicating possible routes for more comprehensive surveys.

Not everyone will feel the need to study Bloomsbury in depth, but nobody interested in the culture of our century can afford to ignore it. Because so much material exists it is now possible to provide a conspectus of the Bloomsbury group as a whole, and this is the present intention. Human beings are less available than their works and always more complex and exciting. There is infinitely more in Lytton Strachey than in *Eminent Victorians*, and Roger Fry's aesthetics are dull compared with Roger Fry. This book then is concerned with people who happened to be writers and artists rather than with the work by which they are well known.

The author's aim in writing his book will now perhaps be clear. But he feels bound to confess that he was also moved to write it by the sheer delight he takes in the characters he has attempted to portray in its pages. Some of this delight he hopes to have been able to convey.

I

Bloomsbury: The Beginnings

DEFINITIONS, to be valuable, should be precise. It sometimes occurs, however, that the more strict a definition is, the more it tends to exclude what properly belongs within it. This is true of any definition but the topographical one of the word Bloomsbury. There is a particular reason why this should be so. The circle of writers, artists and intellectuals to whom the name is attached was an informal group of close friends, and it was nothing more. What made them friends was a similarity—but not an identity—of taste and outlook and a shared rejection of conventional prejudices. They did not subscribe to a common aesthetic or intellectual dogma, and their literary and artistic work has more differences than similarities.

The word Bloomsbury is used nowadays to refer both to an attitude to life and art and to the men and women who, living in Gordon Square and its environs in the early years of the century, personified this attitude. The Bloomsbury attitude need not at this stage be closely defined: it will be demonstrated vividly enough in the lives of those with whom this book is concerned. To define the membership of Bloomsbury is more difficult, since one is here assessing such imponderables as degrees of intimacy—its intensity, its duration and its significance for those who shared it. Was Maynard Keynes, for example, at the height of his world-renown as an economist, still a true member of Bloomsbury? And was David Garnett, Lytton's intimate and the recorder of Bloomsbury in its heyday, ever himself a member? It has been denied by some. If Lady Ottoline Morrell was not one of the circle, why was she not?

Argument, some of it unprofitable, will no doubt continue. It is best therefore to begin with what is certain and build, if possible, on that.

In 1904, Sir Leslie Stephen, the distinguished Victorian man
of letters, died. He left behind two daughters, Virginia and
Vanessa, who had nursed him in his long last illness, their
mother having died some years before, and two sons, Thoby
and Adrian. On the death of their father, the four children, all
aged in their early twenties, sold the family home in Hyde Park
Gate and set up home together at 46 Gordon Square. At this
stage, Virginia had begun tentatively to write; Vanessa was
becoming a painter. Thoby had just come down from Trinity
College, Cambridge; Adrian, the youngest, aged 21, was still
there.

At Trinity, Thoby had been a contemporary and close friend
of Lytton Strachey, Clive Bell and Leonard Woolf, and it was
at Cambridge that they had all got to know the beautiful
Stephen sisters. Lytton had in fact met them briefly in 1901
when Thoby invited him to stay at the school-house at Lynd-
hurst where the Stephen family was spending the summer.

As they all had their homes in London, it was natural that
they should continue to meet, and to do so more often than not
in Gordon Square, where Virginia and Vanessa were their
hostesses. Leonard Woolf left England almost at once for a
seven-year stay in Ceylon as a civil servant, but Clive Bell and
Lytton Strachey remained and were soon on terms of sympathy
and intimacy with the two sisters. Clive fell (hopelessly, as he
first thought) in love with Vanessa, and married her in 1907.
Lytton showed no sign of wishing to marry any woman—
though he did once, a few years later, propose to Virginia and
get accepted. Luckily for them both, they at once came to their
senses and agreed to forget the episode.

Thoby died tragically in 1906 of typhoid contracted in
Greece, and when Clive and Vanessa married, Virginia and
Adrian moved to 29 Fitzroy Square, still in Bloomsbury,
leaving 46 Gordon Square to the newly-married pair. Two
other men were close friends of the Stephen family. Duncan
Grant, a cousin of Lytton Strachey, was an artist with a studio
in Baker Street. Maynard Keynes came down from King's
College Cambridge in 1906 after a brilliant career as an under-
graduate and became for a year or two a civil servant at the
India Office. At Cambridge he had become a close friend of

Lytton's, and it was through Lytton that Duncan and Maynard got to know the Stephen girls.

One other event was to take place before the nucleus of what was to be Bloomsbury was truly formed. In 1911 Leonard Woolf returned to London on leave from Ceylon and in due course (after some hesitation) he resigned from the colonial service. He was welcomed back at once by his old friends. In 1911, Virginia and Adrian moved from Fitzroy Square, where the lease had expired, to 38 Brunswick Square (still, of course, in Bloomsbury). Here they were joined by Duncan and Maynard who shared the ground floor, and by Leonard Woolf who had rooms on the third floor. Leonard was by now deeply in love with Virginia, and in the following year they were married.

With this marriage, the foundations of Bloomsbury were truly laid. It is, I think, clear enough that it is Virginia and Vanessa who must be regarded as the mother-goddesses. It was their marriages with Leonard Woolf and Clive Bell which brought them into permanent association with their husbands' Cambridge friends: it was they who provided the feminine element essential to any healthy human community: and it was in their houses that they could and did all meet and try out new friends.

Marriage, as often as not, weakens or destroys previous intimacies. A husband gradually drops his bachelor friends: either his wife does not share his affection for them or he himself has little wish to provide unmarried men-friends for his bride. For her part, the wife becomes immersed in her new domestic role and has little time for extraneous relationships. Precisely the opposite happened in this case, and the reasons are complex, peculiar and central to the existence of 'Bloomsbury', which flourished certainly until the death of Lytton Strachey in 1932, and, through its younger members, until the outbreak of war in 1939 and beyond. There was certainly no strict identity of taste, talent or professional interest which could have fused these strongly differentiated characters into a stable group, whose component individuals nevertheless resembled each other so much that they could be given a collective nickname. But there was a vague basic community of outlook which made them easy with each other and difficult with almost everybody else. With some of them this outlook took on something of the dignity of a philosophy: it was articulate, explicit and dominant: with others it was passive, latent and barely acknowledged. But it was there, and no new acquaintance who did not have it would ever move into the intimate closed circle of Bloomsbury.

In order to begin to understand what made Bloomsbury possible two things must be clearly appreciated. First, its members were aesthetes—that is to say they were concerned primarily with feelings and the expression of feelings. What was felt was right, however it was regarded by society: if it was felt it was to be expressed, either emotionally in a human relationship, or artistically in words or pictures. Secondly, Bloomsbury was profoundly serious. The reputation it has acquired for frivolity is totally unfounded and rests, if it rests on anything, on malicious interpretations of the childish frolics of friends at intimate parties, and Bloomsbury's deliberate rejection of solemnity as an attitude of mind.

The antagonism (which soon grew up and has never entirely disappeared) between Bloomsbury and conventional society arises precisely here. In conventional society feelings were, and largely still are, with a few agreed exceptions, wrong and must be suppressed. Strong feelings are almost always wrong. Thus it is right for parents to feel love for their children, but wrong for this love to be warmly expressed in actions or attitudes which may 'spoil' them: wrong too for it to be strong enough to prevent the imposition of accepted rules of conduct and social development which may be unattractive to the child. It is permissible for strong feelings to exist between a man and woman in love, but only if they are not publicly in evidence and are quelled in the normal course by marriage. A man, once married, must have no feelings beyond a cool attachment for any woman-friend, however attractive and however intimately associated with him. If a married man or woman is emotionally drawn to a friend of his or her own sex, this feeling must be firmly suppressed: to express it in any overt physical way is unacceptable. To have strong views on social issues, except those which firmly support the existing system, is to be a crank. To have strong views which are sharply opposed to those generally held is to be an extremist, probably a subversive influence and possibly a crypto-communist.

Our present-day society, which we call permissive, has to some extent changed its attitudes. It is, at least superficially, more tolerant of social deviationists. How long it will continue to be so is an open question. Societies, by their very nature, tend to draw up their own codes of conduct and to punish or persecute those who do not conform.

In the last years before 1914, when post-Victorian society had reached its final high plateau of achievement and self-congratulation, there was certainly no permissiveness. In such a world there was no place for the offender. And, in one way or another, all the members of Bloomsbury were offenders. Lytton was a homosexual and made no bones about it. Leonard Woolf was a socialist at a time when even Liberalism was looked on with some suspicion by a large section of society. Clive Bell, a rising art critic, was a vehement admirer of what Roger Fry (a Bloomsbury father-figure) had christened Post-Impressionist art. Vanessa and Duncan were themselves artists in the new anti-traditional mode. Maynard Keynes, in other ways impeccable, was guilty by association.

Rejection was mutual. Bloomsbury rejected with scorn and ridicule the standards and outlook of contemporary society, and were irritatingly content to do without a world which disapproved of them.

It would be wrong to suggest that the break was complete. The Stracheys and Stephens were well-enough connected to be invited out, or even to stay for the weekend, by members of conventional society. The invitations were sometimes accepted if the hosts seemed interesting, and Virginia enjoyed the excitement of parties, even though they left her emotionally exhausted. But such contacts were unsatisfactory and the guests returned with relief to the intimacy of their own circle. A weekend visit to the house of some distinguished person would characteristically be followed by an ironic and uncomplimentary commentary in letters from Lytton to Virginia, or vice versa. Superficially, of course, good manners were generally observed. Bloomsbury was not aggressive in its opposition to conventional attitudes, and its members were of such unexceptionable social status that it would have been disloyal to ostracise them totally. Indeed, when Lytton's writings brought him fame there was a period when he was lionised to an almost absurd extent.

Nevertheless the existence of a profound rift was clear enough. The existence, too, of Bloomsbury as a micro-society which happily dispensed with what London as a whole had to offer became increasingly evident. That a group of otherwise highly acceptable men and women should reject the exclusive world to which they had by birth and upbringing the entrée, and set up their own even more exclusive alternative, was a sharp, and to many an unforgivable, affront. What is more, it was highly suspicious: hidden motives were suspected. There *must* be better reasons than a mere innocent preference for such a procedure. By many people, and for a long time, Bloomsbury was regarded as a kind of conspiratorial group, a pre-Cliveden set, with a sinister, behind-the-scenes political influence. It was a baseless view, and its absurdity is pointed by the celebrated occasion when Vanessa, always liable through absent-mindedness to say something astonishing, asked Asquith, her neighbour at dinner, whether he was interested in politics. He was at the time Prime Minister.

Those who did not share this assessment of Bloomsbury tended to regard them as moral delinquents. This view arose partly because they were all in one way or another artists or involved with artists, and thus by definition loose in their morals. Partly it arose from reports of the highly unconventional and unbridled parties which they loved so much and at which wildly libidinous behaviour and some undressing were tolerated. But partly it was simply, from the conventional viewpoint, true. The marriage of Virginia and Leonard Woolf was, mainly perhaps for temperamental reasons, impeccable. But the relationships of other members of the group tended to be informal, impermanent and, in at least one case, little short of promiscuous. Lytton's love-affairs with young men were not more acceptable because his loves were all gentlemen, and gifted with charm and talent. The girls too were sometimes more fond of each other than they ought to be. What was Dora Carrington's position in Lytton's household, or for that matter

Duncan Grant's in Vanessa's? Could David Garnett—a self-confessed 'libertine'—be trusted with any woman? Was it not shocking that Ralph Partridge should spend the weeks with Frances Marshall and only the weekends with his wife? There were indeed grounds enough for the disapproval of the strait-laced.

One last thing should be said before we look in more detail at the individuals and the relationships which made up Bloomsbury. Eccentrics, misfits and nonconformists are not necessarily either interesting or valuable people. They may be simply inadequate or sick. They may be ludicrous or pathetic. What distinguishes Bloomsbury from such sad or silly people is that they were all gifted, and some very highly gifted, in the intellectual or artistic spheres. They were writers and painters. Virginia Woolf's novels went as far as *Ulysses* in search of the springs of consciousness. Lytton Strachey revolutionised the art of biography. Maynard Keynes and Bertrand Russell, whose spiritual home was Bloomsbury wherever else their talents led them, were respectively the leading economist and philosopher of their day. Roger Fry and Clive Bell opened the eyes of England to the glories of Picasso and Matisse. The painting of Vanessa Bell and Duncan Grant, though not great, can stand confidently on its own merits.

How relevant their attitudes and their achievements are to a world now far different from theirs, and even perhaps radically different from it, is not a question which can yet be resolved. For the present it is enough to know that they were men and women of great interest and value as individuals, and that their lives, in which tragedy and comedy were both deeply inherent, vibrate with the impact of emotions and events against which they had not the common defence of indifference or insensibility.

II

The Strachey Connection

LYTTON STRACHEY was born in 1880, the eleventh child of Lt.-General Sir Richard and Lady Strachey. The Stracheys were an old and distinguished Somerset family, with their seat at Sutton Court in that county. The Grants, his mother's family, were Scottish of the minor aristocracy. His father and maternal grandparents had devoted their lives to the service of India, and Sir Richard was indeed one of the great Indian administrators. It was in India that Jane Grant, a girl of 19, met and married her husband, then a man of 42.

At Lytton's birth, his father was 63 and had been retired for ten years. His mother was 40. They were living in London, and when Lytton was four, moved to a large, forbidding house at Lancaster Gate which was to be Lytton's home until he was nearly thirty.

Since Lytton himself was to become one of the oddest and most unusual men of his age, it is of interest that eccentricity, frequently allied with intellectual gifts of some distinction, was by no means exceptional in the Strachey family. Of his father's brothers, for example, numbering among themselves an explorer and a diplomat, as well as several Anglo-Indians and the third baronet, most had their oddities. Uncle William took matters to the extreme by always living in England by Calcutta time. This involved turning night very largely into day, getting up in the late afternoon and going to bed in the small hours. He was a frequent guest at Lancaster Gate, where the effect of his peculiar life-rhythm on a relatively normal household can be imagined. Dressed always in the style of fifty years earlier, with the addition of galoshes, he was a source of astonishment to the young boy Lytton.

Sir Richard himself was not without his own eccentricities. When not in his room engaged on the study of meteorology or geography, two of his major interests, he read novels, totally oblivious of the enormous din surrounding him—the hubbub characteristically generated by the Strachey family, constantly swollen by visiting cousins and aunts, immensely and endlessly vociferous. Mild and kindly to all, he yet continued to go his own way, ignoring attempts to get him down to meals or up to bed, and sallying forth on foot, though over eighty and very deaf, into the London traffic whenever he wanted to do so.

The conduct, if that is the right word, of this large family and the running of this inconvenient house fell exclusively on Jane. It cannot be said that she was well-equipped for the task, though somehow or other it all worked. Advanced in some of her attitudes—she was a feminist, and, like her husband, an agnostic—she was also deeply interested in literature and music. But she was no intellectual; indeed she was in some ways not even intelligent. She was deeply devoted to her children, but incapable of understanding them. She carried out whatever she saw to be her duty to them with relentless purpose and sometimes calamitous results. Of her, Maynard Keynes penetratingly said, 'How terrible to love so much and know so little'. In spite of the totally unsuitable education she provided for Lytton, and the equally misconceived plans she had for his career, he remained devoted to her, and accepted, with a passivity which was always a part of his personality, all her arrangements and schemes for him. The fact is that, with all her obvious faults, she was a great personality, dominant certainly, even domineering—but, if absent-minded and unpredictable, warm-hearted and vivacious. Carrington's portrait of her, dressed in the sweeping black she always affected, shows something of her formidableness, mitigated by the revealing insecurity of her spectacles.

Instead of sending Lytton to Eton, where his elder brother, Oliver, had gone, Jane entrusted him to a man of magnetic personality, a few embryonic ideas and dangerous stupidity who had recently started a boarding school for boys at Abbotsholme in Derbyshire, run on what were then thought of as new and progressive lines. A sort of ur-Gordonstoun without enlightenment or humanity, it aimed explicitly at producing an improved type of human being, a superman of the German type, fitted by education to hold the reins of Empire more firmly than less lucky men educated elsewhere. That was the idea. The means used to realise it were typical of other later schools of this type—a sadistically spartan physical régime to which the academic curriculum, in the hands of second-rate ushers, took a minor second place.

Lytton just survived two terms. Steadfastly uncomplaining in his letters home and keen to succeed in his first venture into an all-male world, he was constitutionally totally unfitted to withstand the treatment he received. His health broke down and he was taken away.

He was then sent to Leamington, a minor public school of the traditional type. Here, after a shaky start, he settled down well enough, and even, in due course, reached a position of privilege and some distinction.

On the whole, however, Jane made a sad mess of her son's schooling. It is clear that for her his education was essentially a process necessary to prepare him for a career in one of the professions traditionally followed by the Grants and the Stracheys. Lytton's own emotional and intellectual needs had no place in her planning, largely because she did not understand what they were. His physical debility was already a serious problem which she sought to solve by providing large doses of sea air in the holidays and the occasional ambitious expedition to warmer climates abroad.

Admittedly Lytton set her a difficult problem. Obviously an intellectually promising boy, with a capacity for fantasy and friendship that made him both unusual and attractive, he was at the same time dangerously weak physically. On top of it all he was very odd in appearance. He was extremely thin and lanky, with great dark eyes and a huge nose, a marked lack of physical co-ordination and a ridiculous voice. He would never get his rugger colours. He was the kind of boy who inevitably gets bullied as a new boy, but who, at any school where his abilities and gifts are given the opportunity to appear, eventually becomes a 'character' and so is given the licence and the amused toleration which provide the right climate for his proper development. For a boy like him Abbotsholme was a calamity and Leamington adequate only in a negative way. He needed the setting of a big school where his eccentricities would be relatively unobtrusive, where he could choose intimates of his own peculiar kind, and in particular, where his teachers would, some of them at least, be themselves intellectually equipped to recognise and foster the powers of mind and imagination which, as things were, he was not to show to their full until he had reached middle life.

He left Leamington at seventeen and was then sent—yet another wildly unimaginative choice—to Liverpool University in order to prepare for Balliol, where Jane had now decided that he should follow his brother Oliver. At Liverpool he was simply lonely. He passed his examinations, joined one or two societies, but made only one friend—Lumsden Barkway, a future Bishop—and no intimates. Of all the sadnesses of his adolescent life it was the absence of intimate companionship which was the hardest to bear. Strange as he was both in appearance and personality, he desperately required the reassurance which such a relationship would have given him. He wanted to know that he was not irretrievably inferior. More than that, he had a nagging ambition to excel, which arose from some deep inner conviction that he had the ability to do so. But even if he were right in this conviction, he needed as well the encouragement of a friend, or preferably friends, to whom he could freely confide his most intimate and, as he sometimes thought, shameful desires and feelings, and who would, in spite of this, give him the support of their affection. Friends of this kind so far he had not found.

He loyally sat for the examination which would have given him entry to Balliol, though he much preferred the idea of Cambridge, and in due course went up for interview. The outcome was another blow to his self-esteem. On the unconvincing grounds that his command of the classics was inadequate, he was turned down. There can be no doubt, and Lytton himself may have been conscious of this, that he made a very poor impression at the interview, and that this led to his rejection. Nor is there much reason for surprise at the decision. Balliol, under Jowett, was a highly select college, whose students were expected—much as the Abbotsholme boys were, but on far sounder grounds—to go out into the world as leaders of men and to import, as far as might be, Balliol standards into their chosen professions—politics, the law, the church or the universities. The painfully shy, absurdly awkward figure who presented himself for election to this society of outstanding young men of whom worldly success was confidently expected clearly had little to offer.

So it had to be Cambridge. There was no difficulty about selection here. He took his 'Little Go' like anyone else; passed it—who could fail?—and in October 1899 put on, with a shiver of pleasure, the rather jolly blue gown of Trinity College. It was a highly suitable place for him to be. Far larger than any other college of the University, it was academically sound without being vulgarly ambitious. Unlike Balliol, it did not seek to impose an intellectual pattern: its undergraduates were allowed, and encouraged where this seemed appropriate, to develop such abilities as they had without sacrificing the normal interests and pursuits of a gentleman. A high proportion of them were Etonians: all were from the same social class as Lytton, or better. They hunted, roistered and got experimentally drunk in the usual way. They had never seen anyone like Lytton before, of course. Who had? There were some who wished to throw him into the fountain in Great Court to demonstrate their dissatisfaction with him, but on the whole he was allowed to occupy his place quietly as a harmless mutant, regarded more with curiosity than distaste.

For Lytton, Cambridge was a rebirth. The grub wriggling for its life at Abbotsholme, frozen into a miserable chrysalis at Liverpool, emerged at Trinity in imago-form with damp wings admittedly, but with every hope of being able to take off freely into the sunny air he breathed for what seemed to be the first time.

He had always needed love, understanding and success, not necessarily in that order. Love for him meant a deeply emotional, and preferably passionate relationship based both on physical attraction and a joyful community of tastes. As a schoolboy he had focused his affections from time to time on boys who seemed to him to possess all those qualities he wished he had but knew he lacked—manliness, beauty, physical dynamism. His love was never returned in any form warmer than kindly tolerance. By the time he went to Liverpool he knew and accepted with rueful good humour that he was a homosexual. Surely now at Cambridge, in this brilliant world of youth he would find someone who would be worth loving and who would love him: not perhaps straightaway but in due course.

As a newcomer, along with many more, in a society of strangers, he had, however, first to find his feet, which meant finding his friends. In this, Lytton was luckier than most, and far luckier than he, with all his disabilities, was entitled to expect. Within a relatively short while not only had he made for himself a small circle of increasingly intimate friends, but almost without exception they were friends literally for life. For the first time, he had found understanding, and an atmosphere in which he could expand and reveal his powers.

Success, measured by the esteem of his friends, he had thus also begun to achieve. Success in the larger sense, which for Lytton meant not only the approbation of men of merit and judgment, but a public unequivocal recognition of achievement, was something else. He felt convinced that he could win this too, but he seemed to make dismally slow progress towards it and he was frequently in despair. Success in this sense was to elude him for almost another two decades.

Although now happier than he had ever been, Lytton was still not the free man he longed to be. Financially dependent on his parents, he was still rooted in the Strachey household: he had no other base. In University vacations, that is for half of every year, he returned to a world dominated by his mother, littered with peculiar uncles and cousins, a friendly enough world, but busy with its own miscellaneous and rather dreary preoccupations. Here his physical well-being was cared for, from it he was despatched abroad for health-cures, but in it he gasped for the air he had begun to draw in in great lungfuls and which seemed to be found only at Cambridge, and there only in one or two rooms at Trinity.

III

Cambridge

THE precise contribution which Cambridge thought and Cambridge life made to the peculiar character of Bloomsbury has been often argued about. We will not join the argument. We shall content ourselves by telling the story.

Lytton and the future husbands of the Stephen girls, Clive Bell and Leonard Woolf, were exact contemporaries at Trinity. They became friendly during their first term and early in the next term they followed the Cambridge habit of forming a club, with two other members, Saxon Sydney-Turner, and A. J. Robertson. It was a reading club which, as it met in Clive's room every Saturday at midnight, adopted the apt if unimaginative title of the Midnight Society. In sessions which in the summer went on till dawn, the five friends read Shelley and Milton and lesser poets. A sixth member soon joined them. Thoby Stephen, brother of Virginia and Vanessa, whose family had long been on friendly terms with the Stracheys, was also a Trinity freshman. Lytton, meeting him for the first time at this stage, was delighted and charmed by him.

It was in some ways an ill-assorted group. Three, possibly four of them, were predominantly academics, in that their interests were exclusively intellectual. Thoby, though he, like Lytton and Leonard Woolf, was elected to a Trinity scholarship in due course, was at the same time an outstanding athlete. Clive Bell was a member of the hunting set. It is extraordinary that, with the exception of Robertson, who soon drops out of sight, they all remained not only friends, but intimates for the rest of their lives, and that these lives became inextricably entwined one with the other.

Apart from Thoby, who died at 26, and Saxon Sydney-Turner, a vague figure hovering on the outskirts, the other members of the Midnight Society are central to the story of Bloomsbury. There is thus some justification for Clive Bell's later assertion that the Trinity reading club was its beginning. What is beyond question is that Lytton was the club's moving spirit: while he was absent from Cambridge through sickness the society did not meet: when he moved on to other circles, the club died.

Sydney-Turner was a scholarly, well-read and, according to Leonard Woolf, with whom he shared rooms in Great Court, an 'immensely intelligent and subtle' person. He was at the same time extraordinarily static and inert: he seemed to have exhausted his tiny store of vitality in an outburst of high spirits in his first term at Trinity. Thereafter for the whole of his life he was a dim, insubstantial figure, given to endless compulsive talk on specialised topics which interested nobody but himself —technical aspects, for example, of cricket or the opera. After Cambridge he went to the Treasury, a dull enough place in itself, and contrived to create for himself a life of equivalent dullness. His Great Ormond Street rooms were decorated by a huge painting of a farmyard scene which was duplicated on each side of the fireplace and remained there unchanged for thirty years, while in his bedroom paintings by Duncan Grant and others were invisible because of the darkness of the room.

As one of a group of friends who, whatever other qualities they may have lacked, were at least articulate, Sydney-Turner made only spasmodic utterances. His conversation consisted, when he was not monologising on a subject as unexciting as Tacitus's use of the dative, of long silences punctuated by occasional terse comments. As the talk had usually flowed on rapidly between his scattered contributions, they were hard to relate to the context and frequently sounded absurdly irrelevant. Leonard Woolf recalls an extreme example, when he made the firm, but in the context incomprehensible statement, 'He was right'. It turned out that he was referring to a judgment expressed by Thoby in the previous term. There is little doubt that he was, all in all, a bloodless bore: but a man who had earned the respect of Leonard Woolf must have had merit if only of a thin intellectual kind. At all events he remained an accepted member of Bloomsbury society, staying at the same houses and being patiently nursed by its women during his frequent illnesses.

Improbably enough it was through him that Clive Bell, who had neighbouring rooms in New Court, made the acquaintance of Lytton and the rest. Clive was the son of newly-rich philistines. He was well off, passionately devoted to hunting and shooting, full of physical vitality, friendly and cheerful, but no intellectual: 'a gay and amiable dog', Maynard Keynes called him. He had a round pink face, set off by a mass of curly red hair and a strong fleshy frame: the physical contrast between him and Lytton, or even Leonard Woolf, was startling and it is not surprising that it was with the athletic Thoby that he first got on to close terms.

In spite of possessing all the qualities which fitted him to be a Trinity 'blood', he nurtured, somewhere within and behind that hearty, rubicund exterior, a perverse yearning to excel in some more cerebral field. He had, according to Leonard Woolf, an 'eager, lively, intensely curious' mind. He loved argument. The Midnight Society argued about books and authors, and Clive, to whom serious writing came with all the excitement of novelty, acquired a passion for literature. His interest in art, which was to provide him with a career and a permanent niche in the history of art criticism, already existed, but blossomed only some years later when he lived for a while in Paris. Meanwhile, he made his own contribution, and continued through his life to do so, to the animation of the group which he had joined with excitement and enthusiasm. 'Clive's wide reading, quick wit and common sense' said David Garnett later, 'was an essential ingredient in the brilliant talk to be heard in Bloomsbury.' He never became himself a sound creative artist; his books are often clumsily and carelessly written. The truth is that he never quite understood what went on in Bloomsbury and the world of the mind. But what he understood he liked, and even when he was puzzled he remained friendly, jovial and above all, hospitable. He gave Bloomsbury a warmth and humanity which it badly needed. And he could always go away and shoot pheasants, thus making a contribution which had its own value.

Leonard Woolf, his friend and future brother-in-law, was mentally and socially in as wide a contrast from Clive as Lytton was physically. Their backgrounds could hardly have been more dissimilar. One of a large family of Jewish liberals, he was brought up in a narrow world of puritanical culture. There was little money to spare and it was a help when he won a scholarship to St. Paul's and an exhibition, later converted into a scholarship, at Trinity. His physical appearance, with his lean body and even leaner face, accurately suggested the ascetic which he largely was. His mental attitude was essentially that of an observer and critic, with the instincts, but not the committed zeal, of a reformer. He had great mental energy, endless self-discipline and a social conscience that was expressed in life-long political activity. But his real powers lay deeper. Somewhere beneath the tough layers of puritanism, and generally hidden under an air of chilly, impersonal humanitarianism, there was an artist, and a man of deep feeling, sensitive to the needs and emotions of his friends, capable of deep suffering on their behalf and utterly involved in their problems and pursuits. His anguished devotion to Virginia in her illness shows the depth of his emotional personality: his autobiography reveals both his acute and sympathetic understanding of human beings and his outstanding gifts as a writer in whom lucidity amounted almost to genius. It was these characteristics, and not only the keenness of his mind, which made him both an essential part of the small group at Trinity and Lytton's first confidant.

Lytton's Cambridge career, lasting six years in all, falls neatly into two halves. For the first three years, it was mainly centred on Trinity. Then in 1902 he spread his wings; after getting only a second class in his Tripos examination the previous year, he now achieved a Trinity scholarship and went on to win the Chancellor's Medal for an ode on Ely. At the beginning of the same year he was elected a member of the Apostles.

This society, whose composition and attitude to life have close parallels with the later Bloomsbury, must for that reason be described.

Formed in the early years of the previous century, the Cambridge Conversazione Society, to give it its ponderous official title, was a small exclusive group drawn from the whole University, meeting weekly to hear and discuss papers written by its members. Papers were on any and every subject and of any length: so, too, was the discussion which followed. The proceedings of the society—and indeed its very existence—were secret, not for any sinister reason, but because the society shunned publicity. Membership was not a matter of application, but was offered after careful scrutiny by existing members, some of whom were graduates no longer resident in Cambridge, but still in touch with the newer generation of undergraduates. It was through becoming known to some of these, particularly Bertrand Russell and Desmond MacCarthy, that Lytton was elected. Leonard Woolf and Maynard Keynes also became Apostles, but Clive Bell to his deep chagrin was never invited to join.

The best description of the Apostolic attitude of mind is perhaps that of Henry Sidgwick, elected some fifty years before, as quoted by Michael Holroyd: 'Absolute candour was the only duty that the tradition of the society enforced. No consistency was demanded with the opinions previously held— truth as we saw it then and there was what we had to embrace and maintain, and there were no propositions so well established that an Apostle had not the right to deny or question, if he did so sincerely and not from mere love of paradox. The gravest subjects were continually debated, but gravity of treatment, as I have said, was not imposed, though sincerity was.' Apostles were then, by definition and agreement, seekers after truth, and truth at any price. No serious subject was banned from discussion. Religion and sex were discussed with the same uninhibited frankness and freedom from humbug as less sensitive matters like politics or philosophy. Apostles scorned what, in their private language, they stigmatised as the 'phenomenal'—that is whatever held worldly rewards to be gained only by compromise with Apostolic principles.

The Society, as it was called by its members, was an ideal setting for Lytton. Highly select—he was only the 239th name on its register—it flattered his longing to be recognised as a person of merit. More than that, its austere concern for what its members hoped were eternal verities reflected his own attitude of mind. Its close scrutiny of current thought-patterns and the resultant rejection of what was seen as conventional prejudice or half-truth, was to be characteristic of Bloomsbury.

For Lytton too it meant new friends, some of whom, like

those he had made at Trinity, were to be permanent. There was
C. P. Sanger, a rising barrister, formerly of Trinity, a man of
brilliant mind and great kindness of heart, but too modest ever
to claim the success to which his qualities entitled him:
Leonard Woolf summed him up as 'a saint, but a very amusing,
ribald, completely sceptical saint with a first-class mind and an
extremely witty tongue.' He and his wife Dora gave welcome
hospitality to Lytton when he went down from Cambridge
and they moved freely in the Bloomsbury world. It was they
who introduced Lytton to Lady Ottoline Morrell. There was
John Sheppard, a new Apostle with Lytton, runner-up to him
for the Chancellor's Medal, and eventually to become a distinguished Provost of King's College. Lytton fell in love with
him but his feelings were not reciprocated and, after a year or
two of intimacy, they drifted apart. It was another King's
Apostle who was to loom largest in the later life of Lytton and
of Bloomsbury. Maynard Keynes, three years junior to Lytton,
was probably the most intellectually able of his generation at
Cambridge: if ability is measured in terms of its effect, there is
no doubt that this is true. When he met Lytton, the future
inventor of a theory of economics which shaped the world
between the wars was, in spite of a wide acquaintance, in need
of a friend in whom to confide. Like Lytton he had homosexual
tendencies and it may have been this fact which brought into
the friendship which rapidly ripened between them an intimacy
and confidence which survived occasional coldnesses and which
only faded when each, by different routes, reached his own kind
of eminence. He became a member of the inner circle of
Bloomsbury, living for years, even after his marriage, in rooms
at 46 Gordon Square, and becoming the next-door neighbour
of Clive and Vanessa at Tilton, his country house in Sussex. His
intellectual eminence was acknowledged by the most brilliant
of his contemporaries, but it was Bloomsbury which discovered, on the one hand, his great generosity of heart, and on
the other hand, in Leonard Woolf's words, 'some streaks of
intellectual wilfulness and arrogance which often led him into
surprisingly wrong and perverse judgments.' He could be
appallingly rude. And he had, decided Lytton, no aesthetic
sense. As an Apostle he was susceptible to the appeal of the

'phenomenal', but so too was Lytton. Both needed success. The critical note which creeps into Lytton's opinions of May-nard quite early and sounds more strongly as time passes, could have in it an undertone of the jealousy natural in one to whom success came slowly: for Maynard success had begun at Eton, and his later career was an uninterrupted steep ascent to world eminence. Lytton did not grudge him his fame, but the con-trast with his own long drawn-out obscurity was an irritation only to be relieved by drawing attention to feet of clay when-ever for a moment they appeared.

A King's man of an earlier generation with whom Lytton was to have a tenuous but long-lasting association was a frequent weekend visitor to Cambridge at this time. E. M. Forster was in his way as odd a person as Lytton. Self-effacing and impenetrably courteous, he was an observer rather than a participant. He shrank from the eccentricities which Lytton increasingly indulged during his later years at Cambridge, and was nicknamed by him the 'Taupe'—the mole. Forster slips unobtrusively in and out of the later life of Bloomsbury, always in danger of some bitingly critical comment by Lytton, but recognised, and perhaps then dismissed, as a man of sensitivity and gifts.

Bertrand Russell was another constant Cambridge visitor, often in the company of Desmond MacCarthy or of the philosopher G. E. Moore, all Apostles and graduates of Trinity. All three were to be closely associated, each in their different ways, with Bloomsbury; and this association began with their Apostolic friendship with Lytton.

Of the three it was Desmond MacCarthy who was to remain most closely linked with Lytton: he and his wife Mary, known always as Molly, though never fully identified with Bloomsbury were on intimate terms with its members and generally were given its label by outsiders. Indeed it was Molly who, by coining for them the nickname 'Bloomsberries', had first given expression to the notion that such a group existed. Desmond, not yet married when he first met Lytton, was a man of all-embracing charm and affability, with brilliant gifts of mind and heart, and the most delightful of companions. He was at the same time a superbly entertaining raconteur and an intellectual who was the favourite disciple of G. E. Moore. The world in those days was at his feet. Of all the Trinity Apostles of his day he was the one of whom most was expected. He had, said Leonard Woolf, 'wit, humour, intelligence, imagination, a remarkable gift of words, an extraordinary power of describing a character, an incident or a scene.' Instead, however, of writing the great novel which everyone awaited from him, he became a literary journalist; the novel was never written. There was in him a streak of Irish perverseness which was always to make it impossible for him to do what it was obviously right for him to do.

In these early days he was deeply struck by Lytton and he saw more clearly than anyone else the nature of his gifts and character. Writing of these times, much later, he described Lytton's Cambridge role as that of a 'leader . . . not only through his culture, his wit and the discrimination of his taste, but thanks above all to the vehement and passionate nature of his judgements upon character.' There is here something of the wisdom of hindsight, but there is every reason to think that both Lytton and Desmond recognised in each other the dominantly literary character of their gifts at a stage when Lytton at least was contemplating an academic career rather than that of a writer. Lytton reacted less whole-heartedly to Desmond than Desmond to him. He was not sure that he could entirely approve of a man so universally loved and seemed to suspect some concealed insincerity and an improper desire to please: but he succumbed in the end and conceded that Desmond's charm arose from an inner sweetness of character as rare as it was undeniable.

Bertrand Russell who, with Moore, had exerted a strong influence over Desmond when they were all undergraduates, could hardly have been more different from him in personality and, basically, in tastes. Russell was a mathematician with a strong philosophical bent, with little time for the light-hearted nonsense which appealed to Desmond and Lytton. Desmond describes the Apostles of his day, 'We were not much interested in politics. Abstract speculation was much more absorbing. Philosophy was much more interesting to us than public causes. . . . What we chiefly discussed were those "goods" which were ends in themselves . . . the search for truth, aesthetic emotions and personal relations—love and friendship.' In these discussions Russell took a leading part and indeed it was he who persuaded Moore to take the final Moral Sciences tripos and thus launch himself on his career as a philosopher. He had, said Leonard Woolf, 'The quickest mind of anyone I have ever known', and James Strachey, writing to Michael Holroyd, was anxious that he should make clear in his *Life of Lytton* that 'Bertie has the most marvellous mental apparatus, perhaps ever.' With a passionate devotion to philosophic truth as he saw it and to causes which seemed to him to show this truth—a devotion which sent him to prison in the First World War for subversion, which lost him his Trinity fellowship and which took him in the end to Trafalgar Square as a supremely ill-equipped crowd orator in the cause of nuclear disarmament—with all this there was a strange inhumanity in his ruthless pursuit of the good. He did not really care for individuals: love—except in the sexual sense—stopped short for him at respect for those who, to his mind, deserved it. Lytton's gifts appealed to his sense of humour—he shocked the warders at Brixton prison by his loud laughter as he read *Eminent Victorians*—but he mistook Lytton's gaiety for frivolity and never saw beneath it the despair and self-contempt for which it was an attempted compensation. Russell never recognised the emotional needs of others, while accepting his own as self-evidently paramount. He permitted himself in later life a series of sexual relationships of an intense kind, recorded with disarming candour and pursued with no apparent regard for the distress they caused, either to his estranged first wife, or to the objects of his often ephemeral passions. Lytton's homosexual affairs, however, appeared to him 'frivolous and absurd'. Russell was already embarked on his career as a philosopher and lived in a rarefied, dehumanised air of pure cerebration into which Lytton was neither able nor anxious to follow him. They continued, however, to maintain friendly relations, meeting each other fairly often, and Russell found in Bloomsbury, if not the committed intellectualism he would have wished, at least the freedom from inhibition and prejudice which was itself a basic 'good', and he was always happy in their company.

If it was Russell's influence which first persuaded G. E. Moore to make a serious study of philosophy, the influence of Moore and his philosophy on the Apostles, and particularly the Bloomsbury Apostles, was infinitely more profound and long-lasting. He expressed for them their highest aspirations as Apostles and to a great degree personified the ideals they shared. In the endless discussion of issues of every kind which went on at meetings of the Society and at the Easter reading parties which were simply extended sessions of the Society, it was his relentless pursuit of truth and insistence on clarity of expression which forced Lytton, Maynard and Leonard Woolf to examine their own thinking and attitudes with unprecedented and ruthless clear-mindedness. In his company they became, or felt they became, better than without him they ever were. He was, they were convinced, a great man. He was, says Leonard Woolf, 'qualitatively different from anyone else I have ever known'. His utter sincerity, his total integrity, and at the same time his insistence on relevance and commonsense were a revelation and delight to them. His absurdities were the absurdities of Socrates, the sillinesses that go with an unselfconscious and exclusive concern with what really matters. If box after box of matches failed to light his pipe it was because talk was more absorbing and more important than smoking. And his talk, slow because it had to express thoughts strenuously achieved and demanding the most explicit expression, could dispense with the wit which in others was almost a required characteristic. 'A colossal being' Lytton called him later in a letter to Virginia Woolf.

In 1903 Moore's *Principia Ethica* was published. Its effect on Lytton and his friends, and thus ultimately on Bloomsbury, can hardly be exaggerated. Lytton, still far from the success he longed to achieve, was not given to greeting the successes of others with unqualified enthusiasm. But Moore's book reduced him to stuttering, breathless eulogy. In a letter of congratulation which he described as a 'confession of faith' Lytton admits to being 'carried away'. Moore had, he said, 'shattered all writers on Ethics from Aristotle and Christ to Herbert Spencer and Mr. Bradley.' The Age of Reason, he decided, dated from the publication of this book. Leonard Woolf was less lyrical in his

reactions, but no less profoundly affected by it. 'The tremend-
ous influence of Moore and his book upon us,' he says, 'came
from the fact that they suddenly removed from our eyes an
obscuring accumulation of scales, cobwebs and curtains, revealing for the first time to us, so it seemed, the nature of truth and
reality, of good and evil and character and conduct, substituting
for the religious and philosophical nightmares, delusions,
hallucinations in which Jehovah, Christ, and St. Paul, Plato,
Kant and Hegel had entangled us, the fresh air and pure light of
commonsense.' Even Maynard felt the impact of Moore and
described it, not inaccurately, as religious in effect. Moore's
final chapter on 'The Ideal' seemed to him to reduce the New
Testament to 'a handbook for politicians'.

If it was Moore's fanatical pursuit of truth for its own sake
and his rejection of the sanctified irrelevancies of religion and
conventional morality which drew the first deep response from
them all, it was certain oddly bathetic conclusions to which he
came in his book which made the warmest appeal to Lytton.
With what relief after the strenuous intellectual effort demanded
by the book as a whole did he learn that, for Moore, the most
self-evident 'goods' were 'the pleasures of human intercourse
and the enjoyment of beautiful objects'. It was as if after the
difficult and dangerous traverse of a harsh mountain range he
had emerged on to a sunlit meadow, a kind of Islamic paradise.
His loves, of which he had been careful never to speak with
candour at meetings of the Society, were after all not only not
inconsistent with Apostolic ideals but had, at least in principle,
the blessing of the greatest Apostle of all.

If 'bed and boys', to use a later phrase of Maynard's, were not
explicitly recommended they were surely covered by a wide
phrase like 'human intercourse'. So too was the aestheticism
which was to be characteristic of Bloomsbury. Lytton's interpretation of Moore infuriated Russell, who denounced him for
what he regarded as an emasculation of a lofty ethical system.
And he was right: there was a good deal more in *Principia
Ethica* than an argument for love and the arts. But Lytton was
not a philosopher and it remains true that if he did not master
all the material of the book, nevertheless Moore's austere
intellectual method—the almost brutal process of cross-

examination in which every proposition was submitted to
ruthless questioning, every statement analysed word by word—
provided Lytton with a technique which enabled him to arrive
at startlingly new historical judgments.

There is no doubt that, if one of the functions of a University
is to provide an atmosphere, a society and a way of life which
will expand the mind and develop the powers which may be
expected to shape the lives of its sons, Cambridge was a success
for Lytton. But to have suggested this to him when, after six
years' residence, two of them as a graduate, he at last went
down, would have drawn a very bitter response.

What had he done? Apart from the Chancellor's Medal there
were no triumphs: far from it. He had hoped for, and even
expected, a First Class Degree: he got a second. Under pressure
from his mother he had tried to get into the Civil Service: but
here, as once previously, an unsatisfactory interview closed the
doors on him. Undeterred and still inwardly sure of his ability,
he had laboured mightily on a Fellowship thesis on Warren
Hastings: it was rejected. He added a second laborious part to
it, and it was again refused. It was a catalogue of failure. No
career lay before him, except that of journalism: he could
always go on writing book reviews as he had begun to do at
Cambridge. The prospect was desperately dim.

The reality was dramatically different. Not only was there a
brilliant future in store for him, but the Cambridge failures
were essential to it. Lytton as a Civil Servant or a don—he
never really wished to become either—would never have
fulfilled himself and Bloomsbury, whose tone he largely set,
would have been a far different and far duller thing. Equally,
without Cambridge, Lytton might never have risen above the
sense of utter inferiority for which his physical make-up was
largely responsible. At Cambridge the very strangeness of his
appearance and mannerisms suddenly became an asset and he
even cultivated eccentricities of dress and behaviour. At Cambridge he found himself accepted, respected and even liked by
the ablest of his contemporaries. Not only did he become an
Apostle, a mark to him of extraordinary distinction and esteem,
but was undoubtedly in his later years at Cambridge the leader,

with Maynard, of the Society. And he learned through Moore to ask the right questions in order to get the right answers. Most of all he made friendships of two kinds. He fell in love, with 'embryo' Apostles and others; and in Maynard, Leonard Woolf, Sydney-Turner, Sanger, he found lifelong comrades, all men of gifts and sharing in varying degrees his own sceptical, wryly humorous, sensitive awareness of life.

He had, in the widest sense of the word, graduated.

IV

London

THE contrast between Cambridge and London, to which
Lytton now returned, was as appalling as it could possibly
be. A cramped bed-sitting room at Lancaster Gate, where his
parents had now moved, was a dreary alternative to a set of
rooms in Great Court. The company of his mother and sisters
was intolerably different from that of his Cambridge friends.
As Jane argued with her daughters or read out at meal-times
thin jokes from *Titbits*, his heart sank.

He tried to keep in touch with Cambridge by an active
interchange of letters with Maynard, now in his last year, but
it was a thin substitute for living there. He was glad to know of
new 'embryo' Apostles, especially the high-spirited, brilliantly
intellectual Harry Norton, a wealthy old Etonian able to keep
up with Bertrand Russell in argument, who was to be a lifelong
friend and member of Bloomsbury, with a great devotion to
Vanessa Bell.

It was more exciting to have fallen head over heels in love
with his cousin Duncan Grant, who had returned to London
after studying in Paris, and to be able to rhapsodise about him
to Maynard. Good-looking and with a bewitching personality,
Duncan had more of the artistic temperament than any of
Lytton's friends till then: he was vague and childishly irrespons-
ible, intelligent without being at all academic, highly original
in mind and manner, much given to practical jokes, and a lover
of Mozart. He was, said his close friend, David Garnett, 'a pure
artist and nothing else'. He was in fact a very good artist. He
later settled for life with Clive and Vanessa, surviving them
both at Charleston, their Sussex home. Lytton's uninhibited
adoration embarrassed him since he could not whole-heartedly
return it. His own homosexual emotions were aroused and
returned by Edgar Duckworth, a Cambridge man whom

Lytton had also loved, but lost, after a bitter struggle, to Maynard. Soon afterwards Duncan and Maynard themselves fell in love. For a second time and in the same intimate context, Maynard had successfully competed with Lytton. It says much for their friendship that it could survive such episodes which, transient as they were, caused in Lytton the most agonising emotional torments.

There was at least one house in London where he was welcome and where he liked to be. At 46 Gordon Square, Thoby Stephen lived with his sisters and his brother Adrian, and it was the presence of 'the Goth', as Lytton had nicknamed Thoby in tribute to his barbaric physical splendour, which was the magnet. Virginia and Vanessa were indeed beautiful and charming, but there was no falling in love. Lytton, it will be recalled, had met them during their father's lifetime, both as a guest at a house they had in the New Forest and at Cambridge when they visited their brother. Their parents too had known each other well.

Virginia's and Vanessa's childhood had been a strange and tragic one, and Virginia, lacking her sister's temperamental stability, had been marked for life by it. Their dearly loved mother, Sir Leslie Stephen's second wife, had died when Virginia was thirteen, an event of such appalling horror to her that she is said to have attempted suicide. Life with their widowed father was entirely lacking in the warmth which both girls needed: not that he was a cold-hearted person but 'he hated sentimentality and gush', as Virginia says in *The Captain's Deathbed*. Brought up in the austere teachings of the Clapham Sect, his values were strictly intellectual. He gave his children, says Virginia, 'the right to think one's own thoughts and to follow one's own pursuits'. She was given the freedom of his library at the age of fifteen. 'To read what one liked because one liked it, never to pretend to admire what one did not—that was his only lesson in the art of reading.' His care for his children's free mental growth was not matched by any understanding of their emotional needs. He was charming but distant. 'On walks' says Virginia, 'with his dog and his daughter [the order may be significant] he could be silent from Round Pond to Marble Arch.' For the last ten years of his life, during the last six of which he was a bed-ridden invalid, Sir Leslie was looked after by his daughters: thus Vanessa from the age of sixteen, and Virginia from the age of thirteen, grew up in the shadow of a sick old man (he was sixty-three when his wife died) unable to bridge the years which separated them or in any way to join them in their immature gropings for a key to existence. There was fun with their brothers in the school holidays, but otherwise excitement—a major ingredient in the happiness of adolescence—had to be sought in the world of the imagination. Vanessa survived this régime better than Virginia. The tensions which were to make much of Virginia's adult life an agony and were at last to lead her to end it began in the chill silence of a home dominated by a sickroom.

It would almost certainly be wrong, however, to attribute Virginia's ills exclusively to the events and conditions of her life as a child and a young woman. Instability must always have been there. The rift in her character which was widened, and widened permanently, by the deaths of her parents and the ten years of misery which separated these events, was surely there from the start.

Nor would it be right to think of Virginia in adult life as a tragic figure lurching from one bout of madness to another or as an invalid never far from dissolution. She was frequently ill and several times went mad. But more often than not she was psychologically, as well as physically, as sound as anyone else. She was, as long as she was well, gay, sociable, and affectionate. She had the instincts of a woman; deeply envied Vanessa's motherhood, loved and needed love, enjoyed the attentions of lovers; was normal, that is, almost all the way. Only at the point where affection, tenderness, pleasure fuse and ignite into passion and the body is called on to give final expression to emotions which cannot otherwise be expressed, did she fail and turn away. Her aversion from sexual intimacy between a man and a woman must largely be laid at the door of her half-brother George Duckworth. Whatever the precise nature and extent of the liberties which he as a grown man permitted himself with her as a child—and Virginia in writing of them later may have exaggerated somewhat—they shocked and shamed her. The memory of them stood, perhaps permanently, between her and any natural expression of passion for Leonard or any other man.

With women it was rather different. There was common physical ground and little or no danger of disgust. Love, however deeply felt and freely expressed, would not lead on to a point where revulsion took over from delight. Without genuinely lesbian urges, lacking even the frank bisexuality of Lytton's later companion Carrington, she was capable of being stirred by feminine attractions and of taking pleasure in intimate emotional relationships with a woman.

As a girl of sixteen she had fallen in love with Madge, the daughter of John Addington Symonds, who was to marry William Vaughan, a cousin of hers. It was a romantic passion of the kind not uncommon in girls of Virginia's age. Madge was for her a glamorous figure: the daughter of a well-known literary personality and herself a writer, she was beautiful, artistic, emotional and fond of Virginia. Virginia never forgot the intensity of her feelings towards Madge. She was moreover able to let her see her early attempts at writing with the certainty of receiving sympathetic criticism and encouragement. Madge came soon to believe in Virginia's genius.

So too did Violet Dickinson, a very different personality from Madge, and the next woman to touch Virginia's emotions. An intimate friend of her half-sister Stella Duckworth, she was thirty-seven when her friendship with Virginia began: Virginia was twenty. Leslie Stephen was now seriously ill and was to die two years later. Violet was a big person in every way: six feet tall, she had a proportionately large heart. She seemed to understand the confused emotions in whose toils Virginia was struggling as her beloved, self-centred father slowly sank under the weight of his remorseless disease. Violet brought a breeze of fresh air into a house shut up with its grief. She was cheerful, well-balanced, intelligent and lovable. Above all she was strong and could be leant upon. Virginia turned to her, not only for comfort and support, but as to a lover. Her letters to Violet at this time are love-letters, intimate and private, and revealing a passionate affection whose nature Virginia was certainly far from understanding.

Virginia's first breakdown had occurred after her mother's

death. Then for the first time she had heard voices, found her pulse racing madly, suffered alternately from depression and extreme excitement and understood—with what horror it is not difficult to imagine—that she was mad. The second attack came in the summer following her father's death. In that spring Vanessa and Virginia had gone to Venice with their half-brother Gerald and then on to Florence, where they joined Violet. It was for both of the sisters their first real trip abroad. Vanessa, who as her father's housekeeper had borne the brunt of his angers and accusations, was so happy to be free at last that the journey was for her one of simple unbroken bliss; and there were above all the galleries to revel in. Virginia, after the first excitement had faded, fell once more under the sway of the guilt and grief that had dominated her life as she watched her father die. Somehow, she seemed to feel, she should have been able to show more love, and who knows whether that might not have been more effective than the efforts of the doctors? But now he was dead and a wild despair gradually expelled every other feeling from her exhausted heart. On returning home she went mad again. The voices returned. She became violent. A nurse was needed at all times. She was just well enough to be taken to Burnham Wood to stay with Violet. But her illusions remained and even intensified. The birds sang in Greek and there, crouched in the shrubbery, was the King of England uttering obscenities. She threw herself out of a window: but death would not come. Under Violet's care she gradually got better. She was able to go to Cambridge in the autumn and even assist her father's biographer with a selection of private letters and a description of Leslie as a parent. She knew how much her recovery, still not complete, was due to Violet's strength and love. 'I can never tell you,' she wrote, 'what you have been to me all this time—for one thing you wouldn't believe it—but if affection is worth anything you have, and always will have mine.' It was Violet too who, by means of an introduction to the *Manchester Guardian*, enabled her to place her first attempts at journalism and encouraged her to go on writing.

It is difficult therefore to over-estimate the importance to Virginia of the love that existed between her and Violet. It was a love which was to continue but to change as it did so. Affection remained but kindliness replaced passion. A new life in which Violet could not fully share was opening out for Virginia. While she was convalescent Vanessa, Thoby and Adrian had moved from Hyde Park Gate to 46 Gordon Square and she was now able to join them there. The move was not only a rational step following the death of their father but a symbolic act, by which they indicated their desire to escape from the society in which they had grown up. The Postal Districts of London are themselves symbols with their own well-understood meanings. S.W.7 indicated an address at which it was suitable for the upper classes to reside: W.C.2 was something quite different, geographically almost adjacent, but socially remote and inhabited by—but who knew who the inhabitants were? And if one did not know them there was a strong inference that it was not desirable to know them.

Lytton was not moved by such trivial considerations and he soon became a regular visitor. With no inhibiting elders present he could alternate between Apostolic argument with and dumb adoration of the beloved Thoby: Vanessa and Virginia could absorb, and Virginia at least eagerly did so, the new and illuminating ideas which Lytton and Thoby brought with them from Cambridge: they could all be serious or gay together, with Adrian—'mischief-loving and incomparably comic', as David Garnett described him—to inject his own brand of absurdity into the situation as required. Clive Bell, who was established in considerable splendour in chambers in the Temple, was already deeply in love with Vanessa and was to marry her three years later. Duncan Grant floated dreamily in and out from his bare studio in Upper Baker Street.

Meanwhile another household of which they were all to become familiars was being established at 44 Bedford Square, not far away. Lady Ottoline Morrell, half-sister of the sixth Duke of Portland, had married Philip Morrell, an Oxford lawyer and later a Liberal M.P., a few years before and in 1905 moved house from Grosvenor Road to 'my favourite quarter of London, Bloomsbury.' Here she started her Thursday evening parties, to which she invited 'interesting people', that is to say members of the artistic world to which she yearned to belong. Lady Ottoline, one of the most extraordinary personalities of this or any age, deserves, and shall later receive, a fuller description. At this stage it is enough to say that she had already met Lytton at the home of Charles and Dora Sanger and found him 'most sympathetic', and knew Desmond MacCarthy, whom she claimed as 'for a time one of my closest friends'. Charles Conder, one of her earliest artist-friends, introduced her to Augustus John, whose nudes shocked her, and it was while sitting to him that she met Clive and Vanessa. Ottoline's attitude to artists was highly romantic: feeling herself to be one of them, prevented from proving it only by her ducal, philistine upbringing, she cast herself in the role of a feminine Maecenas. If she could herself not be a poet or painter she could at least give inspiration and encouragement to painters and poets, especially, as she said, 'to those who had not yet arrived'. It is doubtful whether any of those who accepted her hospitality without returning it were much encouraged by the experience. Some of her male guests were shocked by her rather predatory advances: others were not. All had their sexual inhibitions and relationships examined and discussed, and strenuous if clumsy efforts were made to cure or improve them as necessary. Somehow art took a second place to those more personal considerations. This was perfectly acceptable to the Bloomsbury friends she now easily acquired, but while taking every advantage of her generosity, they mocked her without mercy afterwards.

For Lytton and Virginia, the twin hubs of the Bloomsbury circle, the period from 1906 to the outbreak of war was a strangely unsatisfactory one. Both conscious of latent ability, neither had found the form in which to express it. Neither had the independence and security of a true home of their own. Lytton still lived under his mother's roof. Virginia left 46 Gordon Square to Clive and Vanessa when they married in 1907 and, with Adrian, took a four-year lease of 29 Fitzroy Square. In the same year Lady Strachey moved to Belsize Park Gardens, where, after his father's death in 1908, Lytton found existence increasingly intolerable. His work too was by now a drudgery. He was reviewing regularly both for Desmond MacCarthy's *New Quarterly* and his cousin St. Loe's *Spectator*, activities which gave him a welcome degree of financial independence, but at the same time prevented him from embarking on any major work. He also contributed articles on French literature to G. M. Trevelyan's *Independent Review*, and these were to lead him on to his first important work— *Landmarks in French Literature*.

Meanwhile, his health was if anything worse than ever. He had gastric troubles, and piles, and took fierce cures in Sweden with only temporary benefit. His love affairs ended in rejection. Duncan had set up house with Maynard and Swithinbank, an Oxford favourite, disappeared to India as a civil servant. On a visit to King's he met George Mallory, a young mountaineer later to meet his death on Everest, and gave him the adoration he had previously reserved for Thoby.

Rupert Brooke, with whom it was pleasant to spend a holiday at Lulworth in default of an exciting invitation to Paris by George Mallory which Lytton was unable to accept, was on the whole a disappointment. The great reputation which had followed Rupert from Rugby to King's was not, Lytton felt, supported by his performance as a companion and fellow-Apostle. He certainly cut a romantic figure with 'his pink cheeks and bright yellow hair' but this was not enough for Lytton, though James, now at Trinity, adored him. Lytton thought him 'egoistic and intellectually inadequate'.

In a vain effort to recapture the life he had loved at Trinity, he spent long periods at Cambridge, taking Mallory's old rooms for a term, and for a short while toying with the idea of living at the Old Vicarage next door to Rupert Brooke at Grantchester. But even the company of the Apostles, whose meetings he attended regularly, failed to re-create the old atmosphere. He felt out of it, and old. 'Am I altogether passé?' he asked Clive, at the age of 28. Writing to Duncan in 1908, with whom, in spite of his love affair with Maynard, Lytton was still on terms of emotional friendship, he said, 'I feel all topsy-turvy and out of place, as if I were a handkerchief dropped on the top of Mont Blanc.'

In a different and more sinister way, Virginia too was out of place. For her the sense of *déplacement* was a darker, deeper thing. Lytton was to find himself in the course of time and to

learn to accept, with a certain mocking humour, the pattern
which his strange personality imposed on his life. For Virginia,
it was to be an anguished, endless and unsuccessful search. And
whereas Lytton sought happiness in emotional human relationships, Virginia's search was for her own identity and had to be
pursued in solitude. For Lytton, love and friendship were
integral to his existence. For Virginia they were a relief from
the agony of self-examination.

While Thoby was still alive, regular Thursday evenings at
46 Gordon Square had begun, and Virginia continued these at
29 Fitzroy Square, the rather bare house where Adrian's neat
quarters contrasted sharply with Virginia's untidy upstairs
work-room. Virginia's hospitality was austere. 'Whisky, buns
and cocoa were the diet' said Duncan, served in Adrian's study.
Her manner with those with whom she felt out of sympathy
was equally austere: a limp, unsmiling handshake, a wide-eyed
angry astonishment at an insufficiently intelligent remark, a
fierce rejection of commonplace or insensitive attitudes. This
manner succeeded in excluding undesirables: they did not
return a second time. What remained was a small close circle
with whom she found it safe to relax. Here she radiated gaiety,
wit, fancy and affection. She was self-confident, expansive.
Only sometimes was there an air of rather too hectic excitement. She had, said David Garnett, the gift of sudden intimacy.
It is not surprising that Lytton chose her, in talk with Clive, as
the person he would most like to see coming along the street
towards him in a lonely town.

At these Thursday evenings, the only entertainment was
talk. 'Conversation' said Duncan. 'That was all.' 'Talking,
talking, talking' wrote Virginia later. 'As if everything could
be talked.' But it was talk among friends with whom it was at
least permissible for 'everything to be talked'—uninhibited,
irreverent, seriously gay, or just plain absurd. An extraordinary
characteristic of Bloomsbury talk must here be mentioned
since it struck all who heard it. It should first be explained that
all or most of the Strachey family shared a highly distinctive
quality of voice and manner of speech. 'The Strachey voice'
was well known. Lytton possessed it in a notable degree. It so
amused his Bloomsbury friends and, with its high-pitched

tones and idiosyncratic use of emphasis, seemed so well-adapted as a vehicle for the eccentric conversations in which Bloomsbury delighted that one by one they found themselves copying it. It became an identifying mark and a member of the Bloomsbury circle could infallibly be recognised by the use of it. As an affectation it aroused marked irritation in its hearers, diluted only rarely, as in Osbert Sitwell's case, by amusement. He wrote: 'the tones would convey with supreme efficacy the requisite degree of paradoxical interest, surprise, incredulity: in actual sound, analysed, they were unemphatic, save where emphasis was not to be expected; then there would be a sudden sticky stress, high where you would have presumed low, and the whole spoken sentence would run, as it were, at different speeds and on different gears and contain a good deal of expert but apparently meaningless syncopation.'

Lytton and Virginia now became close friends. Virginia got from Lytton a warm uncensorious friendship which she appreciated; and which she returned. With her he was never conscious of his physical ugliness or the absurdity of his mannerisms. By 1908 they were writing to each other frequently: Lytton described to her reading parties with Moore and his life among his mother's family on visits to Rothiemurchus. 'Hundreds of dead relations lurk behind every bush. They are all varieties . . . and all eminently repellent.' Virginia thought of him on holiday on the Lizard as 'a kind of Venetian prince, in sky-blue tights, lying on your back in an orchard, or balancing an exquisite leg in the air. . . .'

The letters at this stage show much affection, mutual confidence and admiration, expressed in the fanciful, whimsical style which they knew amused each other. The warmth of feeling between them might in other people have been expected to lead to a passionate relationship. They assumed for a while, for epistolary purposes, the bogus-romantic names of Eleanor Hadyng and Vane Hatherley. But Virginia's sexual needs were buried deep in a thicket of nervous and psychic confusions, and were probably in any case minimal, while Lytton's could be met only by another man. Virginia's attitude to Lytton was made clear when Hilton Young (later Lord Kennet), a devoted member of the Fitzroy Square circle, proposed marriage to her. She refused him and confessed that Lytton, with whom she was also not in love, was the only man she could think of marrying. Lytton at this time was suffering acutely from having lost Duncan to Maynard. To Leonard Woolf, still his confessor, though far away in Ceylon, he expressed the nearly intolerable anguish he was suffering. It was in this context that one of the most extraordinary episodes in the lives both of Lytton and Virginia occurred. Lytton describes it to his brother, James. 'On February 19th [it was in fact February 17th, 1909] I proposed to Virginia and was accepted. It was an awkward moment, as you may imagine, especially as I realised, the very minute it was happening, that the whole thing was repulsive to me. Her sense was amazing, and luckily it turned out that she's not in love. The result was that I was able to manage a fairly honourable retreat.' The retreat was not in fact contrived until the following day, and it is easy to imagine the chill horror of the intervening hours when each understood the ghastly mistake they had agreed to make. For marriage was no way out of their problems and both knew it. By an extraordinary coincidence at the very moment of Lytton's proposal a letter was on its way to him from Ceylon in which Leonard confided his intention of proposing to Virginia himself. Lytton replied to this letter, as might be expected, with alacrity and joy. He was sure, he said, that Virginia would accept him and that Leonard was just the man for her. 'You'd have,' he added, 'the immense advantage of physical desire.'

In this absurd way Lytton's dream of domestic peace, which had turned into a nightmare as soon as he attempted to make it a reality, blew away on a scented breeze from the East. It was neither the first nor the last time that an emotional crisis in his life turned into farce. Perhaps because of some deep-seated ineptitude, there seemed always to be a ludicrous element in his affairs of the heart. The same was not true of Virginia. But she too was relieved to escape from an undertaking she had hardly had any intention of making. Tacitly they agreed to understand that the whole episode was an expression, not of the emotional commitment which could provide a basis for marriage, but of the deep sympathy and unity of outlook which is the stuff of friendship. This friendship continued unbroken for the rest of their lives.

Meanwhile the problems remained. Virginia was writing her first novel, *The Voyage Out* (which was not to be published until 1915) and attempting in this way to call forth and exorcise the dark spirits against which her whole life was a battle. Lytton, whose reading at this stage largely consisted of the French classics, was about to give up his weekly *Spectator* essay in order to write *Landmarks in French Literature*, published in 1912.

Thus Lytton and Virginia were in the same state and at approximately the same stage in incipient authorship: that period in which fears and hopes, tremulous optimism and black despair alternate, and when the self-confidence without which no writer can begin is sapped both by the inherent difficulties of composition and by the absence of the encouragement which only publication can give.

Their literary purposes could not have been more different, and expressed totally different needs. Without too much over-simplification it can be said that Lytton simply needed success. He needed it for many reasons: on the practical level he needed the money which success would bring. Without it he was condemned to go on living in what he now felt to be the airless domesticity of his mother's home. He and his friends were agreed that to do so would stifle his gifts. But there were more profound reasons. It was necessary for Lytton to demonstrate to himself as well as to others that he was not the failure which he felt himself to be. A reputation, which he had already begun to achieve as a literary journalist, was not enough: anything less than a splendid, resounding success was for him the same as failure. To this extent he was no more a genuine Apostle, scorning the lure of the 'phenomenal', than Maynard. From the worldly point of view, however, Lytton's literary ambitions were normal and healthy.

Virginia's desire to be a writer, which was a burning fire within her at all times, was much more Apostolic than Lytton's: she needed, not spectacular success, but the acclaim of those people, however few, who were able by their acuity of judg-ment and delicacy of sense to assess the quality of good writing.

She would strive to win it by wringing the very life-blood from her veins and forcing it into the prose she would write. All of her personality—mind, emotion, desires, fears and longings—would go into her novels. There would be nothing left. As time went on more and more of her life would be absorbed into writing, until it became not merely the main occupation of her life, but in a real sense, existence itself. She lived in and through her writing: anything else—social life, her friends, her later work as a printer and publisher—became either a holiday or an escape from the true business of living, the laborious, agonising process of creative writing. There were deep psychological reasons for this. It is tempting to regard Virginia's life and death as a symbolic expression of her guilt-complex for having failed to keep her sick father alive. But a woman who has attempted suicide as a child has deep-seated conflicts and intolerances of which later unbalanced attitudes are only the expression. There can be no doubt that the intellectualism and high moral tone of her childhood home, and a lack of warmth which may have been there even before her mother's death, had a profound and irreversible effect on her. When it became her task as an adolescent girl to nurse her father through years of sickness she yearned to show him the tenderness which she deeply felt but which could not be expressed without some reciprocal show of love. In these circumstances it is not surprising that a feeling of guilt was added to the long pain of watching a beloved father die. But, however deep this feeling was, it was merely an additional agony for one who found so much unbearable. It was life itself which was incompatible with her. Her writing was an effort, appalling in its intensity, to create a world constitutionally tolerable to her and in which she had a place as an actor as well as an observer. The effort was in the end too much for her, as inevitably it had to be.

For both Virginia and Lytton, friendship with other like-minded people was a consolation and a need. Social life of the ordinary kind was not enough: it was not the same as, indeed it was in many ways the reverse of, a confident, approving association with those who did not find one ridiculous. Lytton, in company with strangers or mere acquaintances, that is with people who had not aroused or did not deserve his interest, betrayed his indifference or his inability to believe that they could really exist by ironic or amazed utterances in his unique falsetto. Or he lapsed into long silences, sometimes refusing through a whole dinner to take any part in conversation at all. Thursday evenings in Fitzroy Square were so different. Here talk flowed freely and was never dammed or retarded by lack of understanding or approval. Virginia could take off on flights of fantasy which were a delight to her and to those who listened. The indecencies with which Lytton was liable to lighten a literary argument were accepted joyfully. The Greek or the French way of life could be discussed with knowledge and understanding, but without solemnity or pedantry. What was demanded was a respect for aesthetic and intellectual excellence expressed with as much gaiety or wit as possible. It was necessary to be both literate and articulate. What was assumed was a quite intolerant rejection of any attitude, how-ever hallowed by convention, which could not stand up to the kind of questioning which Moore had taught, and which people like Virginia and Duncan did not have to learn.

Lytton, and to a much less extent, Virginia, had also found another set in which they were accepted and which they found acceptable. Lady Ottoline Morrell was already known to both of them, and their circles intersected both with each other and with those in which Augustus John, Roger Fry and other artists moved. Ottoline's admiration for Virginia—'This strange, lovely, furtive creature' as she described her, this 'Diana of the mind'—was full of the yearning she felt towards all artists. It was romantic and therefore, in the eyes of Bloomsbury, false. Virginia never took, as Lytton said, to the 'caviare' offered by Ottoline. Lytton himself, however, was rather shamefacedly attracted. Not only was her hospitality immensely generous to gifted people whom he liked, but she herself was a larger-than-life flamboyant figure whose exuberance and self-assurance were in fascinating contrast to his own diffidence and gaucherie.

Lytton's assimilation into her circle of intimates began when, meeting him at Cambridge, she invited him to her country cottage at Peppard. His acceptance of the invitation owed a good deal to the fact that Henry Lamb, a good-looking young

artist and protégé of Ottoline's, whom Lytton had admired at
a distance at an earlier party at 46 Gordon Square, would be a
fellow-guest, not certainly under the same roof but at the
village inn, the Dog, and using a studio the Morrells had found
for him. Henry Lamb was the younger brother of Walter
Lamb, a Trinity contemporary of Lytton's, who, while moving
in the same Cambridge circles as the later Bloomsbury friends,
was never fully accepted by them. Like Clive, Walter had
never succeeded in becoming an Apostle and was nicknamed
by Lytton 'the Corporal' with reference to his air of insensitive
self-importance. He was tolerated now at Bloomsbury parties,
was an habitué in Bedford Square, and had introduced Henry
to these circles. Henry had very considerable gifts as a painter,
although they were constantly overshadowed by those of his
friend and mentor, Augustus John. He copied both the latter's
flamboyant style of dress and his enthusiastic pursuit of
attractive women.

At Peppard an extraordinary situation was now created.
Ottoline's attitude to Lamb was ostensibly maternal: she felt,
as she felt with so many other artists and with as little justification, that she could help him. She took him for walks in the
woods, where she probably failed to recognise her disappointment that he did not make love to her. That kind of intimacy
developed later, and there was a ludicrous episode at Garsington, her house near Oxford, when she was discovered in a hot
embrace with him which she explained by saying that she was
'giving Henry an aspirin'. Lytton was in no doubt about his
feelings for the dazzlingly handsome painter. He was utterly
in love, and was to remain so for several years. Ottoline
noticed that his 'sensations were tickled by Lamb's beauty' but
did not perhaps realise how deeply he was affected.

From now on Lytton would be a frequent guest of Ottoline's.
He was attracted by the strange exuberance of her dress and
manner, pleased by her obvious admiration, and not at all
averse from having made such a strong impression on the
sister of a Duke. Through her he had met not only Henry
Lamb, but the great Augustus John himself and other painters.
Although he never appreciated contemporary art—he considered Clive Bell's admiration for Picasso and Matisse simply

absurd—he liked the Bohemian style of its practitioners. Partly in order to make himself more acceptable to Henry, but partly, too, for his own pleasure, he now adopted a more exotic appearance. He wore a black cloak and an extraordinary wide-brimmed, high-crowned hat. He had his ears pierced, wore ear-rings and let his hair grow. If he never succeeded in looking like a painter, he achieved a highly unusual Dracula-like effect which was most striking. The last and most permanently characteristic contribution was added by the beard which he grew while recovering from mumps in an hotel at Corfe in 1911. Until now all he had dared was a rather dreary moustache: now he appeared with a splendid luxuriant growth, a bright reddish-brown in colour, which was greeted with enthusiasm by Ottoline and all his friends.

For the first time he had succeeded in turning his bodily defects into assets. If he could never have the physical splendour of Thoby or Mallory he could, he now realised, have as striking an appearance and even, in terms of individuality, a more remarkable one. It is perhaps a mark of the strong feminine streak in his make-up that his growing of a beard did as much for his self-confidence and thus his happiness as a new hair-style is said to do for a woman. From now on Lytton at least *looked* distinguished: he knew he did. But was he really? He still had to find out, and there was depressingly little evidence.

In 1912, after a good deal of wrestling both with the task of authorship and frequent attacks of ill health, *Landmarks in French Literature* at last appeared. There was, and is, no doubt of its excellence. His love of and judgments upon French writers are those of a Frenchman: his style is his own. It is a sensitive study of a literature which, though superficially familiar to most educated Englishmen, is generally misunderstood by those for whom Racine compares unfavourably with Shakespeare and Rabelais is incomprehensible as well as indecent. It is still, and still deserves to be, in print. Lytton was glad to have finished it, modestly content with it as a piece of writing, and happy at the *succès d'estime* which it achieved. But it was a little book, and what was literature compared with life? How could he use his talents to express his identity with the main stream of human development, with the emotions, desires and unconfessed impulsions which make men and women—and he was almost as much one as the other—act, feel and make their impact? He had written a good deal of verse: that was easy enough, too easy no doubt. Lytton's love-poetry was no better and no worse than could be produced by any young man with a soft heart and a feeling for words. No sooner was *Landmarks* in print than he turned his hand to play-writing. By the end of the year *The Son of Heaven*, a melodrama about a Chinese count, was going the rounds of the actor-managers. It had an enthusiastic reception: Granville-Barker in London and Max Reinhardt in Moscow both thought that it had every prospect of becoming a great success on the stage. But no one would go quite as far as accepting it, and in fact it was never produced until Lytton's fame was already established, when in 1925 there were two charity performances at the Scala.

Lytton had hoped to make some quick money from the play: he was therefore once more disappointed. He could hardly have regarded it as the great work he longed to write. To Ottoline, after he had finished the play, he expressed his passionate desire 'to achieve something—not unworthy of my hopes, my imaginations and the spirit I feel to be mine . . . Oh to bound forward and triumph!'

'Bounding forward' was a bold procedure quite out of keeping with Lytton's nervous and tentative personality: it was almost by accident, and as a product of a plan that had started off quite differently, that Lytton at this stage, in one of the numerous country cottages to which he retired to write, began a study of Cardinal Manning, which was to lead directly to *Eminent Victorians*. He told Ottoline that he thought a series of short biographies of eminent persons 'might be entertaining', written, as his first effort on Manning was, 'from a slightly cynical standpoint'. To Virginia, however, he confided openly his growing conviction that the Victorians were, by and large, a 'set of mouthing, bungling hypocrites'.

The year 1912 was thus a turning point for Lytton. The new 'persona' which his beard and exotic clothing had given him—his wardrobe now included a striking yellow coat worn over

corduroys, an orange waistcoat and—incredibly—a peaked
cap and striped breeches to mark his mastery of the impossible
art of hacking—was one of self-confidence: he felt that he was,
and began to act as if he were, somebody. No doubt other
factors—increasing maturity, the support of friends, a firm
reputation as a literary journalist—contributed to this development, and perhaps his new appearance merely expressed the
fact. But the expression itself was critical—it committed him
to the personality his clothes suggested. He had to have the
courage of his wardrobe and, no doubt to his own astonishment, he found that increasingly he had. He began to sign his
essays and reviews, not with the modest, almost anonymous
'G. L. Strachey' ('Who might he be?') but boldly and confidently 'Lytton Strachey' ('*Lytton* Strachey, of course'). There
were fears and doubts and even despairs ahead, but never
again the blank, black hopelessness of his first London years.

    For Virginia too 1912 was a landmark. In the previous June
Leonard Woolf had returned from Ceylon on a year's leave.
Now he carried out the intention he had already expressed to
Lytton and proposed to Virginia. She asked for time to
consider his offer, and Leonard asked for an extension of his
leave so that he might await her decision. His application was
refused and he at once sent in his resignation. Virginia's reaction
to his proposal of marriage had in fact crystallised Leonard's
growing sense that he was not cut out for a career in the
Colonial Service. He had, as he records, enjoyed his work in
the 'remote, backward district' where he had hitherto served,
and had earned a high reputation: as a consequence he knew
that he had to expect, on his return to duty, to be posted to an
appointment near 'the seats of power in Colombo'. The
prospect became increasingly distasteful to him. Not only was
the 'Kiplingesque society' of Ceylon unattractive to him, but
he had no wish, by the successful exercise of an authority he
did not enjoy wielding, to end up, as he had good reason to
expect, as a Governor, with all the trappings of office, cut off
from the simple people he liked to serve but did not wish to
rule. Now Virginia had solved his problem for him, and he
gave up what would certainly have been a distinguished career
for an uncertain future in some yet unspecified literary field.

For his first six months in England he divided his time between Cambridge and London, finally taking rooms at 38 Brunswick Square, where Virginia and Adrian now lived, and where Maynard and Duncan were also lodgers.

At Cambridge he re-entered the circle of the Apostles and within a month went to stay at Beckey House on Dartmoor with Lytton and G. E. Moore, who were both busy writing. Lytton was groaning over *Landmarks*, Moore adding qualification after qualification to sentences laboriously composed for his new book on Ethics. Leonard himself was planning a novel with a Ceylon background, *The Village in the Jungle*, which he began to write soon afterwards.

He had already renewed contact with Clive, and had dined alone with him and Vanessa in Gordon Square. After dinner they were joined by Virginia, Duncan and Walter Lamb. This evening was for Leonard the starting-point of a new life, the life which was from then on to provide his natural setting. There was for him, as they sat talking, a sense of emotional and intellectual intimacy, of complete freedom of thought and speech, deeper and easier even than among the Apostles. It was above all the presence of Virginia and Vanessa which gave this additional quality. He noticed that Christian names were now used—a significant change from 1904 when Apostles used surnames only.

Leonard, who, with his love of accuracy and order, was concerned in his autobiography to date and document the past, gives this dinner-party as, at least for himself, the first beginnings of what was to become Bloomsbury. 'Bloomsbury' he writes, '. . . did not exist in 1911: it came into existence in the three years 1912 to 1914'. He lists its members—Vanessa, Virginia and Adrian; Lytton, Clive, Maynard, Duncan, E. M. Forster, Saxon Sydney-Turner, Roger Fry, the MacCarthies and himself. He points out that at this time only Clive and Vanessa and Saxon lived, strictly speaking, in Bloomsbury, whereas ten years later all except the MacCarthies had their homes there. This is all a little too dogmatic and definite and contributes to the false view that Bloomsbury was an entity, almost a formal body, whose foundation, location and membership could be precisely dated and listed. Leonard is not really entitled to judge such an intangible thing as the development of friendships during the years preceding his return from Ceylon. What for him was a sudden, delightful dawn had been shedding its light for some time on those who had remained in England: for them it was, if not noon, already mid-morning.

Leonard recalls vividly the impression made on him by the two women who gave charm and brilliance to the circle of which they were the centre. Vanessa he thought the more beautiful, her 'form of features more perfect, her eyes bigger and better, her complexion more glowing'. She was physically splendid, with a 'most beautiful speaking voice'. Although he thought he could trace in her an extreme sensitivity and a nervous tension rather like Virginia's, there was too 'something adamantine in the content and language of her judgments', a 'lapidification of character' noticeable in other members of her family—her father, for example, Thoby, and her aunt, the formidable Principal of Newnham! Her great charm did not exclude an occasional outburst of caustic humour.

What impressed him most about Virginia (with whom in his autobiography he does not yet admit to being in love, in spite of his earlier correspondence with Lytton) was, apart from her beauty and charm, a nobility of manner and appearance which arose in part from her emotional awareness and was in part morbid (as later became clear) in origin. 'Even the shape of her face changed with extraordinary rapidity' he wrote, 'as the winds of mental strain, illness or worry passed over its surface'. In conversation she might suddenly take flight with a fantastic, dreamlike description of some event or place or person.

Writing long afterwards, Leonard recognises this as evidence of the genius she certainly already possessed, defining genius as a faculty employing fundamentally non-normal mental processes. She lived a good deal in an inner world of unreality, to an extent which could affect her physically. There was even a faintly unreal quality in her dress and appearance as she went 'with a slightly shuffling movement along the streets in the shadow of a dream'.

Leonard's identification with Bloomsbury was registered by

his membership of Virginia's Brunswick Square household. It was a boarding-house, if that is the word, like no other. Although its inhabitants were all close friends, privacy was fanatically respected. Meals, excellent in quality and preparation, were deposited on trays in the hall and taken to individual rooms to be eaten. It was accepted that everyone should work in solitude according to a programme which might be strict, but which allowed periods of delightful relaxation in one or another's room. It was on one of these occasions in May that after lunch in her room, Virginia at last, and quite suddenly, told Leonard that she loved and would marry him.

Leonard had long since confessed his love to her, and had been urging his suit with assiduity. Lytton, when he heard that it had succeeded, was delighted; so too was Duncan who, according to Lytton, fell flat on the floor at the news. Lytton could not resist adding his own fictitious embroidery to the story of the love-affair. He wrote to Ottoline with an absurd account of one of Leonard's unsuccessful proposals. He alleged that this occurred on a train journey, and that this time Virginia actually accepted him. Owing to the rattling of the train, however, Leonard did not hear her reply and, assuming it was probably once more negative, took up his newspaper. 'What?' he asked, whereupon Virginia, suddenly taking flight, replied, 'Oh, nothing' and the matter was dropped.

Meanwhile, Virginia had taken the lease of Asheham House at Firle in Sussex, which she had discovered on an earlier visit with Leonard, and throughout the summer he was regularly there, usually with Adrian, Vanessa or Roger Fry, occasionally with Lytton or Lytton's sister, Marjorie. Four miles from Lewes, Asheham stood by itself, overshadowed by elms with a steep down rising behind it. It was a romantic and melancholy house, with its own ghost, said to have been seen by Clive, and even by contemporary standards primitive. A pump was the only water supply, cooking was by oil stove, and candles provided lighting. There was an earth closet. It was to be their country home for seven years.

At the time of their marriage, Virginia's and Leonard's financial position and prospects were precarious. Leonard was writing his novel but had no other employment. He had, however, won £690 in a sweepstake, enough in those days to keep him for two years. Virginia had an invested income of £400 a year and was writing and re-writing *The Voyage Out*. She also wrote reviews, but her output was limited by the constant need she felt to re-write them five or six times before allowing them to go for publication. Her income from her novels was to remain negligible, although her reputation grew steadily, for the next 15 years. Leonard's novel, and a second one written shortly after the first, brought him practically nothing.

They were married in August 1912 at St Pancras Register Office. An absurd episode, of the kind one learns to expect at solemn moments in the life of Bloomsbury, interrupted the ceremony when Vanessa broke in to ask the registrar how she could change the name of her two-year-old son from Claudian to Quentin. The honeymoon was largely spent wandering through Provence and Spain, where Virginia wrote to Lytton that 'several times the proper business of bed has been interrupted by mosquitoes. . . . They always choose my left ear, Leonard's right ear. Whatever position they chance to find us in.' Back in London they lived at Clifford's Inn where, through the winter, Virginia wrote, re-wrote and wrote again the last chapters of *The Voyage Out*. When at last in March it was finished Leonard took it to her half-brother, Gerald Duckworth the publisher, who accepted it on the advice of Edward Garnett.

An appalling pattern, to be repeated with varying intensity with the completion of each successive novel, now revealed itself for the first time. Although the process of creative writing was often agonising to Virginia, and was carried out against constant self-criticism, leading to bouts of despair, she was able, as long as the book she was engaged on was incomplete, to work on it day by day, and even to enjoy hours of relaxation. When it was finished, however, and went out of her hands, to be published and read and to be subjected to review and criticism, Virginia became sick with horror. The prospect that a novel which had become an integral part of her existence, which she had destroyed and re-written half a dozen times

which she could not, however imperfect, make any better by
any power at her disposal, should now be read and criticised
by strangers was intolerable to her. What in a normal writer
would have been a natural sensitiveness to the possibility of
adverse comment, became in Virginia a horror which she could
not control. From insomnia and headaches the horror grew
until it became madness. By the summer of 1913 it was clear
that she was seriously ill and for a year she suffered a manic-
depressive breakdown. In the manic phase she was violent with
her nurses, four of whom were for long periods required, and
was subject to delusions. In the depressive phase she barely
spoke or ate and had suicidal tendencies: she took an overdose
of veronal that autumn. She was well enough to be moved to
Asheham in November, and stayed there until the following
summer. But the improvement was only a temporary reprieve.
By the following February she was as ill as before, with long
periods of incoherent, unbroken talking ending in coma. It was
not until the end of 1915 that the symptoms at last disappeared.
Thus for two and a half years, with an interval of a few months,
Virginia had been severely ill, and for considerable periods
actually insane. It was a high price to pay for the writing of a
novel. It was the price, perhaps, which she had to pay for living
at all. Whereas most people, even the most gifted and sensitive,
have periods of calm and areas of indifference, which provide
both the strength for creative effort, and the stability needed for
it, Virginia, while she was working, had no such resources. On
the other hand, not to have written, not to have spun from her
imagination a fabric of words and images and people, would
have been as much the death as that which she eventually found
for herself.

V

Developments and Departures

THE period between Vanessa's marriage to Clive and Virginia's to Leonard had been an emotionally charged one for the two sisters. For Vanessa there were first the joys of motherhood: in 1908 Julian was born, and two years later, Claudian, to be re-named Quentin. She was absorbed by her babies almost to the point of obsession, and was to remain all her life a passionately devoted mother. Clive was in principle a proud father and happy for Vanessa's happiness: in practice, the noise and nastiness inseparable from infancy were highly repugnant to him and he was glad of, and perhaps needed, the opportunity to get away when he could.

An opportunity was at hand. Within weeks of Julian's birth, Clive, Vanessa and Adrian joined Virginia for a stay at St Ives. Virginia had always understood that Vanessa's marriage would involve a change in their relationship, although in fact they remained on terms of intimacy rarely found among sisters. She now felt both cut off from Vanessa who could think of no one but her baby and jealous of a happiness and fulfilment from which she was in the nature of things excluded. It suited both her and Clive to go for long walks alone together. For Clive, they provided relief from domestic exasperations and for Virginia they suspended the necessity of observing those of Vanessa's joys she was unable to share. Clive, always ready to admire an attractive woman, had a particular admiration for Virginia. It was natural to him to offer gallantries to his sister-in-law and, when they were accepted, to flirt with her. It is certain that she offered him no lures, but equally certain that she was warmed by his attentions and happy to receive them. Her reaction was by no means only an expression of the affection she felt for him: it revealed some of the dark side of her character. She was seizing in fact the opportunity which offered itself to open up a breach in Vanessa's self-contained happiness. There was, as there almost invariably was in Virginia's closest relationships, malice in it. It is interesting that, running alongside this titillating sexual relationship, and almost completely independent of it, there was a literary one almost amounting to collaboration. Virginia was engaged on the novel, called at this stage *Melymbrosia*, which was to become *The Voyage Out*. For the first and last time in her life as a writer she wanted criticism. She sent her manuscripts to Clive for his opinion, putting herself, in a phrase hardly recognisable from Virginia's pen, 'into [his] hands with great confidence'. He responded at some length and with a frankness which in later years might have made her ill. He thought the novel 'wonderful' and praised it with the kind of understanding that Virginia was delighted to recognise. At the same time, she accepted humbly and happily his damnation of unsuccessful passages— 'the dull apparent', in his phrase, that at times concealed 'the thrilling real'. Much later she was to remind him that he was 'the first person who ever thought I'd write well', a statement which seemed to Clive, as he told Leonard 'the finest feather I shall ever be able to stick in my cap'.

Meanwhile, there were kisses as well as criticism, and admiration expressed, not in writing, but in tentative caresses. Vanessa was thoroughly alive to the situation, and deeply pained by it. In the following year, Virginia, Lytton, Clive, Vanessa and others joined in a fanciful letter-writing game, in which they all took different names and tried to construct an epistolary novel between them. The letters from Clive, writing as James Philips, to Virginia as Elinor Hadyng, were so openly amorous that Lytton felt it appropriate to chide Virginia, pointing out the pain they caused to Vanessa. Virginia wriggled: she could conceal from him neither the discomfort nor the satisfaction she felt.

When in 1909, Virginia went to Florence with Clive and Vanessa, the flirtation continued. Virginia's coquetry and evasion began to annoy Clive, just as his occasional gestures of love towards Vanessa irritated Virginia: she left after a fortnight and made her way home alone.

However pained Vanessa was by the situation, she understood Clive and Virginia well enough to keep a cool head, and it was part of her generous nature to sympathise with Virginia's bleak sense of loneliness. She wrote at this time to Margery Snowden, an intimate friend: 'I am sometimes impressed with the pathos of her position . . . living with Adrian who does not appreciate her . . . I have come to think that in spite of all drawbacks she had better marry'. Virginia showed little sign of wishing to do so. Walter Lamb was to be no more successful with her than Hilton Young had been.

In 1910 an event occurred which was to lead to solutions, for Vanessa and Clive, if not for Virginia. Clive and Vanessa travelled from Cambridge to London with Roger Fry: it was their first meeting. The impact on them all was strong and immediate. Clive was delighted by this man at the height of his eminence as an art critic and connoisseur, who had rejected the Directorship of the National Gallery in order to become Curator of Paintings at the Metropolitan Museum of New York, but was yet entirely without pomposity or conceit. The gap in age—he was some fifteen years their senior—might not have existed. Their views on painting matched astoundingly well. Roger's professional life, and Clive's part in it, will be dealt with in a later chapter. The state of his personal life is, however, relevant here. His wife Helen, mentally unstable for years, had just been confined to a mental home from which she was never to emerge. He himself, after the last of a series of differences with J. Pierpont Morgan, the Chairman of Trustees of the Metropolitan Museum, had just been dismissed from his post there. It was the end of his career as an official, and the beginning of a more uncertain but more exciting life as a free lance. His chance meeting with Clive and Vanessa came therefore at an interesting moment. The parting of the ways was behind him, but the road ahead was not clearly marked. His whole life, both personal and professional, had now to be reconstructed, and he had scarcely begun the process. He was therefore delighted when Clive and Vanessa introduced him to their friends in London, and they were equally delighted to find him one of their own kind. No expert at this stage on English painting, he was interested and excited by the work Vanessa and Duncan Grant were doing. Clive and Vanessa, for their part, gave Roger enthusiastic help in mounting the first Post-Impressionist Exhibition which took place later that year.

In 1911, Roger accompanied Clive, Vanessa and Harry Norton to Turkey. Here Vanessa, after a miscarriage, fell ill and she and Roger fell in love, perhaps in that order, for Roger took masterful charge of the sick-room. Virginia, who hurried out to join them when she guessed from Clive's letters that Vanessa was more ill than he wanted to admit, considered that Roger saved her life. However that may be, it was Roger's entry into her life that enabled Vanessa to come to terms with her marriage. In theory an advocate of sexual licence, she had found in practice that Clive's excursions in this field with a beloved sister, though falling far short of what she regarded as permissible, distressed her deeply: much more deeply, she realised, than his taste, which she must by now have recognised, for emotional adventures with women at large. Roger provided what Vanessa at this stage needed—passion to which she could, and did, respond and an emotional satisfaction which masked her distress over Virginia. Lytton, never an admirer of Roger, was sceptical as to the intimacy of the relationship and the extent to which Vanessa was involved. Roger's letters, however, leave no room for doubt. He writes to her of their 'extraordinary intimacy which leaves nothing to be said, scarcely anything to take form in the mind'. 'You give me', he wrote, 'more than I would ever dare to ask, and that so freely with such a gesture of boundless generosity that I can find no room in me for the least prick of jealousy.' Roger's enthusiasms always led him into language more notable for ecstasy than accuracy. But if he could rhapsodise over 'your torso that's hewn in such great planes and yet is so polished, your "squareness" beneath the armpits' he was expressing an artist's clear visual memory of a physical experience. 'Oh Nessa,' he wrote, 'it was good, our little married life.'

It was at this time, and through this experience, that the marriage of Clive and Vanessa gradually came to take its permanent form—what Quentin Bell calls a 'union of friendship'. Clive would move through a series of loves and would live his own life largely in London. Vanessa would be happy in her motherhood and, later, in her lifelong love for Duncan

Grant. But the affection felt for each other by Clive and Vanessa remained. Clive was always a member of the family, staying under the same roof in Sussex or Bloomsbury, going on joint trips abroad, making his own contribution of wit, charm and unfailing good humour, on excellent terms with everybody.

It was not quite so simple for Roger. When after three joyful years Vanessa turned from him to Duncan he was profoundly distressed. For some time he did not fully appreciate what had occurred. In 1915 he could still complain to her 'You work with him constantly, you're his usual and constant pal, you play with him, you can spend a week in the country alone with him. He gives you everything except love. . . .' It was not quite like that, and he eventually had to admit that he had lost her. When at last he was reconciled to the facts, he remained on terms of friendship both with Vanessa and Duncan, and was later to write an appreciative book on Duncan's painting. Clive's flirtation with Virginia came to nothing: it remained what it had always been—for Clive it was both his normal reflex to an exceptionally charming woman and an expression of true admiration for her gifts as well as her charm, and Virginia continued to take a wicked but cautious pleasure in the attentions of her sister's attractive husband.

While Roger was awakening London to the merits of the modern French painters and constructing what became a rather top-heavy structure of aesthetic theory over and around their work, Will Rothenstein had assembled at the Slade School of Art a scattering of gifted young English artists. Like all young artists, they were obsessed with their art, alternately made desperate by technical problems that seemed to have no solution, and elated by sudden successes achieved by means they tried in vain to repeat. Most of them were poor, but at least they were poor together and could offer each other the comforts which cost nothing. They fell in and out of love in much the same way as they loved and hated their art, and with the same intensity. As apprentices with little finished work to show, they did not expect patrons. They were nevertheless obvious targets for Ottoline's hospitality. By definition they qualified for her encouragement, and some, the handsomer and more attractive, began to find themselves at her parties. If they were puzzled to find themselves made much of, and baffled by Ottoline's incomprehensible efforts to show that she, too, was at heart a fellow-artist, they were soothed by her generosity and enjoyed the company of the writers and art patrons they met at her house.

Mark Gertler, one of Ottoline's particular favourites, was the youngest child of a Spitalfields furrier, a Jew of Austrian and Polish descent, whose talents had been recognised by Rothenstein. At his prompting, the Jewish Educational Aid Society had given him a grant to enable him to study at the Slade. It was a good investment and he was to become a painter of distinction. A fellow-student was C. R. W. Nevinson, later to achieve renown in his specialised field as a war artist. Through Nevinson, Mark met Dora Carrington, one of a small group led in a vague, gentle way by Dorothy Brett, daughter of Lord Esher, the courtier who was at the same time a behind-the-scenes political force and the able editor of Queen Victoria's letters. Both girls used only their surnames and continued the habit life-long. Paul Nash, a fellow-student, had been struck by Carrington, whom he first saw in the antique class, with her very blue eyes and 'incredibly thick pigtails of red-gold hair'. She was, he found, the dominating personality in the Brett group, a quaint, amusing and striking figure, with turned-in toes and a stutter which only added to her charm. When she cut her hair into a heavy golden bell, her appearance was even more entrancing. Mark fell in love, deeply, lastingly, and very simply. For Carrington, love was never to be simple. Her childhood had been filled with complex relationships and she emerged with tangled senses and an emotional confusion from which she was never to escape. She had loved her father, a sensitive affectionate man, practically confined to his invalid chair. Of her brothers, Teddy was a charming, good-looking, superbly masculine boy, while Noel, equally charming, was intellectual and artistic. Carrington was fond of Noel, and adored Teddy. There was an elder sister, but she married young and faded from the picture. Her mother was a hectoring, insensitive and demanding woman. She was totally incapable of understanding, still less of sympathising with the needs either

of her husband or her daughter. Carrington's passionate love
for her father was constantly frustrated by her mother's lack of
feeling, and intensified by his patient acceptance of her short-
comings. The contrast between the men of the family, with
their sweetness and intelligence and the one other woman, so
markedly their inferior, may have contributed to Carrington's
dislike of being a woman, amounting at times to fierce disgust
and self-contempt. She hated in particular the physical evidence
of womanhood—menstruation and the inability to react with
automatic regularity to sexual stimulation. When in adult life
she had charming women friends, it is not surprising that they
aroused strong lesbian emotions in her. Her love affairs with
men were almost never satisfactory. Some of the complex
reasons for this will emerge later in her story, but always
beneath them was the, to her, inexcusable inferiority of being
a woman. Since at the same time she was easily sexually excited
by male beauty and equally susceptible emotionally, there
would be little tranquillity in her love life.

In 1912, when Gertler first confessed his love for Carrington,
she was Nevinson's girl. Gertler's persistence, however,
together with his physical beauty and Jewish charm, won as
much of Carrington's heart as she was able at this stage to give
anyone and they became, in everything but the final physical
sense, lovers. Carrington's refusal to become his mistress drove
Mark to despair, and she, too, was distressed by her inability to
respond to his passion. Gilbert Cannan, the novelist, a close
friend of Mark's, observed the relationship with professional
interest and angered them both by making it and them the
subject of his novel *Mendel*. It was a poor novel. Cannan was
an habitué of Ottoline's Bedford Square soirées where, with
his good looks and astringent humour, he had a strong temporary attraction for Lytton. It was at Cannan's insistence that
Ottoline made the acquaintance of Mark: she invited him, and
with him Carrington, to the opera. She also went to Spitalfields
to see Mark's paintings, which impressed her so much that she
made him bring his 'Fruit Stall' to Bedford Square for Sickert's
inspection. It passed muster and Ottoline bought it for the
Contemporary Art Society of which she, with Roger Fry, was
a founder.

At Bedford Square, Carrington and Mark now joined a circle which included their fellow-students, Dorothy Brett, Paul and John Nash, and Barbara Hiles, who was to be a life-long Bloomsbury friend. Augustus John was a regular member too. And it was here that Carrington first made the contact with Bloomsbury that was to shape her whole life.

It is perhaps no longer proper to refer to the group who appeared regularly at the Bedford Square soirées as 'Ottoline's circle'. A circle is a very satisfactory shape: the group of people whom Ottoline had gradually assembled formed at best an irregular and unstable polygon. All distinguished, or at least gifted, in one field or another, they were not always compatible. There could be little common ground between Winston Churchill and Arnold Bennett and still less between Lord Henry Bentinck and Stanley Spencer. Some of Ottoline's guests, like David Garnett and D. H. Lawrence, became incompatible with their hostess. Others, after a trial, were dropped. Fluctuations of this sort soon make the geometrical metaphor inappropriate.

The immediate pre-war years were formative for Bloomsbury. Not only had Ottoline established her position in a pattern that was to be valid for twenty years but new friendships were born which were to permanently enrich the lives of what had hitherto been a tiny côterie based on Cambridge and the Stephen and Strachey families. Lytton and Virginia, Clive and Roger, all in this period took the first steps on the paths they were to follow lifelong.

In 1913, Virginia, now married to Leonard, had finished *The Voyage Out* and was in a serious state of psychic disintegration which was to repeat itself as later novels were completed and offered for publication. Lytton, in the same year, succeeded at last in freeing himself from the suffocating atmosphere of his mother's household at Belsize Park Gardens and was beginning to work on the biographies which became *Eminent Victorians*. He was in love with Henry Lamb. In 1913, too, Ottoline decided to leave London and live in the country.

It was an exciting year in many ways. The Bloomsbury parties were at their wildest. There was Oliver Strachey's fancy dress affair, with Duncan as a pregnant whore and Saxon Sydney-Turner as a eunuch. At Adrian Stephen's party most of the guests seemed to undress, Duncan reducing his costume to bathing drawers, and Marjorie Strachey (according to Lytton) wearing a miniature of the Prince Consort and apparently nothing else. Vanessa shed so many clothes while dancing that she ended up naked to the waist. At a party given by Karin Costelloe, later to marry Adrian, the highlight was a farce based on the complex love-relationships of men disguised as women and vice versa, in which Duncan, Clive, Vanessa and Marjorie played leading roles: it was all highly amusing and most improper.

The important artistic event of the year was the appearance of the Russian Ballet, with Nijinsky and 'Le Sacre du Printemps', Stravinsky's new work. Lytton was horrified by Stravinsky's music but excited by Nijinsky and eager to meet him. He got Ottoline to arrange a meeting early in the following year, and bought a purple suit and an orange stock to wear for the occasion. He found Nijinsky very attractive, in spite of the impossibility of talking to him. Ottoline found no such difficulty, since she, unlike Lytton, was prepared to use French as the medium. Lytton overheard her, tête-à-tête with the dancer. 'Quand vous dansez, vous n'êtes pas un homme—vous êtes une idée. C'est ça, n'est-ce pas, qui est l'art? . . . Vous avez lu Platon sans doute.' It is not surprising that Nijinsky could find nothing but a grunt in reply.

Lytton, meanwhile, had decided that he must, like Leonard and Virginia, find a country cottage. Having failed to find what he wanted, he toyed for some time with the idea of building one, and while searching Wiltshire for a suitable site, stayed with Hilton Young at the Lacket, his cottage near Marlborough. When, in the spring of 1913, Hilton offered to let it to Lytton, he snapped up the offer and the Lacket became his main home until 1915. Here he was able to make a serious start at writing *Eminent Victorians*. Here he was at last free from his family.

The Lacket was a lonely, thatched cottage, separated from the road by a high box hedge, and sheltered at the back by a hillside scattered with large sarsen stones known in Wiltshire as 'grey wethers'. It had five bedrooms and was thus large enough to accommodate the stream of Lytton's guests, whose numbers and frequency so upset old Mrs Templeman who looked after him.

He paid Hilton Young £30 a year for the Lacket. With what was left of a £100 gift from Harry Norton, with another £100 from his mother, the interest on his East India stocks, the fees for his essays and reviews, and at least the prospect of royalties on *Landmarks in French Literature*, Lytton contrived to do on a modest scale almost all he wanted to do—to make the occasional trip abroad and frequent visits to London, and, best of all, to entertain his friends under his own roof. Desmond came to stay, as far as ever from writing anything important, but with all his old charm undimmed. Leonard took advantage of a temporary improvement in Virginia's condition to spend a week there in the spring of 1914.

The first Christmas party he held after the outbreak of war was notable for the beginning of his friendship with David Garnett, who had been invited as a friend of Francis Birrell. Francis was the son of Augustine Birrell, leading politician and occasional essayist, and had attracted Lytton when they met a few years before at Cambridge where Francis was a King's undergraduate. David Garnett, now aged 22, was doing a year's research in zoology at Imperial College. As the son of Edward Garnett, Duckworth's reader who recommended the publication of *The Voyage Out*, and Constance, the brilliant translator of the Russian classics, his background was, however, entirely literary and artistic, and he was completely at home with Lytton and his other guests—James Strachey, and Duncan, for example, and two of the beautiful Olivier girls from Cambridge.

At the Lacket, David observed his host. 'Lytton,' he wrote, 'was tall and rather emaciated, with a reddish beard and lank dark hair which hung in a long lock over his forehead and was cut off squarely, in pudding-basin fashion, at the back of his head. His nose was large with a high bridge; he wore gold-rimmed spectacles and was obviously rather short-sighted.' He was struck by Lytton's gentleness and the warmth of his hospitality, and at the same time warily conscious of his capacity for boredom. Before the visit was over he had emerged successfully from the searching examination to which Lytton submitted any potential new friend. He was perhaps a little boisterous—Lytton disapproved of young men diving through box hedges on Christmas morning out of sheer high spirits—and he did not share Lytton's sexual tendencies, but he was charming, sensitive and probably gifted. He was, later, with the publication of *Lady into Fox* to achieve overnight much the kind of triumph that Lytton longed for. Meanwhile, he had written nothing and was very ready to listen to Lytton reading his own short story, *Ermyntrude and Esmerelda*, a deliberately lubricous account of the awakening of sexual desire in two young women. (David claimed later that it was this story which revealed to him his own deep need to be what he called 'a libertine'—that is one who, in his relations with women, was untrammelled by the shackles of conventional morality—and determined him to follow his instinctive desires wherever they might lead. They led him in fact into innumerable love affairs as well as two marriages.) As well as gaining Lytton's approval, he at once got on to terms with Duncan. A long walk which they took together was the beginning of a lifelong friendship.

The impression David made at the Lacket that Christmas was enough to open the doors of Bloomsbury to him, and he was soon on terms of intimacy with them all. Duncan did a portrait of him.

Vanessa took tea with him in his dingy rooms in Pond Place, and kissed him. David describes her as she appeared to him then. 'Vanessa was a very beautiful woman, tall and striking in appearance. She had a lovely sensitive mouth, strangely innocent grey-blue eyes, with hooded lids, and straight brown hair, parted in the middle, which swept over her ears and was worn in a bun on the nape of the neck. Her face was a perfect oval and recalled that of a Gothic madonna sculptured at Chartres or Reims.' He was charmed by her humour and spontaneity: she was, he thought, as intelligent as Virginia, but without the vanity and self-obsession that marked her sister. 'Her brain,' he says, 'was original and logical, and she was a quick reasoner, never hesitating to put forward her views. She never produced the same impression of being such a brilliant conversationalist as Virginia, but she was witty and very fond of making bawdy jokes. Like Virginia, she often showed her teasing affection by jokes at the expense of those she loved.' At the same time, he recognised her way, shared to a large extent by Virginia and Lytton, of dividing her acquaintances into two groups—a small closed circle of intimates and a large mass of outsiders. Very few—David was one of them—would ever graduate from the larger to the smaller group.

David, in later years, regarded Duncan as the most original man he had ever met. He was, he thought, 'pure artist and nothing else'. Not everyone would have agreed. Duncan's love of practical jokes, combined with a permanent air of vacuity and vagueness led some to regard him simply as an idiot. But no idiot could have succeeded, as he did, in disguising himself so successfully as an old lady as to deceive his own aunt, Lytton's mother, when he called on some manufactured pretext of acquaintanceship. Some of his more cleverly constructed jokes were disquietingly successful. There was the occasion when Lytton received through the post a French poem, implying that he had been seen in a compromising situation with a youth and ending, in a version quoted by David, with the couplet:

'C'est toujours plus discret de monter en fiacre,
Tel est le conseil de votre ami Delacre'.

Delacre was a rather solemn French actor whom Lytton had met at Ottoline's. On receiving the poem Lytton, although he could recall no incident which could have occasioned it, was panic-stricken. It was just the kind of morsel Ottoline would delight to regale her friends with. Summoning his courage, he called on Delacre at his hotel, and begged him not to let Ottoline see the verses or hear the story. Lytton's manner and the matter of his request, which bewildered Delacre utterly, made him conclude that Lytton was out of his mind. He made an excuse to leave the room and never returned. Lytton waited nearly an hour before realising that he had been stranded. It was David who suggested that Duncan was the author, and Lytton at once recognised his cousin's work. This was the end of the story for him, but not for Delacre who, whenever he saw Lytton at Ottoline's parties in future, showed every sign of apprehension and stayed as far away from him as possible.

Before his visit to the Lacket, David was already on friendly terms with literary figures like D. H. Lawrence, Middleton Murray and Katherine Mansfield. So was Mark Gertler, and it was while on a visit to the Lawrences at their borrowed cottage near Chesham that David met Carrington, who arrived with Mark while he was there. She took no part, it seems, in all the talk that went on, but sat silently observing the others.

Bloomsbury had little or nothing in common with Lawrence and his friends: only Katherine Mansfield was to interest Lytton, and later to be involved in a strange love-hate relationship with Virginia. They were, however, qualified by their status as writers to form part of Ottoline's collection. David, who met her at one of Vanessa's parties in the new year, also qualified, both as a friend of Bloomsbury and as an attractive and handsome young man. Lytton cautiously contrived not to meet Lawrence at Bedford Square parties, but there was inevitable contact between Lawrence and other 'Bloomsberries'. Guest or not, Lawrence had no inhibitions about lecturing Ottoline on her choice of friends. Intellectuals and aesthetes drove him into a frenzy of contempt and disgust, and most of Ottoline's friends were one or the other.

Her Bloomsbury friends were both and aroused him to a high pitch of blind fury. He made his feelings very clear. Having been invited by Duncan to see his paintings, along with Frieda and E. M. Forster, he treated the artist to a stream of venomously destructive criticism in which arrogance and ignorance did duty for informed judgment. Only Duncan would have tolerated it. Lawrence followed up this performance with a letter to Ottoline full of turgid nonsense, condemning Duncan's work root and branch. No doubt he felt, on the strength of his own painting, qualified as a critic. A visit paid a few months later by David Garnett and Francis Birrell to the Lawrences at the cottage in Greatham which Wilfrid Meynell had lent them, led to another outburst of rage in a letter to Ottoline. 'To hear these young people talk fills me with black fury: they talk endlessly, but endlessly—and never, never a good thing said. They are cased each in a hard little shell of his own and out of this they talk words.' In a further effort to void from his system the bile of Bloomsbury, he wrote to David: 'I feel I should go mad when I think of your set,

Duncan Grant and Keynes and Birrell. It makes me dream of beetles. . . . I could sit in a corner and howl like a child.' David decided to break off the acquaintance. There was clearly no possibility of contact with a man who rejected so totally and with such violence the whole world of intelligence and art and respected only the instincts of the body. In spite, however, of Lawrence's offensive attitude to Bloomsbury, it was Bloomsbury which took the lead, when Lawrence's next novel, *The Rainbow*, was banned, in the agitation to have the ban removed. Lytton tried hard, without success, to get the *New Statesman* to take up the case, and Clive tackled the rest of the press. Whether Lawrence was grateful or not, there was no resumption of contact between them.

The war had now begun. The mould upon which life had so far been shaped was smashed for good. Society shuddered under the impact of change brutally forced upon it, and unstable elements disappeared. The small world of Bloomsbury was later said by some on its outskirts to have been irretrievably shattered. It was not so, and it was not so because Bloomsbury consisted of friendships and was not dependent on the social facilities and conveniences which the war removed. They were friendships which survived the upheavals and dislocations of war, in many ways were even strengthened by them. Bloomsbury, when it was all over, found itself better equipped than ever to live the life it desired.

VI

Ottoline

LADY Ottoline Morrell, though never in the true sense a member of the Bloomsbury circle, knew them all, was on terms of intimacy with a number of them, and was their hostess for many years at her houses in London and Oxfordshire. The reasons for her lack of acceptance emerge as one examines her life and character.

She was brought up at Welbeck Abbey, the family seat of the Cavendish-Bentincks and lived there mainly until her marriage at the age of 29. Welbeck is one of the great estates of the Dukeries, and the Abbey is princely in scale, style and eccentricity. Largely of seventeenth century construction, it was given its particular character by the fifth duke, who created a huge underground ball-room and a sort of private underground railway for the carriage of food and supplies along the complex network of passages and alleys under the house. The same duke, when the railway came to nearby Worksop, would not, when he had to go to London, leave his carriage. It was simply unharnessed and hauled on to a railway truck with the duke still on board. He could thus take advantage of the railway without the need to travel in public, and he considered himself well repaid for the considerable expense and inconvenience to others involved. It was in such an atmosphere, of domestic splendour and aristocratic self-absorption, that Ottoline grew up. There was a total lack of interest in the arts, no cultural activities, and, for a girl, no education worth talking about. She hated it. The country pursuits of the nobility did not interest her, and aristocratic society bored her. When she was sixteen, her brother married and for a few years she lived with her mother in London. But when her mother died she returned to Welbeck, a frustrated girl of barely twenty, full of yearnings for the fuller life she knew was possible, highly sexed without being aware of it, conscious of her own deficiencies in the cultural field, romantic in the extreme.

She did what she could for herself. She arranged courses of study at St Andrews and Oxford. She travelled in Italy and Sicily where, if she missed the significance of the splendid ruins of Greek and Roman civilisation, she reacted appropriately to Pan-like goatherds, and nightingales and roses at Hadrian's villa. She fell in love with Axel Munthe on Capri but he, though attracted to the point of considering her as a possible wife, was offended by her prudery and decided that she was a 'nerve-case'. Back in London she achieved a safer and more culturally gratifying intimacy with H. H. Asquith with whom she found she could discuss 'poetry, religion and the ways of life of Wordsworth, Tennyson and Browning.' There is no evidence, however, that she opened the Thucydides he had given her for her trip to Sicily.

After her marriage to Philip Morrell, she and her husband set up house in London, moving in 1905 to Bedford Square. Here Ottoline was able for the first time to entertain, and to do so on the lavish scale to which her upbringing had accustomed her. Soon enough her evening parties were crowded with a heterogeneous collection of guests, leading political figures, writers and painters mixing as well as they might with young artists with their names yet to make. Her circle rapidly widened. Lytton Strachey and Desmond MacCarthy, as we have seen, joined it. Charles Conder the painter was a particular favourite, wildly romanticised by Ottoline, who compared him, not necessarily in this order, to Villon, Giorgione, a child and a troubadour. He painted her, and it was in his studio that she met Augustus John. Later she sat to John in a 'dull violet dress with green sleeves' and soon afterwards she and Philip were escorted by Augustus and Dorelia John to one of Virginia's weekly parties in Fitzroy Square. 'We have just got to know' said Virginia in 1909, 'a wonderful Lady Ottoline Morrell, who has the head of a Medusa; but she is very simple and innocent in spite of it, & worships the arts'. It was a crucial visit, not only for Ottoline. From now on Ottoline's most frequent guests at her Thursday parties would be from Bloomsbury, and though some, like David Garnett, enjoyed her friendship for only a short time and others, like Virginia, remained ironically aloof, others—Lytton Strachey and Bertrand Russell in particular— became her intimates. Even Virginia, meeting her again in 1915 for the first time after her long illness, was momentarily carried away once more—at least by her marvellous appearance. 'I was so much overcome by her beauty' she wrote to Vanessa, 'that I really felt as if I'd suddenly got into the sea, & heard the mermaids fluting on their rocks. How it was done I can't think; but she had red-gold hair in masses, cheeks as soft as cushions with a lovely deep crimson on the crest of them, & a body really shaped more after my notion of a mermaid's than I've ever seen; not a wrinkle or blemish, swelling, but smooth'. Even her conversation had its merits. 'She didn't seem so much of a fool as I'd been led to think; she was quite shrewd, though vapid in the intervals.' The thrill soon evaporated and she was later to refer to 'the despicableness of people like Ottoline'.

The close association which grew up between Ottoline and Bloomsbury was as improbable as it was in a sense fatally inevitable. A woman who could write 'Life lived on the same plane as poetry and music is my instinctive desire and standard. It is the failure to accomplish this which makes me discontented with myself,' and who could speak of 'my power of loving people . . . the only touch of genius I possess' was the very personification of the flatulent romanticism which was anathema to Bloomsbury.

She was, however, a persistent and generous hostess and Bloomsbury had always enjoyed parties. Moreover she was, both in appearance and personality, a striking and highly unusual figure. David Garnett describes her—'tall and lean, with a large head, masses of dark Venetian red hair which, when I first knew her, she had not rashly begun to dye, glacier blue-green eyes, a long straight nose, a proud mouth and long jutting-out chin . . . her lovely, haggard face.' Leonard Woolf, never an admirer, writes of her 'drifting about . . . in strange brightly-coloured shawls and other floating garments, her unskilfully dyed red hair, her head tilted to the sky at the same angle as the birds, and her odd nasal voice and neighing laugh.' Bertrand Russell writes 'Ottoline was very tall, with a long thin face something like a horse, and very beautiful hair of an unusual colour, more or less like that of marmalade, but rather darker. Kind ladies supposed it to be dyed, but in this they were mistaken. She had a very beautiful, gentle, vibrant voice, indomitable courage and a will of iron. She was very shy.' Peter Quennell describes her on the lawns at Garsington, her Oxfordshire house. 'She seemed to trail as did the bird [a peacock, of course] she followed—in a dress of bottle-green that swept the lawn, trimmed with thick white swansdown bordering the square-cut neck. The large feathered hat that she often assumed was both regal and pleasantly proletarian; for it suggested a portrait of Queen Henrietta Maria but also recalled an Edwardian photograph of a Cockney *élégante* on Hampstead Heath.'

Writers seeking to place Ottoline in an appropriate historical period are as likely to settle on the Renaissance as on the gothic or baroque: but they all agree that flamboyance was the dominant characteristic of her style.

It was never enough for Ottoline to be on terms of easy friendship with the artists whom she so assiduously cultivated. Her need, and it was a profoundly felt one, was for acceptance and identification. At all costs, and by any available means, she had to be one of them. Here was the difficulty, for the plain fact is that she was, for all her remarkable qualities, a woman without talent or taste, who combined a generalised enthusiasm for the arts with an almost total insensitiveness to art itself, and whose worshipful reverence for artists was never modified by understanding or critical sense. When, in her memoirs, she writes of the artists she knew, she has nothing to say of their work. Of Henry James, with whom she claims to have been on close terms, she recalls that he was ill-mannered towards young people and could not easily be placed in the pattern of conventional society. Matisse struck her only as 'a commercial business man'. Not a word of writing or painting: they might as well have been stockbrokers.

The gap that yawned between hostess and guest in Bedford Square or at Peppard, her cottage near Henley, was thus deep and daunting: and yet it had to be bridged.

It had to be bridged for a commonplace reason which Ottoline certainly never recognised and would have rejected with scorn. There seems little doubt that the 'discontent' of which she constantly complained was rather more sexual than aesthetic. She describes herself on her marriage as 'full of potentialities, large and unfinished, rather Michelangesque'. It is, in the light of her later life, not unreasonable to interpret this naïve statement in simple sexual terms. It is a fact that her most favoured guests were almost exclusively male: Leonard Woolf notes that during all his visits to Garsington, the only women of distinction there, apart from Virginia, were Katherine Mansfield and Margot Asquith.

When Ottoline wrote of 'my power of loving people . . . the only touch of genius I possess' she was again dressing her instinctive urges in inappropriate garments. The fact is that her characteristic approach to the artists who attracted her was predatory and promiscuous. If intimacy could not be achieved at aesthetic levels, there were easier and more obvious routes to similar ends. It may even be, as has been suggested by some of those who knew her well, that she was, unknown to herself, a nymphomaniac whose enthusiasm for the arts was a sublimation of dominant instinctive needs. However that may be, there are examples enough of her *affaires* to indicate her tastes. Not all of them progressed very far, but no doubt with a little more co-operation they would have done so. She even made a routine attempt to seduce Lytton, whose homosexuality she never quite accepted at its true value. She succeeded only in making his lip bleed. Henry Lamb was much more amenable. Walks in the woods at Peppard led to nothing, but there were hot embraces at Garsington and in the end he fell seriously in love with her.

When not engaged on her own account, she was tireless in forwarding the affairs of others. Many of her match-making activities were simply crude and clumsy attempts to force together couples who were obviously incompatible. Brett was thrust hopefully together with Bertrand Russell: Maurice Bowra, then a rising young Oxford don, was urged strenuously to marry a young woman whom in fact he barely knew and rather disliked. His unwillingness to do as he was told was taken rather amiss. Perhaps her greatest efforts in this direction were directed towards Carrington. An abortive scheme to get her into bed with Harry Norton was only a minor skirmish in a sustained siege of the stronghold of her virginity. Mark Gertler, whose wild virile beauty added an exciting lustre to his undoubted talent, was at the time one of Ottoline's most adored guests. He had confided in her his love for Carrington and his frustration at her persistent refusal to surrender to his passionate demands. Both Ottoline and Philip were indignant to the point of outrage at what seemed to them her senseless and stubborn stand on a minor technical point. Philip walked her round the pond at Garsington after dinner one night and treated her to a fifteen-minute lecture on her cruelty to Mark. Then Ottoline took over and gave her an hour and a half on the same subject in the asparagus bed. She was rather more understanding than Philip had been, but no less determined. She went so far as to admit to Carrington that she was herself having an affair with Bertie Russell, a fact that was widely suspected in Bloomsbury but not hitherto admitted.

Ottoline's affairs, often so disappointingly innocent, with artists and similar folk, formed part of the romantic life she had constructed for herself. They also probably had in them a strong element of aristocratic condescension: if they were talked about she did not greatly mind—there were plenty of precedents for generous relationships between great ladies and gifted men of low birth. But Bertie was, as well as being a leading intellectual, himself an aristocrat. A liaison between the grandson of an Earl and the half-sister of a duke was different in kind from a romance with handsome commoners like Henry Lamb or Mark Gertler. It had almost dynastic overtones. It should not therefore be a matter of gossip among the lower orders, and Ottoline was careful to keep it as dark as possible.

Bertie had been married since 1894 to Alys, the sister of Logan Pearsall Smith and of Mary, the second wife of Bernard Berenson; but they had been estranged since 1902 and, though by Alys's wish they lived under the same roof, the marriage was at an end. In 1910, Bertie got to know the Morrells when he helped Philip in his campaign for re-election as the Liberal M.P. for South Oxfordshire. He had no high opinion of Philip and his puritanical tastes were at first offended by Ottoline's use of rich scents and powders. When Philip lost his election and became a candidate at the Burnley by-election in the same year, Bertie continued to see them both in London. One night when he was their guest in Bedford Square, Philip was called away and Ottoline and Bertie spent the evening alone together. Risking a few timid advances, he received, to his surprise, a clear welcome. They decided then and there to become lovers, and did so. 'My feeling' says Bertie in his autobiography, 'was overwhelmingly strong, and I did not care what might be involved. I wanted to leave Alys and to have her leave Philip. What Philip might think or feel was a matter of indifference to me.'

When Bertie told Alys what had happened and what he wished, Alys flew into a rage and swore to divorce him, naming Ottoline. Ottoline, for her part, could not leave her four-year-old daughter Julian to marry Bertie. Bertie, in face of Alys's reaction, threatened suicide. He could still, however, behave rationally. 'After she had stormed for several hours' he says, 'I gave a lesson in Locke's Philosophy to her niece Karin Costelloe who was about to take her Tripos. I then rode away on my bicycle, and with that my first marriage came to an end.' He did not see Alys again until a year before her death in 1951.

Bertie's affair with Ottoline came at the end of eight years of celibacy: it was to be followed by a series of passing affairs and hardly less transient marriages which reveal an emotional susceptibility he may not hitherto have recognised as having a sexual basis.

There were almost inevitably absurd aspects to their relationship. Alys had been persuaded by her brother Logan to give up her intention to divorce Bertie. At the same time Philip, also under pressure from Logan, laid down for Ottoline the conditions under which he would accept her relationship with Bertie. Of these, the most important was that, whatever they achieved in the daytime, they should never spend the night together. The agreement represented both a concession to public morality, which conferred symbolic significance on the sharing of a bed overnight, and a broadmindedness on Philip's part which was worthy of Bloomsbury. Neither Bertie nor Ottoline was wholly faithful. He was quite ready to spend a happy night in the arms of a gynaecologist's wife whom he met at Lake Garda when he and Charles Sanger were on a walking tour. Ottoline manipulated complex relationships with Lytton Strachey and Henry Lamb.

It is satisfactory to record that Philip, too, dull and conventional as he appears in the writings of the time, had at least one fruitful love-affair. None of Ottoline's amorous excursions upset her love affair with Bertie. The only impediment here was his bad breath. Until he managed to find a cure for his pyorrhea, the relationship was suspended. It then continued happily for a year or two until by 1916 it was all over.

Looking back on it, Bertie found it good. 'Ottoline had a great influence on me, which was almost wholly beneficial. She laughed at me when I behaved like a don or a prig. . . . Her sense of humour was very great, and I became aware of the danger of rousing it unintentionally.'

Ottoline's affair with Bertie had begun in London. Two years later, when she was in poor health, her doctors advised a country life and she and Philip began house-hunting.

In the following spring a house in Oxfordshire which she had already identified as 'the only country house' she could live in came up for sale and Philip bought it at once. Garsington Manor was a Tudor stone mansion set in spacious grounds a few miles from Oxford. Robert Gathorne-Hardy describes its setting. 'The house faced southward on to a level lawn, beyond which the land sloped to a rectangular pond, with a white temple at one end, and ranged formally around it, against a hedge of yew, old statues. To the left of the slope was a great ilex tree. The view extended across the wide Thames valley to the Berkshire downs, and in front of them, beech-crowned, the twin, lovely Wittenham Clumps.'

Lytton was desolated at the prospect of the move. Ottoline's London house 'was the one centre' he wrote to Henry Lamb, 'where I had some chance of seeing amusing and fresh people— my only non-Cambridge point of rapport in London'. The move did not in fact occur until the summer of 1915, by which time Ottoline, paying little heed to the restraint Philip tried to impose, had had the house redecorated and furnished according to her own eclectic taste. Writing of this time, she says 'his

[Philip's] taste was so architectural and accurate, at first it was quite bewildering to me, who was not accustomed to so much care in details of furnishing and house decoration, but I soon learnt my lesson and was stimulated to many developments of my own, more romantic and wilder inventions, he curbing and pruning'.

The result was, of course, pure Ottoline, and it is Garsington which will, for as long as she is remembered, express the style and exuberance of her unique personality. 'Places explain people' David Garnett once said, and Garsington certainly provided a key to Ottoline's character. Leonard Woolf's thought on the same subject—'What cuts the deepest channels in our lives are the different houses in which we live'—was perhaps less true of Ottoline than of himself. Ottoline was too strong and headstrong a person to be so affected: she would do the cutting of any channels that were to be cut.

Leonard and Virginia first visited Garsington in 1917 and this and later visits gave him plenty of scope for his powers as an observer and recorder of human oddity. He understood the sexuality which infused Ottoline's aesthetic emotions, but he recognised the validity of the latter. They were, he saw 'strong and persistent if erratic and sometimes deplorable'. He acknowledged that she was at least partially successful in providing a congenial setting for the 'intelligent, imaginative, creative people' whose intimacy she craved. But at the same time his sardonic eye missed nothing of the 'disorderly flamboyance' both of Garsington and its hostess. It was, he thought, the 'compromise between good taste and her own taste [which] gave a peculiar and sometimes incongruous aspect to her rooms and a strange and sometimes ludicrous aspect to her parties'.

Lytton, Vanessa and Duncan Grant had paid their first visit to Garsington in June 1915 and Lytton described his impressions to David Garnett. 'The house is a regular galanty-show, whatever that may be; very like O. herself, in fact—v. remarkable, v. impressive, patched, gilded and preposterous.' The tasteless exuberance of Garsington had also struck David. The dignity of the Elizabethan manor had, he felt, been overwhelmed with oriental magnificence. To paint fine oak-panelling 'peacock blue-green' exemplified Ottoline's urge to enrich her setting and in the process to ruin it. Even the air was improved with the aid of innumerable bowls of pot-pourri and orris root. The walls were thickly hung with paintings by her friends— Augustus John, Duncan, Henry Lamb, Mark Gertler and Conder. Ottoline herself, magnificently overdressed for the country, and accompanied by a pack of small pug dogs, dominated the scene, imposing unlikely activities on her guests ('acrobatic dances on the lawn' are mentioned ironically by Lytton), gathering to her those with whom she wished to hold uplifting discussions on art and literature, pairing off others she thought romantically suited to each other. Philip Morrell's contribution to the gaiety of Garsington was to play the pianola and occasionally to give dim support to Ottoline's match-making efforts. He was all in all a sad figure, quite out of place, and cruelly described by Aldous Huxley in *Crome Yellow* as looking like 'a grey bowler hat'. He did not really count for very much. Even when his mother was dying and he brought increasingly serious news of her condition to Otto-line, she barely interrupted the charade she was engaged upon for a perfunctory word of consolation. In her defence, it should be said that she had a Spanish duke playing the part of Napoleon, a role which demanded her close supervision.

Neither Leonard nor, still less, Virginia fell under Ottoline's spell. The Garsington diet was much too rich for Leonard's austere palate. Virginia was able to admire, at a distance, the baroque splendour of Ottoline's façade, but was not interested in the complex, pathetic character it was constructed to conceal. The bogus aspects of her personality and behaviour attracted her ridicule. She disapproved too of her sexual extravagances. Writing to Lytton after a party at the Sitwells where everyone had conspired to isolate Ottoline, she commented '. . . even in vice what magnificence she has . . . got up to look precisely like the Spanish Armada in full sail.' She was careful not to give full expression to her distaste in Lytton's presence, for he was at this time a confirmed Garsington addict.

Virginia never understood Lytton's relationship with Ottoline which, with whatever irony he chose to refer to it in his letters, was nevertheless a close and valid one. She could not understand how Lytton could stay so often at Garsington and afterwards tell her how he had hated it. 'Garsington was terribly trying . . . Ottoline I really think is in the last stages—infinitely antique [she was 46], racked in every joint, hobbling through the buttercups. . . . She is rongée too by malevolence.' At the time of this letter Lytton was established in a comfortable home of his own and thus perhaps less easily charmed than before by the luxury of his quarters at Garsington. But a letter two years earlier had struck the same note: 'Lady Omega Muddle[1] is now I think almost at the last gasp—infinitely old, ill, depressed and bad-tempered.' She was in fact suffering from necrosis of the jaw, a painful and potentially dangerous condition, which was only to be cured by an operation which left the lower part of her face pitted and scarred and made it necessary for her to cover it with scarves.

Lytton's readiness to accept Ottoline's hospitality and then to sneer at her behind her back was no different in kind from the attitude of the rest of Bloomsbury. Carrington noticed it on her first visit to Asheham in 1915, when they all—Lytton, Vanessa, Clive, Duncan and Mary Hutchinson—ridiculed her. 'I think it's beastly of them,' she wrote to Mark 'to enjoy Ottoline's kindnesses and then laugh at her.'

It is of course true that Bloomsbury, much given itself to absurdity, had a sharp eye for the absurd in others, and made it almost a matter of policy, in their intimate circle, to dissect and laugh over the ridiculous characters of outsiders. And Ottoline, however much she tried to be one of them, was always an outsider.

How was it then that Lytton, of all people, could not only spend so much of his time under her roof, but admit her to an intimacy as close as, and in some ways closer than, that which he shared with his natural family of Bloomsbury friends? For intimacy there was. Not only did he take her into his confidence about his love-affairs—he was fairly open about these with other friends—but he allowed her to see into the innermost recesses of his heart, dark areas of unworthy yearnings—

[1] A nickname Lytton often used for her, with the same brand of humour that produced for her the name 'Lady Vaseline Mulberry' among Eton schoolboys.

unworthy, that is, by Apostolic or Bloomsbury standards—which he would never have dared to reveal to Virginia, with her malicious eye for her friends' defects, or to Maynard or Duncan, or even to James or David Garnett, his chosen confidants. It was, it will be recalled, to Ottoline that, as early as 1912, he confided his passionate desire 'to bound forward and triumph!' A confession of this sort would have had a ribald reception in some Bloomsbury quarters and would have been subjected to sharp and painful analysis in others. The fact that he knew that Ottoline would understand and sympathise provides a key to their relationship.

The truth is that they were both romantics, as their friends were not. It is significant that Lytton took romantically successful figures—Queen Elizabeth, Gordon, Florence Nightingale, for example—as the subject of his biographies; the attraction he felt for them was then transmuted by the ironic habit of his mind into a ruthlessly sceptical assessment. Only Queen Victoria defeated him: she emerges almost undiminished from beneath his microscope. As for Ottoline, a synthetic creation in which pre-Raphaelite and Renaissance elements were joined in an unstable compound, she saw herself as a heroine of romance. Her exotic dress, the luxuriant furnishing of her houses, and even her friendships with poets and artists were designed as a setting for the character she imagined herself to be. They both really believed in the possibility of dreams coming true, by way of some flawlessly perfect event, or relationship, or setting. Lytton was clear-minded enough to see that the event might never happen, the relationship never ripen, the setting nowhere exist. But his scepticism was not strong enough to prevent him from labouring stubbornly for a literary triumph, from seeking the ideal, ultimate lover, or, at a less intense level, from pursuing his search for the country cottage of his dreams.

Ottoline, entirely lacking Lytton's capacity for critical intro-spection, had dreams and longings as intense as his. Her romanticism was whole-hearted, and when the facts were against her, her reaction was not irony but self-pity. Like Lytton she felt, deep within herself, that she was a person of distinction; unlike him, she was not. She longed to be, not an

artist in any real sense, but what she conceived an artist to be—
a romantic Shelleyan figure such as schoolgirls dream of.
Unable to produce any evidence of her own powers as an
artist, she could at least surround herself with artists and thus
win a kind of distinction by association. There is no doubt that
her hospitality had an exclusively self-regarding aim, and that
it achieved this aim. One by one, most of the leading literary
and artistic figures of her day, and many of the statesmen and
politicians, became her guests and often her friends. Personalities as dissimilar as Henry James and Arnold Bennett, Walter
Sickert and Stanley Spencer, D. H. Lawrence and Aldous
Huxley formed part of her circle for longer or shorter periods.
She understood almost none of them, and in her memoirs is
able to describe little more than trivial aspects of their appearance or personality. With the more attractive she contrived to
achieve varying degrees of physical intimacy, a consolation for
her failure to share their artistic emotions.

With Lytton, somehow it was different. There was no
possibility of an 'affaire' with him. But whereas her yearning
romanticism seemed to irritate her lovers until, one by one,
they turned away from her, Lytton, with gentle melancholy,
accepted and understood it. He read to her, in the deep voice
which on such occasions replaced the high-pitched Strachey
squeak. No sooner had he left her roof than he would propose
himself for another visit. He would stay, not for the ritual
weekend, but long periods. It was no good for Lytton to sneer
at her, as he constantly did in his letters to Bloomsbury friends.
The fact was that he was drawn to her by a temperamental
similarity powerful enough to smother his intellectual disapproval. It is clear, however, that Lytton made use of Ottoline,
and the scorn he showed for her to others gives a cynical
character to his relationship with her. Significantly, the time of
their greatest intimacy occurred before *Eminent Victorians* gave
him the triumph he longed for and before Carrington had
created for him a domesticity in which he could be pampered
and adored. When in these ways his dreams had come true, he
no longer needed someone like Ottoline in whom to confide
them. When at last he arrived, he found that he had left
Ottoline behind. During the twenties, when he was at the

height of fame and fortune, their friendship cooled, the visits grew less and less frequent.

Ottoline's obsessive cultivation of writers and artists exposed her to dangers of which she was largely unconscious and which, when they became realities, she never understood. Her fantastic appearance and personality made an almost irresistible appeal to those whose business it was to record human character on paper or canvas. Moreover, only the slightest touch of pen or brush was needed to produce a caricature woundingly recognisable to all who knew her. Her hospitality, generous and even relentless as it was, offered endless opportunity for observation and study of the hostess. Her gifted guests ate her dinners, enjoyed the company of their friends in her drawing-room, and then, in the privacy of the bedrooms she so thoughtfully provided, made their notes or drew their sketches.

It was the novelists who inflicted the sharpest wounds. Her physical appearance after all had a wild majesty which no artist's caricature could conceal, and an eccentricity which gave serious portraits an air of caricature. It was an appearance she cultivated and exaggerated and so could not properly complain of. There are many caricatures and some posed portraits, of which Augustus John's unfinished full-length is the finest. In all of them she appears extraordinary and in John's portrait her unique physical distinction is brilliantly recorded. On the whole she was not much disturbed by the way her artists saw her.

But novelists are more concerned with character than appearance. A verbal portrait enters territory almost entirely beyond the reach of the visual artist. The novelist describes personality in action and adds his own commentary. The result, when the character is drawn from life, can be devastating. So when Ottoline appeared as Priscilla Wimbush in Aldous Huxley's *Crome Yellow* and as Hermione Roddice in D. H. Lawrence's *Women in Love* she was horrified and deeply hurt. Both authors had been her guests and to varying degrees possessed her confidence. In return she found herself held up to ridicule and contempt: for both portraits are cruel as well as unmistakable, and executed with acrimony as well as brilliance.

Ottoline, in her memoirs, records in a moment of insight,

the compulsion she felt to 'batter one's wings against other people's cages, they look so lovely inside, so variegated and attractive . . . and then when one approaches them with dainties in one's hand, one is wounded by their beaks'. It is the experience of any keeper of wild creatures. Eagles are not doves and cannot be made so by treatment however kind. Ottoline's hospitality could not protect her from the sharp talons of her more gifted guests. They were, in their way, as predatory as she was, and she was as much their proper prey as the fieldmouse is that of the harrier.

Ottoline's relationships with Bloomsbury are thus ambivalent and, however explained, still puzzling. They were aesthetes and creative artists: she was neither. She was a ravenously hot-blooded female of the species: Bloomsbury regarded sex as a source of delight and, while enjoying it in every variation, kept it in its place. Bloomsbury's attitude to life was cool and sceptical: Ottoline's whole-heartedly romantic. Bloomsbury consisted of intellectuals: no one ever accused Ottoline of being one.

What then was the bond? It must at once be said that it was a loose one, and that, even where it was firmest, it always snapped in the end. But it existed and had its own validity and effect. Basically the relationship was of course that of guest and host. It is unlikely that it could have existed without Bedford Square, Garsington and later, Gower Street. But there were other hostesses, equally generous and persistent, like Lady Colefax and Lady Cunard, whose parties were attended by the more distinguished members of Bloomsbury, without intimacy developing. Neither guest nor hostess of course wished it.

So it must be said that part of the basis for Bloomsbury's relationship with Ottoline was her sheer determination to create it. She set out deliberately to be irresistible, and largely succeeded. In the face of her persistence, and tempted by the quality of her hospitality, Bloomsbury found it easier, and pleasanter, to accept invitations than to refuse them. The company would certainly be interesting and, generally speaking, congenial. And if the food was sometimes meagre, the setting was lavish. Some ludicrous event or situation would almost certainly occur, to be enriched when it was described afterwards. Most of all, however, it was Ottoline herself who was the attraction. She was so strange, so fantastic, so absurd, so vivid a person that to observe her at close quarters, to submit to her questioning, to catalogue her changes of costume, was an experience to be repeated until some tiresome event revealed an underlying incompatibility, or until one simply became bored. Even those who, like Virginia, were not fascinated by her, were glad, as Quentin Bell with insight points out, that such an improbable person existed.

Almost all descriptions of Ottoline tend to become unfair. It is not necessary to exaggerate in order to produce a picture of an absurd, and even, from certain aspects, a rather undesirable character. Indeed it is almost impossible not to do so. But such a picture omits qualities which, though less striking than those which Aldous Huxley or Lawrence chose to bring out, were there and were an essential part of Ottoline. Her generosity as a hostess has been mentioned. She was, too, a warm-hearted and immensely human person. She was, says Julian Huxley, who was a frequent guest at Garsington and later in Gower Street, 'generous in understanding and forgiving of human foibles'. She was open-minded as well as strong-minded. And although her judgment of art in any form was faulty, her judgment of the artistic or intellectual potentiality of individuals was uncannily sound. Clever young Oxford men visited Garsington in streams. Some came once or twice and were not again invited. Those for whom her doors remained open were, amazingly often, men whose later achievements vindicated her measure of them. It is here that the sensitiveness and insight which she certainly possessed, but which were obscured behind the fantastic front she presented to the world, is most clearly seen.

She was, as a personality, built on a grand scale, dwarfing many of those who laughed at her. She had no defence against their ridicule, of which she was often enough aware. But she had the courage to nourish friendship with men and women of outstanding gifts, accepting the risk that these might be turned against her.

Ottoline never truly understood herself. Her introspective vision was blurred by longings which could not, in the nature

of things, be satisfied and were often irrelevant to her real
needs. Her world of fantasy, created in the unknowable depths
of her character, invaded the world of reality and to a large
extent took over from it. The setting which she constructed for
herself and the glamorous figure which formed its centrepiece
were at the same time both artificial and essential to her. It was
her naïve confidence in the actuality of this dream-world and
of her place in it which made her seem ridiculous to those who
did not understand or could not sympathise—which made her,
in fact, often ridiculous.

But when all has been said, and the laughter and mockery
are still, Ottoline remains—a superb, unlikely figure of high
romance, bravely denying the dreary facts of life, unique and
inimitable. She was not necessary to the times in which she
lived—their life and work would have proceeded in much the
same essential way without her—but she gave them an extra
panache, a touch of outrageous, marvellous magic of which she
only had the secret. The secret died with her.

VII

Carrington

CARRINGTON and Lytton met in the late autumn of 1915: it was the beginning of a strange intimacy which lasted until death. Their relationship was to have at various stages all the ingredients of a marriage. But it was both more and less than this. After a brief unsatisfactory period of sexual intimacy, each recognised that this was impossible and indeed unnecessary between them. Their relationship had some of the quality of a warm love between father and daughter, but with the added intimacy only possible between near contemporaries —Lytton was thirteen years older than Carrington. It was a relationship which permitted each to fall in and out of love with others while remaining deeply faithful to each other. Carrington's marriage to Ralph Partridge, after four years of living under the same roof as Lytton and running his house for him, only strengthened the bond between them. Her husband became the third member of the household and Lytton's house was their only home. While Lytton moved from one homosexual infatuation to another, and Carrington enjoyed a series of affairs with one attractive man (or woman) after another, they never wavered in their love for each other. Carrington gave Lytton's life a permanent foundation of affection and care: for Carrington the event was to show that life without him was impossible.

At the time of their first meeting Carrington was involved in her long and unsatisfactory love-affair with Mark Gertler. For three years Mark had been begging insistently that she should become either his wife or his mistress. Carrington as persistently refused to give in: 'I do love you' she wrote on one occasion, 'but not in that way'. Sexual intercourse on any terms at this stage was repellent to her. Any attempt in that direction left her, she said, feeling ashamed and unclean inside. She sympathised with Mark's frustration, but would not

permit the step required to cure it. At the age of 22 she confessed to him that she had never experienced sexual desire for
a man. As for marriage, she was convinced that this would
destroy her independence as an individual and her freedom as
an artist, and she was rootedly opposed to entering into any
such contract. If Carrington had not been so enchanting a
person, Mark would have been happy to turn his attentions
elsewhere. But it was no good. Making love to Katherine
Mansfield when they were both rather drunk provided no
relief. Sometimes he lost heart. 'I know that, if I am to get
something satisfactory out of life, it's to be from my work and
not from you', he wrote. But he was still enslaved.

In many ways, Carrington is the most fascinating personality
in the whole Bloomsbury story. She had derived little benefit
from her schooling and was, by Bloomsbury standards, without
education. She had acquired a taste for literature, and reading
was one of her abiding pleasures, but she could never see life,
as Bloomsbury so readily did, in literary terms. She had a
remarkable gift as a painter without the dominant creative
need of the artist. Her urge to paint, which produced work
only now beginning to be appreciated at its true worth, was
not strong enough to compete with the claims of life. She was
sorry when other activities filled her day, but she never felt it
her duty to develop her talent, which in any case she consistently
underrated. She was in no sense an intellectual, and often
appeared to be unintelligent. There is no doubt that, had it
not been for her relationship with Lytton, she would never have
found a place in Bloomsbury. She seemed to possess no single
one of the qualities required for membership of the group—
except perhaps an impish sense of humour and a disrespectful
attitude towards the conventions and those who lived by them.

But although it is true that without Lytton she could never
have established herself on her own merits as a member of the
closed circle of literary intellectuals which Bloomsbury
essentially was, it is equally true that there was in her personality
something which had a strong attraction, for Lytton certainly,
but also for the others in the group. They were charming to
her because she herself was charming. The mere fact of being
Lytton's companion could not have made her acceptable. It

Roger Fry

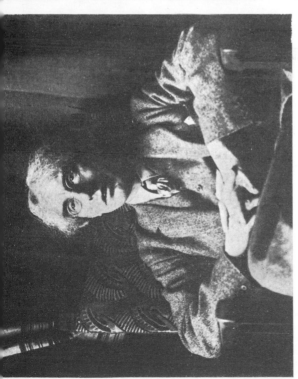

Vanessa Bell

Carrington

Carrington, Lytton Strachey, Vanessa Bell and Duncan Grant

Clive Bell and Francis Birrell

Virginia Woolf

Leonard Woolf

Maynard Keynes

Duncan Grant

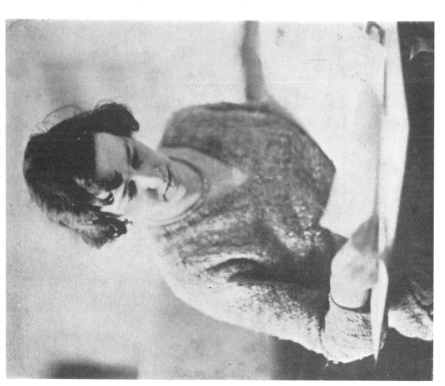

Frances Partridge

Ottoline Morrell by Duncan Grant

The Sitting-room at Charleston

(*The painting above the mantel is by Duncan Grant*)

was the warmth of her personality, an abundance of ingenuous charm, her impulsive friendliness, and perhaps, above all, her gay vitality which attracted them to her. She had a zest for life which Bloomsbury found delightfully refreshing. While their concern as artists was to write books about, or paint portraits from, life, she—also an artist—participated with energy and enjoyment in the vulgar business of everyday life, actually taking pleasure in growing vegetables and cooking meals. Ottoline called her a 'wild moorland pony', a description which David Garnett thought 'quite good', but which ignores more than it suggests.

Leonard Woolf describes the impression she made on him at more length. She was, he writes, 'one of those mysterious, inordinately female characters made up of an infinite series of contradictory characteristics. . . . She had a head of the thickest yellow hair that I have ever seen, and as . . . it was cut short round the bottom of her neck, it stood out like a solid, perfectly grown and clipped yew hedge. She had the roundest, softest, pinkest damask cheeks and large, China blue eyes through which one was disconcerted to glimpse an innocence which one could not possibly believe really to exist this side of the Garden of Eden—in 1920 in the Berkshire house of the author of *Eminent Victorians*. . . .'

Carrington was an original in the way that a child is original. She retained as an adult the child's inability to be or pretend to be anyone but herself. In a letter to Rosamond Lehmann, she wrote '. . . really I think it's NO good being anything but what you are and the great thing is never to do anything one doesn't feel genuinely inside oneself.' Although she adds that this was 'Lytton's creed, not *my* invention,' it was her own, too, not consciously thought out, but imposed upon her by her own personality. It was this inability to act inconsistently with her emotions which made it impossible for her to react physically to Mark Gertler's love-making. It was because she acted consistently with them that she was able to remain essentially faithful to Lytton while passionate love-affairs with others came and went. They supplied an emotional satisfaction he was unable to give. She discussed them freely with him and he understood and sympathised perfectly.

Carrington met Lytton first at Asheham as the guest of Clive and Vanessa, who had borrowed the house temporarily from Virginia. Duncan, and Lytton's favourite cousin Mary St. John Hutchinson, were fellow-guests. The invitation was a surprise to Carrington, who did not expect to enjoy the visit and could not understand why she had been asked. She reported afterwards to Mark: 'It was much happier than I expected'. She helped Vanessa with the cooking and walked over the downs with Lytton. Mark at this stage provided the only direct link between Lytton and Carrington. Mark, a wildly handsome figure, had attracted Lytton when they met at Ottoline's, and Lytton had taken his education in hand. Under his guidance, Mark was reading Dostoevsky, Spinoza and Bertrand Russell, and, if truth were told, finding the going rather difficult. Nevertheless he was grateful to Lytton, whom he liked and admired. He would be interested therefore in Carrington's reaction to him. 'Lytton is rather curious,' she wrote. It was not till later that she expanded this statement with an account of what had occurred on a walk they had taken together. To Carrington's astonishment, and perhaps too to his own, Lytton had suddenly kissed her. Carrington had at this stage the conventionally contemptuous attitude to homosexuals and may have known that Lytton was one. She was affronted that he should attempt what appeared to her to be an indecent intimacy. She determined on revenge and very early next morning she crept into his room with a pair of scissors, with the intention of snipping off his beard. At the critical moment, however, Lytton opened his eyes. At his glance, Carrington was made powerless by emotion and she stole from the room: Lytton's eyes, a deep spaniel-brown, were always his best feature. It was on this absurd note—Carrington's schoolgirl revenge frustrated by Lytton's lucky awakening—that their love-story began.

Although the temperature of their feelings for each other rose rapidly, neither was anxious to admit the fact to others nor even, too openly, to each other. Carrington continued to deceive Mark into believing that he was the only man in her life while firmly refusing to relinquish her virginity and explaining her attitude to a sympathetic Lytton. Lytton was

both embarrassed by Carrington's undisguised adoration and
warmed by the attentions of such a charming creature. He was
nervous too, of any situation developing which might endanger
his fragile independence; and he was trying to work on his
study of Dr. Arnold, the second of the Eminent Victorians.
Mark meanwhile encouraged their friendship in the absurd
hope that Lytton's high opinion of him as an artist (it was in
fact not quite so high as he imagined) might sway Carrington
in his favour.

All three, together or alone, were frequent guests at Garsington and Carrington began to move freely in Bloomsbury
circles. From now on Carrington would write to Lytton,
sometimes almost daily, whenever they were apart, and every
letter would express, more explicitly as time passed, her love
for him. Her letters to Mark at this period were a mixture of
innocent gossip designed to lull the jealousy of Lytton he was
already beginning to feel, and protestations of love. 'The
intimacy we got at lately makes other relationships with people
strangely vacant, and dull . . . How amazing it is to be able to
write so little of what I want to you', she wrote to him, adding
naïvely, 'But it always seems rather false directly I put it
down'. The truth was that within weeks of their first meeting,
the fascination that Carrington felt for Lytton had developed
into an absorbing passion. But she wished neither to hurt nor
to give up Mark. She therefore embarked on a policy of
duplicity which became increasingly difficult until the final
inevitable showdown. Carrington, like the child she essentially
was, never accepted the necessity of choice between two
alternatives both of which gave her pleasure.

In August 1916 she spent a fortnight at a cottage in North
Wales with Lytton and Barbara Hiles (her Slade friend) and
Barbara's fiancé Nicholas, who was convalescing from a war-
wound. It was from here that she wrote Mark the letter from
which the quotations above are taken. From North Wales
Lytton and Carrington went off alone together for a few days
at Bath and Glastonbury. Carrington wrote enthusiastically
descriptive letters to Mark. What she did not describe were the
physical intimacies which took place: intimacies which, if
Lytton had been as anxious to play a part as Carrington, might

have led to the loss of her famous virginity. It was from Glastonbury that Lytton wrote to Maynard, on the back of a letter to him from Carrington, the following revealing lines.

> When I'm winding up the toy
> Of a pretty little boy,
> —Thank you, I can manage pretty well;
> But how to set about
> To make a pussy pout
> —*That* is more than I can tell.

Carrington was by now largely reconciled to Lytton's homosexuality and tried to excuse it to Mark. 'When one realises it is there—a part of them [homosexuals] and a small part—it is worthwhile overlooking it for anything bigger and more valuable,' she wrote.

Much of the autumn she spent searching for a cottage for Lytton, a search in which Barbara took an equally active part. Barbara, a 'nice, springy and gay girl' as Ottoline called her, was now married to Nicholas Bagenal, who had returned to his unit in France. She was always ready to devote herself to others; she nursed Saxon Sydney-Turner, who was in his ineffectual way in love with her, through his innumerable illnesses, and many years later looked after Clive when he was dying. Some of her friends found her unfailing solicitude irritating. Lytton, however, was grateful to her, not only for trying to find him a cottage, but for joining with Saxon, Maynard, Oliver Strachey, Harry Norton, and others in a scheme by which he could afford one. Under this scheme the participants, with Barbara as treasurer, would contribute towards the rent, with the right to use the cottage when they wanted to, while recognising it as Lytton's home.

Carrington carried on the search from temporary homes in London and from Hurstbourne Tarrant, her parents' home in Hampshire, until in October she moved with Brett, Middleton Murry and Katherine Mansfield into Maynard Keynes' home in Gower Street, where she could be nearer to Lytton in Belsize Park Gardens.

Proximity to Lytton also involved accessibility to Mark, and he was now able to meet her regularly, either in her attic room in Gower Street or his studio at Hampstead. 'How can people ever know', he wrote to her in November, 'what goes on between us on Mondays! Heavens! How wonderful it all is'. Perhaps as compensation to Mark for the time she spent with Lytton, and as an unconscious admission of guilt for concealing from him her feelings for Lytton, she was clearly now allowing him intimacies she had previously refused. By one means or another, however, it seems that she avoided completely succumbing to his relentless pressures until in December they spent a week alone together at Gilbert Cannan's windmill house at Cholebury. Here at last the citadel fell. As a lover, Mark was direct, potent and insensitive. Carrington recognised the importance to her of the experience, but any enthusiasm she might have felt was killed by Mark's violence and by her hatred of the contraceptive apparatus he provided for her use. She only liked 'sugar in her coffee', she told him, 'sometimes, not every week and every day'. She rationed him to three lumps a month, which meant 'no more until next year'. Mark's victory was thus a fairly empty one.

For Carrington it was a miserable winter. In November her adored brother Teddy had been reported missing on the Somme, but it was not till February that his death was confirmed. She could not expect much comfort during these months of anxiety and loneliness from Mark, with his monotonous sexual demands. Only Lytton seemed able to understand. Mark's frustration and resentment at her coldness, which it was beyond her power to overcome, led to quarrels. A crisis was clearly coming. It was precipitated by a stay which Carrington made in April at her friend Alix Sargant-Florence's attractive home near Marlow. It was a characteristically Bloomsbury occasion. The other guests were Lytton, James Strachey (whom Alix was later to marry), Maynard and Harry Norton. They read Shakespeare together or listened to James playing Bach. Carrington read Plato with excitement. The atmosphere was one of intellectual culture and relaxed intimacy. The contrast between the serenity of these few days with Lytton, the congenial company of the circle to which he belonged and in which she felt herself welcome and the misery of the emotional scenes with Mark, was decisive. Before leaving she wrote to Mark and to Lytton, arranging to meet them both separately in a few days in London and giving Mark some idea of what was in her mind. Her meeting with Mark in his studio was all the more shattering because, instead of raging at her, he was very quiet and at last, when he understood that this was meant to be the final break, wept. Strangely, Lytton's name was barely mentioned, but Carrington was only too aware that she was giving up Mark's love, which to a great extent she returned, in exchange for the 'unreality and coldness of Lytton'.

When she talked with Lytton in her flat later that night, the awareness was intensified. Carrington records their conversation in detail in her diary. Lytton seemed unconscious of the anguish through which she was going. 'Aren't you being rather romantic?' he asked when he learned that she had given her love for him as the reason for breaking with Mark. It was hardly an adequate reaction, though she had expected little more. They discussed the sexual difficulty of their relationship and Carrington dismissed it as unimportant. She rejected similarly Lytton's fears of their friends' opinions, and was hurt when he pointed out that he could not afford to 'keep' her.

It was a strange, painful conversation. They were both in their own ways thoroughly realistic. Carrington recognised her overwhelming need of Lytton and was determined to mould her life round him. Lytton, less committed emotionally, saw the difficulties. 'He was', recorded Carrington, 'so wise and just'. To strangers it would have appeared as if she were throwing herself at his head and he were tactfully putting her off. But it was not so. The affection between them was already so deep that they could talk as they did without misunderstanding. In the end, she wrote, 'he sat on the floor with me and clasped my hands in his and let me kiss his mouth, all enmeshed in the brittle beard and my inside was as heavy as lead, as I knew how miserable it was going to be'. Next day she gave Mark an edited version of the conversation, and he was scornful of Lytton's unmanly part in it. He told her that he did not want to see her again as long as she felt as she did for Lytton. 'And so it all ends like this' she wrote, 'about as crooked as it could be'.

It was not, of course, the end. For Carrington, relationships did not end like that, by a mere verbal agreement. As long as any feeling remained she clung to them, regardless of new loves and inevitable duplicities. Almost immediately after her ostensibly final meeting with Mark, she became his mistress on a regular basis. She was still as unsatisfactory as ever in bed, and for Mark there was the added frustration of knowing that their meetings had to be fitted into her programme of engagements with Lytton. She was still looking for the elusive cottage for him and had every intention of sharing it with him when they found it. She denied this to Mark, just as later she tried to conceal the fact from her family, but it was so. The lies she readily told in defence of her emotional necessities were never, to Carrington, more than mildly regrettable expedients.

For Lytton, 1917 was a crucial year in more ways than one. He completed *Eminent Victorians* in the summer and by the end of the year it was ready for the printers. His difficulties with the military recruiting authorities appeared at last to be over. As a conscientious objector his first brush with them had occurred in the previous year. His appearance before the tribunal at that time resulted satisfactorily in his exemption on medical grounds, but the dignity of the occasion had been marred by Stracheyesque absurdities. Lytton was suffering at the time from piles: he was therefore no doubt entitled to use an air cushion: but it was not in keeping with the importance of the occasion that he should make the tribunal wait while he blew it up in front of them. The fact that it was a delicate pale blue in colour added nothing to the propriety of this performance. When he was asked what he would do if he saw a German soldier attempting to rape his sister, he replied with owlish solemnity 'I should try to interpose my body'. It was a memorable reply whose monstrous ambiguity was fully appreciated by Lytton's three sisters, who, with other relatives and friends, were present to support him. Now he had to appear again, like everyone who had gained previous exemption. Once more, after a hearing by the tribunal and a medical examination lasting six hours, he was given exemption, not on grounds of conscience, but of physical unfitness: he was awarded the lowest possible medical grading—C4. Six months later, the exemption was to be made absolute and permanent.

Lytton and Carrington had spent much of the summer and early autumn together, in Sussex with Clive and Vanessa and later in Cornwall, accompanied by James Strachey and Noel Olivier, who as a girl of fifteen had been the object of Rupert Brooke's romantic affection. Carrington was ecstatically happy. She painted a great deal, producing a portrait of old Mrs. Box, their hostess at Welcombe near Bude, as well as a number of landscapes. In the evening, Lytton would read aloud—from Morley, Gibbon or his own writings. Carrington confided her joy to Barbara Bagenal: if she got exhausted it was from 'simply loving so hard'. She wrote to Mark constantly too, tactlessly telling him how happy she was, but at the same time, with no apparent consciousness of inconsistency, saying that she longed to be back with him, begging him not to leave her, making plans to do things together.

In fact her plans were quite different, and they did not include Mark. By the time she returned to her parents at Hurstbourne Tarrant she knew that her life and Lytton's were bound together—at least she hoped beyond all else that this was so. Almost at once the first step towards this life became possible. On October 20th she visited three houses on Lytton's behalf: two were unsuitable, but the third, the old millhouse at Tidmarsh, a little village a mile from Pangbourne, was exactly, she thought, what was wanted. She could not wait to tell Lytton. Sitting in a teashop at Newbury that afternoon on the way home she wrote to him, describing the house. It stood in an acre of grounds, with an orchard, a large lawn and gardens with a river running through them. It had two large and four small bedrooms, three large rooms downstairs, and a bathroom and electric light. It seemed in good condition. It was available on a three-year lease at £52 a year. It was, she told Lytton, 'very romantic and lovely' with its gables and lattice windows. 'I'm wildly excited' she said, and sent him a sketch of the house from the orchard. Lytton in his cooler way, was equally pleased, and negotiations were at once put in hand. By November it was all settled: settled, that is, except for the explanations that were required on all sides. The inevitable Bloomsbury gossip had to be stilled. Lytton wrote a detailed letter to Clive to assure him that everything was 'above board' and 'quite devoid of mystery': he simply needed a quiet place outside London where he could work and for this purpose female companionship on a 'certainly by no means romantic basis' was essential. Ottoline would undoubtedly be furious at losing Lytton to a nondescript young woman who had made life so difficult for her dear Mark. Lady Strachey, although she might not say anything, was bound to disapprove, and did so.

But Lytton's difficulties were nothing compared with Carrington's. She had somehow to satisfy, not only her own utterly conventional parents, but Mark himself. She solved both problems simply by lying. She told her parents a preposterous tale about Tidmarsh being planned as a country retreat for girl-artists from the Slade, and this story was good enough to enable her to extricate her own furniture and also to make off with various items which would come in useful at the Mill House. The procedure was made easier by the fact that her father and mother were at this time moving to a smaller house at Cheltenham. It was this fact that enabled Carrington to explain to Mark her frequent absences from London. But his suspicions were not easily allayed and while the furniture was being installed at Tidmarsh in November she wrote, 'No, I am not going away with Lytton'. She tried to give colour to this statement by seeing as much as possible of Mark and his friends in London, and for a time she succeeded. He was 'charming and gay', she told Lytton after a visit to Garsington, and quite unaware, it seems, that Brett was at the same time giving Carrington furniture for Tidmarsh. There were noisy parties with Monty Shearman, Mark's friend and patron, at which D. H. Lawrence and Frieda mixed with Carrington's friends Barbara Bagenal, Alix Sargant-Florence and 'Bunny' Garnett. Mark's friend Koteliansky, the strange Russian who looked like a 'Major Hebrew prophet' and whom everyone, including Virginia, loved and admired, was always present and always charming. It could not, of course, go on. Carrington's last effort to keep up the deception came at the end of November when in a letter to Mark (she was writing to him almost every day at this stage) she said 'Oliver Strachey has taken an old water Mill House near Reading, so I am going to let him keep all my furniture for me. Until I have a place in London of my own.'

In December Carrington, aided by Barbara Bagenal, spent three hectic, happy weeks, bringing the Mill House under control, so that Lytton might spend Christmas there. Rooms were cleaned and painted, the furniture—still woefully inadequate in spite of numerous gifts from friends and large-scale looting at Hurstbourne Tarrant—disposed to the best advantage, the garden was tidied up and planted with bulbs, potential maids and charwomen were interviewed. Lytton was instructed to steal some electric light bulbs from Belsize Park Gardens as Carrington found it tedious to carry one in her pocket and fit it in each room as she came to it. Lytton's arrival coincided with a cold spell which burst all the pipes. But there was at least a fire in front of which he could read Queen Victoria's letters (edited and annotated by Brett's father, Lord Esher) while Carrington hammered nails, unpacked, repaired carpets. Although he wrote to Virginia that he was in 'considerable agony' because of the general discomfort, he added that he hoped to be able to work in the seclusion the Mill House offered. 'Ah, la vie' he said, 'It grows more remarkable every minute'.

It must indeed have been a remarkable Christmas. Harry Norton, James and Alix arrived as the first house-guests. Carrington's talents as a cook were still largely latent and would always be erratic. But with the help of good fires and good wine all passed off well enough. Perhaps Lytton was relieved that he had to be in London most of January negotiating the publication of *Eminent Victorians*, while Carrington stayed at Tidmarsh to do battle with the domestic side of his new life. Her letters to him, reporting such varied matters as the engagement of outside help and a purely unpractical idea to cope with the rats ('Buzzards in Wellington Boots' she called them), which were noisy at night, expressed her happiness in every line. To Mark, however, she wrote 'I find being Mary [she meant Martha] and looking after a house, a confounded bore'.

Any belief Mark may have had in Carrington's fictions about her place in the Tidmarsh household was wearing dangerously thin. Neither Lytton's sincere efforts to be more than usually friendly, nor Carrington's invitations and promises to spend time with him in London, could for long disguise the fact that the two had set up house together for good. He at last saw what had happened. Lytton had stolen his mistress from him. Mark's emotions were too primitive to admit the possibility of a triangular relationship of the kind which, as later events showed, seemed peculiarly fitted to Carrington's character. With him, at least, she could not have her cake and eat it, though later and with other lovers she found this difficult feat perfectly possible. The inevitable explosion occurred after a party given in February by Mary Hutchinson in Hammersmith. Mark, not unusually, got drunk. As Lytton and Carrington left the party together, he was overcome with rage and set upon Lytton with both fists. Before much damage was done Maynard, efficient as ever, dragged Mark away, while Carrington took refuge with Sheppard and Harry Norton took charge of Lytton. Mark was forgiven by Carrington in a note the next day, and a week later Mark apologised to Lytton whom he saw by chance at the Eiffel Tower restaurant with David Garnett. Lytton accepted the apology with a light remark and an embarrassed giggle: David felt that Mark found this response rather inadequate.

At no time did Carrington spell out to Mark what the Tidmarsh arrangement was. No doubt she knew that her explanation would never be accepted. Her tentative offers to tell him 'more about herself' were rejected. She still felt warmly towards him, however, and they continued to correspond and to meet, though Carrington broke more appointments than she kept. They were drifting apart. Mark spent more and more time at Garsington, Carrington less and less, as Tidmarsh increasingly absorbed her time and interest. But she could not let him go completely: three years later, within a few weeks of her marriage to Ralph Partridge, and when she was already emotionally involved with Gerald Brenan, she made another effort to renew contact with him. This time it was too late: Mark was suffering from incurable tuberculosis, and, apart from occasional letters, nothing more passed between them.

Carrington never really understood her own emotional make-up, although she knew too well what difficulties it caused to others. The nearest she ever got to an explanation was in a letter to Gerald Brenan at an early stage in their relationship. 'I believe if one wasn't reserved, and hadn't a sense of "what is possible" one could be *very* fond of certainly two or three people at a time—To know a human being intimately, to feel their affection, to have their confidences is so absorbing that it's clearly absurd to think one only has the inclination for one variety. The very contrast of a double relationship is fascinating. . . . One has to abandon some people and the difficulty of choosing is great. Don't you find it so? Honestly when I get to London, and meet old loves, and friends, I can hardly bear the feeling of being away from them.'

It is certainly true that Carrington passionately yearned for permanence in her emotional relationships, the kind of permanence a child feels in the love of its parents, and which, for most people, is refound in marriage. Carrington resisted the biological imperative to pair for life. She retained the child's need to love and be loved by more than one person at a time. Sex was an intrusive element, which she resisted vigorously until she discovered, almost ashamedly, that she too was subject to its force and was capable of enjoying it. By that time her shame at being a woman was transmuted into a form of lesbianism which partly compensated for the unwilling pleasure she took in sexual activities with men. But however many lovers came and went, her basic need for permanence remained. If only they had not insisted on exclusive rights, all might have been well, and she could have had joyous simultaneous relationships with them, as she had with her brothers in childhood, and they could all have gone on and on happily together. Only Lytton seemed to understand. Only they two could, as loving friends, discuss, freely and sympathetically, their emotional affairs with their other lovers. Carrington never saw that this perfect relationship was possible only because they were not themselves lovers: she would have married him at any time if he had asked her. She did not see that this would have been fatal: it was of the essence of their association that it should leave each other heart-free to pursue new loves as they appeared.

It is reasonable to explain Carrington's unconventional emotional relationships by saying that they express a consistent, unconscious need to recreate in idealised form the conditions of childhood. In this explanation, Lytton plays the rôle of her father, and her lovers that of her brother Teddy, while the intense attraction she felt for some women represents the love she had never been able to feel for her mother. There is so much truth in this analysis that it may, in its seductive simplicity, be taken for a complete explanation. No human being, however, fits totally into any classical psychological category. When all the explanations are given there remains a part of Carrington which is original, unpredictable and beyond classification. And however un-normal her emotional constitution was, it was never identifiably morbid. Even her suicide after Lytton's death was the act, not of a sick person, but of one who, taking everything into consideration, decided against life.

Meanwhile life was good. In the midst of the chaos of moving into a new house, in no way reduced by Carrington's enthusiastic but not invariably successful attempts at housekeeping, Lytton not only found it possible to work but was convinced that he had found a lasting solution to his problems. Although to his friends he enjoyed describing, with the irony natural to him, the rigours of rural life and the strange activities of his 'female companion', he knew that his life was now firmly based. He could sally forth into London society, go on foreign jaunts with a current favourite, submit for a while to Ottoline's intense hospitality, and then return, not to a cramped bedsittingroom in Belsize Park Gardens, but to a house where his study and library awaited him, a house warmed by Carrington's gay affection and the fires she solicitously lit to welcome him.

Carrington, for her part, when Lytton did not need her, could keep contact with her friends in London by making quick trips to Gordon Square, could go to Virginia and Leonard in Sussex, and while there, get excited over Vanessa's and Duncan's painting.

In the spring of 1918, *Eminent Victorians* appeared and Lytton became overnight, as he had for so long dreamed of becoming, a famous literary figure. The reviews were immensely flattering. There was no doubt that the book, with its brilliant deflation of Victorian idols, corresponded exactly with the mood of a public bored with the windy rantings of war-time writers. By the summer it had gone into a third edition, and the American edition a month or two later was sensationally successful. Only the denunciations of the Old Guard, represented by Edmund Gosse and Mrs. Humphry Ward (Arnold's grand-daughter) relieved Lytton of the fear that he had failed in his objective of stirring up the conventionalists.

VIII

Clive and Roger

UNLIKE Lytton, Clive when he left Cambridge had neither the practical need nor perhaps the inner impulsion to make a career for himself. Nor were his eyes turned in any particular direction. His imagination and his literary taste had been aroused by his Cambridge friendships. But there was little evidence, at the time he took his degree—like Lytton's it was a second class—that his nascent interest in painting would develop into the dominant passion of his life. Indeed, having been awarded an Earl of Derby Studentship, he began to prepare a dissertation on British policy at the Congress of Verona. For a year he engaged himself in researches at Cambridge and the Record Office. It is not conceivable that this work was to his taste or that Clive would ever have become a political historian. He soon decided that it was necessary to consult the National Archive in Paris and in 1904 he set himself up in Montparnasse with this ostensible object. There is no evidence that he made any serious study of historical documents while he was there. Certainly, if he did so, nothing came of his work.

He had gone to Paris with an introduction to Gerald Kelly (later Sir Gerald Kelly, P.R.A.) who had left Cambridge a year before Clive to study painting in Paris. Through this introduction he entered a new world of a great deal more interest to him than the National Archive could offer. In the 'Chat Blanc' and the 'Closerie des Lilas' he met artists and their models. Montparnasse had not yet succeeded Montmartre as the artistic heart of Paris. But a number of English and American artists lived there and Rodin himself made very rare appearances at one or other café. It was a fringe world and Clive was on the fringe of it. To say that he was intoxicated by this second-hand contact with the life of the painter suggests a loss of judgment which is unfair to him, but he was certainly deeply thrilled by it. At Cambridge, the Midnight Society had introduced him to literature, but the Apostles would not have him, and the life of a literary intellectual was clearly not for him. Painters, Clive discovered, were artists without necessarily being intellectuals. Their gifts owed little to education: some of them were hardly literate by Cambridge standards. Their amusements would have bored or disgusted the aesthetes of Trinity or King's. They drank too much and the models who seemed to inspire them were vulgar tarts. The work they produced, however, was as truly art as that of his literary friends; perhaps more truly. Clive could not paint; he could never therefore fully enter into the essential life of the painter. His point of view would remain unalterably that of an onlooker. But the fascination he felt as he sat at the same café-table as these strange, untidy, gifted men was to remain with him all his life. He saw, or thought he saw, that he could make his own contribution: not this time in unhappy competition with brilliant thinkers like Maynard, or literary aesthetes like Lytton, but in a field where they were largely foreigners. Clive had found his future. As an art-critic, he could play an important role in obtaining recognition for painters who might otherwise never become known; as a theoretician he could increase the understanding of modern art, and even perhaps indicate new directions in which it might move.

His marriage to Vanessa in 1907 meant that his home was a painter's household of which Duncan Grant was to become a permanent member. Further visits to Paris brought him into close contact with Derain and his circle, he became a friend of Segonzac, got to know Cocteau and at the Deux Magots saw, but perhaps only saw, Braque himself. Through Gertrude Stein he met Picasso and was invited by him to call whenever he liked. And he had a slight acquaintance with Matisse. There is little reason to think that he was ever on intimate terms with any of this brilliant group, though he called Derain 'tu'. He moved, it seems clear, still on the fringe. But from his place on the rim of the circle, he could see into it and comment on what he saw.

For him the most important event of this period was the beginning of his friendship, in 1910, with Roger Fry. Roger was to become a sort of elder brother of Bloomsbury: listed by Leonard Woolf as an original member of 'old Bloomsbury', he was, in terms of age, the odd man out. He was at this time 45, and looked a good deal older. Nevertheless he had an immediate welcome when Clive and Vanessa introduced him to their friends, few of whom were much more than 30.

Like Lytton and the Stephen girls he had grown up in the repressive atmosphere of a home dominated by strong-minded parents, with the difference that Sir Edward and Lady Fry were strict Quakers. Lady Fry in particular conceived it to be her duty to exercise the most rigid control over the lives of her two sons and five daughters, going to absurd lengths to ensure that they were protected from any remote possibility of moral infection, and directing their conduct in detail long after they were adult. Roger alone rebelled. By virtue of his sex he was allowed to go to the university. (Of his sisters, all able and some brilliant, only Margery was reluctantly permitted to go to Oxford where she later became Principal of Somerville). At King's he read science and shared rooms with his school-friend, the philosopher J. E. McTaggart, formed a romantic association with 'Goldie' Lowes Dickinson, then a young King's don, and became, like him, an Apostle. At Cambridge he experienced for the first time the intellectual excitement essential to his temperament. He also found his career.

It was at Cambridge that his interest in art developed into a passion and that he determined to be himself an artist. There were difficulties. His narrow religious upbringing made it seem necessary for him to reconcile the function of art with the doctrines of Christianity: his taste, too, was still unformed and enthusiasm often did duty for judgment. While his mother bombarded him with a stream of moralising letters, his father expressed strong opposition to his desire to be a painter, particularly since it would apparently be necessary for him to contemplate the female nude. Help was fortunately at hand. J. H. Middleton, the gifted and eccentric Slade Professor of Art, became his friend. While Apostolic discussion cleared his mind of the irrelevancies implanted by his home life, Middleton persuaded Sir Edward to withdraw his objections

to Roger becoming an artist, pointing out, rather dis-
ingenuously, that although it was essential for a painter to
work on figures as well as landscapes, the male body was really
rather more suitable for the purpose than the female.

So Roger was allowed, while reading biology for his degree,
and in the intervals of dissecting frogs, to work on the male
nude under the Slade Professor. He obtained his First, but
failed, to his parents' chagrin, to win a fellowship. His course
was now set. On leaving Cambridge he worked in the studio
of a minor artist in London and two years later began the
visits to art galleries in Italy and France which were to form a
major part of the pattern of his future life. Not only was he now
painting hard but he was studying pictures and the history of
art and had begun work as a lecturer, reviewer and critic. He
became a connoisseur of early Italian painting, but was un-
moved by the Impressionist work he had seen in Paris. His
taste had begun to develop and would never cease to do so.
His own painting was at first rejected by the New English Art
Club, but his excellent portrait of Edward Carpenter, now in
the National Portrait Gallery, was exhibited at the Walker
Gallery in 1894 and two years later his work was shown at the
N.E.A.C. In the same year he married Helen Coombe, a
charming and witty fellow-artist. Predictably, as she was not
a Quaker and had no money, his parents disapproved of the
marriage.

The following decade saw Roger's rise to a position of such
eminence that in 1906 he was offered, but could not accept, the
post of Director of the National Gallery. He was by now an
authority on the Italian School, had written a notable book on
Bellini, and was a regular contributor to the *Burlington
Magazine* and the *Athenaeum*. For a time too it looked as if
his dearest desire, to be an acknowledged painter, might be
within reach: in 1903 twenty-five of his paintings were sold
at a single exhibition. He never repeated this success. Nor did
he ever become, as he might have become, a serious rival to
Berenson as an expert on Italian art.

The fact was that he was the true Renaissance man: his
interests and enthusiasms were too varied and too easily
aroused for him to become a narrow specialist. He could write

with equal verve and expertise about French medieval painting and the Victorians, could apply his scientific mind to abstruse problems of attribution, and was constantly being excited by new theories of aesthetics, developed in articles, lectures and controversy. He had, said Virginia Woolf in her biography, 'a great capacity all his life for laying himself open, trustfully, optimistically, completely, to any new idea, new person or new experience that came his way.' One such experience came in 1906 when he became Curator of the Department of Painting at the Metropolitan Museum of New York, of which the Senior Trustee and dominant figure was the redoubtable J. P. Morgan. Two years later he became the Museum's adviser on European painting. There was little prospect of two strong characters like Fry and Morgan, with such utterly opposed characters and attitudes, working in amity and the inevitable clash led to Roger's dismissal in 1910.

Meanwhile, his domestic life had collapsed. Helen had had a serious attack of mental illness within two years of their marriage, and recurrent attacks, each more severe than the last, culminated in her permanent confinement in a mental home in 1910.

It was at this crucial point in his life, when he was unemployed and had no money and was effectively a widower with two young children to bring up that he met Clive and Vanessa. It would be an exaggeration to say that the Bloomsbury friendships which resulted from this meeting were a life-saver for him. Roger was never a man who needed such assistance. But there is no doubt that Bloomsbury brought joy and delight into a life sadly lacking in emotional, as distinct from intellectual, satisfactions. What made him acceptable to his new friends was the zest and originality of his mind, his total lack of prejudice, his erudition and his great charm. In conversation, so important to Bloomsbury, his deep rich voice was an added attraction. Bernard Shaw once said that only Roger's voice and Forbes Robertson's could be listened to for their own sake. Virginia describes him at this stage as 'worn and seasoned, ascetic yet tough'. Bloomsbury was none of these things, but could offer uncensorious affection, sensitive understanding, and a kind of moral ease and freedom which for Roger, still not entirely free from the intellectual confusion created by his childhood upbringing, was immensely refreshing. While he still had at the back of his mind a nagging concern with the relationship between artistic achievement and the eternal verities, which to him had still a largely moral content, his new friends had no such preoccupations. They were essentially rationalists, sceptical, disrespectful, mocking and, above all, gay. They were not immoral: on the contrary they were all engaged in their different ways in the pursuit of the good. But they had rejected those definitions of the good which would not stand up to strict intellectual tests. They were left with an interpretation of life and a code of conduct which enabled them to follow freely natural impulses which society suppressed. And so they were happy, and free of all but the limitations imposed by their own emotional and intellectual morality. They lived, not by a set of regulations laid down by society, but by general rules arrived at in the light of the total human need. These rules had kindness as well as strictness. Greed, ambition, cruelty, jealousy came under their ban, but conventional sins and breaches of the social code were forgiven wherever in a rational light they were comprehensible. In such a circle, Roger felt himself liberated and happy.

With Clive the growth of intimacy was hastened by their common interest in modern French art. Roger had long been excited by it and had already given expression to his views in a long letter in the *Burlington Magazine* in 1908, in which he contrasted the Impressionists, concerned only to render 'the totality of appearance' with their successors—'neo-Impressionists' and 'proto-Byzantines' as he called them—who understood the importance of contour and design, 'the relation of one form to another'. The concept to which Clive was to give, a few years later, the title of 'significant form' was thus already dominant in Roger's mind. There were other, profounder, ideas which were fermenting in his mind. He was particularly preoccupied with the identification of the type of emotion aroused by a work of art and the way in which this was different from, and even independent of, the emotion aroused by beautiful objects in nature. He recognised that the sight of a beautiful woman and the contemplation of the portrait of a beautiful woman caused reactions in the viewer which were as much different from each other as they were similar. This being so, the function of the artist should not be limited to the artificial reproduction of beautiful objects, indeed it was hampered and even vitiated by such an interpretation. A work of art aroused emotion on its own merits, whether or not it was a faithful image of an emotive natural object—a sunset or a nude girl or a stag at bay. What in any case was beauty? There was of course no completely satisfactory answer to this question. Luckily Tolstoy in his *What is Art?* had removed the need to seek for one. He had suggested, in Roger's paraphrase of his views, 'that art had no special or necessary concern with what was beautiful in nature'. The suggestion came to Roger with the force of divine revelation. At once the work of the new French school fell into place. They were not after all anarchists nor even heretics, but followers of the true religion. Cézanne had shown the way. He had used nature, not as a model to copy, but as material for his own perception and in particular for his own sense of design. He reorganised the Mont Sainte Victoire, or a plate of apples, in accordance with his own vision and produced works of art whose emotional appeal depended on the genius of the artist rather than on the intrinsic attraction of the objects they seemed to represent. He had not gone far enough, perhaps, but he had gone much further than the other Impressionists, whose aim had still been merely to represent what they saw, though with a new vision. Van Gogh demonstrated the truth of Tolstoy's views when he took a commonplace kitchen chair as a model and made from it a painting of marvellous beauty. The works of Van Gogh and Cézanne were short but important steps towards the ultimate liberation of the artist from the duty of representing nature. With Manet and Matisse and even more emphatically with Braque and Picasso, the artist had become a true creator and not a copyist. Roger saw his duty quite clearly. He must educate the British public in the appreciation of the new forms of art. He must show that what appeared to the uninformed to be a distortion and mockery of nature, ugliness for its own sake, was in fact a development of the essential role of art along quite classical lines. The only thing to do was to bring a

representative collection to London and to exhibit it, with a
catalogue which would have to be didactic as well as descriptive,
at some suitable gallery. Roger persuaded the Grafton Gallery
to agree to house such an exhibition and he now needed help
in collecting the pictures for it and in conducting the business
side of the venture. Clive agreed at once to go with him to
Paris for this purpose, and Roger enlisted Desmond MacCarthy
as his secretary and man of business. The choice of Desmond as
an administrator was a strange one and lends colour to Clive's
comment on Roger: 'a poorer judge of men I have seldom
met'. Desmond had no knowledge of the world into which he
was now plunged. In some ways this turned out to be an
advantage: by sheer ignorance he obtained for the gallery a
20% commission on sales—nearly twice the normal figure
for that time. In Paris Roger, in cautious deference to English
prudery, gave Desmond the task of vetting nudes, rejecting
for the exhibition those whose frankness might have antagonised
a public which still found Ingres' expurgated versions of female
anatomy rather bold. Gradually the pictures were collected.
The artists best represented were Cézanne, van Gogh and
Gauguin, but Vlaminck, Derain and Rouault were shown
and there were two Picassos. Desmond wrote an introduction
to the catalogue. The problem of a title for the exhibition was
solved by Roger, who invented the term Post-Impressionist.
He chose the name as being 'the vaguest and most non-
committal' he could think of, recording the mere fact that his
artists followed the Impressionists in time, but not necessarily
in anything else. It was a good name, sufficiently unspecific to
include artists of widely different styles and gifts and, since it
had no partisan implications, capable of being adopted by
opponents as well as supporters of the new art.

The exhibition was scandalously successful. The crowds who
thronged the gallery, attracted by curiosity and the hope of
being shocked, no doubt got their money's worth. So did
Desmond, who was delighted to receive £460 as his share of
the profits. Roger got nothing except the satisfaction of having
succeeded in bringing modern French art to the attention of
London. He was reviled in the press and his reputation as a
reliable art critic shuddered under the most violent attacks.

Even the supporters of the Chelsea school of Augustus John were antagonistic. Lytton came down on their side, partly because of a genuine failure of visual perception, partly perhaps, too, out of intellectual snobbery. If Post-Impressionism could gain the impassioned support of people of the modest intellectual calibre of Clive Bell, he may have felt, it could not be worth much.

The success of this first tentative exhibition made clear that another more comprehensive showing was required and in 1912 the second Post-Impressionist exhibition was held, again at the Grafton Gallery. This time Picasso and Braque gave a strongly Cubist flavour to the exhibition, and Matisse was well represented. So, too, were Duncan and Vanessa, and Henry Lamb's full-length portrait of Lytton was shown. Augustus John still refused to take part, and Lytton, though the brilliance of Matisse's colour excited him, was as unimpressed as before. He was intensely irritated, too, by Clive's air of ownership, and by the patronising way in which, in a loud voice, he lectured the bystanders on the qualities of the paintings on show. 'I had to disown him', he wrote to Ottoline. He had sympathy for Leonard Woolf, who, being short of money, had taken Desmond's earlier post as secretary, and was now the patient target of furious attacks by 'irate country gentlemen and their wives', purple in the face with the indignation which Picasso or some other exhibitor inspired. Nor was Lytton particularly pleased to have been mistaken, on a visit to the exhibition, for Augustus John, simply because of his beard and Bohemian clothes. He had to go and stand in front of his self-portrait to demonstrate his identity.

Lytton was not at the moment feeling very friendly towards Roger whom he described as 'a most shifty and wormy character'. There were complex reasons for this antipathy. Roger had by now assumed a leading place in Bloomsbury, both by his general qualities of mind and personality, and for Clive, Vanessa and Duncan, by his enthusiastic understanding of art. In 1911 he had gone to Istanbul with Clive, Vanessa and Harry Norton, a most successful expedition from which he returned as Vanessa's lover. Virginia admired and was fond of him. Undoubtedly, Lytton was jealous.

Roger had also offended Lytton at a more sensitive level. When Henry Lamb hurt his hand sufficiently badly to prevent him from painting, Roger's reaction was to express the hope that the injury would not affect his piano-playing! On top of this he had quarrelled with Ottoline. Only Ottoline's account of this episode exists. According to this, Roger accused her, on his return from Istanbul, of spreading the story that he was in love with her. There was, it seems, an extremely ugly scene which led to a permanent break. The event occurred at a time when Ottoline was cultivating Lytton with assiduity and success. She showered him with gifts—a snuff box (he did not take snuff), a gaily-coloured stock (he did not know how to put it on), a huge bottle of hair-water (whose use he did not understand), a large embroidered handkerchief and some aromatic leaves intended as book markers. She pressed invitations on him, using Henry Lamb as an additional lure. Lytton basked in the warmth of her attentions, so much more comforting, he felt at this time, than the austere intellectual companionship which was all that Bloomsbury seemed able to offer.

How much truth there was in Roger's intolerable accusation —or whether in fact he made it—it is impossible to say. Ottoline was at this time involved in her lengthy and spirited love-affair with Bertrand Russell. But her appetite was large, both for men and artistic reputations. The lions she hunted were meant, if they were attractive enough, as trophies as much for the bedroom (when she could lure them there) as for the salon. And it would not have been out of character for her to hint at intimate relations with a man of distinction whom she admired. On the other hand, Ottoline attracted slander, and it may merely have been a malicious invention which Roger heard. A further possibility which cannot be excluded is that Ottoline, writing some twenty years after the event, edited the episode in her own peculiar way to show Roger in a very bad light and herself as the innocent victim of malice. What is certain is that there was a serious breach between Roger and Ottoline and Lytton is bound to have been aware of it. For Roger it meant the loss of an influential patron, who had been a member of the executive committee of the first Post-Impressionist exhibition, and whom he would continue to meet, with some embarrassment at the Contemporary Art Society, where they were both committee members.

Roger now carried his sense of the importance of design from the sphere of fine art into the everyday world of the decorative arts. The theory of significant form had for Roger functional as well as visual relevance. 'Why must the potter,' he asked in a review of *Art*, the book in which Clive first spelt out the doctrine, 'who is to make a superbly beautiful pot not think only of its significant form, but think first and most passionately about its function as a pot?' The answer seemed to include the notion that it was the genius of the artist that made form significant and that this genius could be applied with advantage to what was to be used as well as looked at. Within a few months of the Second Post-Impressionist exhibition he opened the Omega Workshop. Here artists worked, anonymously and for a fixed weekly wage, at the design of fabrics, pottery and furniture which then became the property of the Workshop. They also undertook complete schemes of interior decoration on commission. Duncan and Vanessa collaborated enthusiastically from the start, but artists are egoists and relatively few were content with anonymity. Partly because of the impact of war, the Workshop was never the success Roger hoped it would be and he closed it down in 1920. But as long as it functioned it had distinguished patronage, and it had a powerful effect on later attitudes to interior decorating and the design of domestic objects. Like William Morris fifty years earlier, he taught the lesson that useful things could be made beautiful under an artist's hand, and in the postwar period it was clear that the lesson had been widely understood.

Roger's future career as an artist and critic is outside the scope of this book. The range of his activities seemed to widen with age, to include children's painting, lithography, pottery, handwriting, the translation of Mallarmé's poems, photography, Russian icons. He continued to paint, and was disappointed by the lack of response he obtained: his other disappointment, that he was several times rejected for the Slade

Chair of Fine Art, was resolved when in the year before his death he was appointed Slade Professor at Cambridge.

In 1922 Roger fell in love with a fellow-patient at Coué's clinic at Nancy. Unhappily, Josette Coatmellec was as unbalanced as his wife, who had died in 1913, and after two years of mutually intense but anguished emotion she committed suicide. In the only letter to her which survives, a letter delivered only after her death, his feelings for her are agonisingly expressed. In the following year he met and fell in love with Helen, the wife of Boris Anrep, the distinguished Russian mosaicist. She fell as deeply in love with him; she left her husband and for the rest of Roger's life they lived together in great happiness. In Helen he at last found true feminine companionship and understanding.

Roger was an individualist and a man with a mission. Both these aspects of his complex character appealed to Bloomsbury. Roger saw it as his vocation to bring enlightenment to the heathen. These were, by Roger's definition, the philistine gallery-goers and the worshippers of the lifeless images of the Victorian artistic tradition. The enlightenment he wished to bring to them emanated from his own theories of art. These were liable to change, but as long as he held them, they had for him, as Clive pointed out, the force of principles, almost the expression of the will of God, whereas the views of others where they conflicted with his own, were 'unworthy prejudices'. One recognises here once more the traces of Roger's Quaker background. He was a man who needed doctrine: cubism was to supply for him the deficiencies of Christianity. Even his interest in Mallarmé arose partly from his view that he was a cubist poet, who, by a process of poetical analysis broke down and then reconstructed his themes, 'not according to the relations of experience, but of pure poetical necessity.' The key word here is 'pure'. The cubists were pure because they stripped from their subjects what was casual or fortuitous—almost what was in Apostolic language called 'phenomenal'—and organised what remained into relationships that had 'order and inevitability', that is, relationships in which purity and truth produced a beauty uncluttered by superficial charm. Lord Clark has pointed out (in his introduction to Last Essays) that this was ultimately a mystical aesthetic. There was little prospect of the heathen following him far along the difficult path he mapped towards a true understanding of art, but he could set their feet upon it, and he held it to be his duty to do so. Bloomsbury approved, and if they too were sometimes lost in the still fundamentally religious subtleties of his aesthetic there was matter in them for endless exciting discussion.

Missionaries and theorists are not always attractive and Roger's energetic activities and difficult doctrines would not have gained him his special place in Bloomsbury's affections. But his argumentativeness was sweetened by charm as well as learning. And he looked so extraordinary with his bushy eyebrows and thick spectacles, his goblin face wrinkled into a boyish grin, his shapeless brown Jaeger homespuns enlivened by brilliant shantung ties, sandals and a broad-brimmed hat. He looked, in fact, like what he was—a bohemian Quaker eccentric—and when he talked his deep impressive voice gave a richer significance to the profundities which he uttered.

Naturally they loved him (Lytton apart) and forgave him his faults, which were as remarkable as his appearance. He was stubborn to the extent of driving his car into a field because that was where the map showed that his route should be. He overrode the wishes of others. He was unscrupulous in small matters: he would accept an over-large contribution to a cab-fare and pocket the change. He came as near as is possible to cheating at chess.

In spite of his training as a scientist, which enabled him to make accurate attributions of paintings whose authorship was in question, he was absurdly and constitutionally credulous. 'A champion gull' Clive called him. Leonard Woolf records that he sent a drop of his blood to America for analysis by the notorious 'black box' and that he believed, from some nonsense that he read somewhere, that there was a certain characteristic in the intestine of birds which would lead to their survival of man. In later years, Clive's son Julian cherished memories of Roger laying paintings on the floor and swinging a pendulum over them to establish their authorship.

While it is easy to see how Roger, his gifts and qualities far outweighing his defects, found a permanent place in the

Bloomsbury circle, it is less easy to imagine how Clive fitted into it. That he did so is quite certain and it is interesting to examine the reasons.

He had, of course, as Vanessa's husband, a pre-emptive right to membership. But intimate relationship with a member of Bloomsbury, whether formal or not, was not automatically a passport to acceptance. Neither Lydia, Maynard's wife, nor even, for different reasons, Carrington, was in the full confidence of this carefully exclusive group; in Carrington's case a degree of snobbery and a resentment at her intimate relationship with Lytton—a relationship that was almost ownership—must have created the impediment. For Carrington lived out the philosophy of Bloomsbury more naturally and single-mindedly than some of the original members. Clive, however, had characteristics that would have prevented others from being accepted and largely lacked the qualities Bloomsbury admired. The Apostles, significantly, would have none of him, though he knew them all and they liked him. When he married Vanessa, Virginia felt that he was not good enough for her. There was, however, at no time in his life any doubt as to his total acceptability within the Bloomsbury group.

His inadequacies were plain enough to see. Both by upbringing and temperament he had many of the tastes and qualities of an eighteenth-century country squire. At Cambridge he had been a member of the hearty hunting set. At Charleston, he devoted two or three days a week to shooting, as David Garnett reported to T. H. White in 1944, when Clive was 63. He was fond of the social life of London, as fond as Virginia but without her ironical, deprecatory attitude to it. He had mistresses, none of whom was acceptable to Bloomsbury, apart from Mary Hutchinson with whom, exceptionally, he was in love for nearly ten years. He was a name-dropper. He had a red face and, according to Virginia, 'a bawling voice'. He had, it was felt, a second-rate mind. Any one of these characteristics would have been enough to close the doors of Bloomsbury to otherwise possible candidates.

David Garnett suggests some of the reasons for Clive's acceptance. 'Clive's wide reading, quick wit and common sense was an essential ingredient in the brilliant talk to be heard in Bloomsbury.' When Clive was not shooting or being the host at smart luncheon parties in London, he was, in fact, reading. And his mind, if neither brilliant nor original, was, according to Leonard Woolf 'eager, lively, intensely curious'. He loved argument and was educated by it. More than anything, his warm, friendly personality and his concern for the comfort of others earned him deep affection from those who knew him well. 'He saved Bloomsbury' wrote David Garnett, 'from being another Clapham Sect, devoted, in the same cold unworldly way, to aesthetics and the pursuit of abstract truth instead of to evangelical religion.' So Clive 'jolly, and rosy, and squab, a man of the world', as Virginia described him, held his place easily among a group of friends all abler and more gifted than he. He philandered with Virginia, who encouraged him. Lytton was for years a constant correspondent. Vanessa soon understood that he was rather unselectively susceptible to women and she found herself comfortable in a marriage in which friendship and easy confidence had replaced passion. When Clive did not wish to follow his friends into the rarer regions of intellectual or aesthetic speculation he teased them all, Virginia in particular, and sometimes in ways that hurt more than he intended.

It was one thing to be liked, quite another to be respected for one's own qualities or achievements. It was necessary to provide some evidence of distinction and Clive had strong ambitions in this direction. The way was shown to him by his early association with French painters and finally made clear to him by his friendship with Roger. Already by the time of his marriage he was something of an expert on the new art-trends in Paris and thus had some standing as an aesthete. Virginia was, as we have seen, sufficiently confident both in his friendship and judgment to let him see her early drafts of *The Voyage Out*. She accepted his lengthy and detailed criticisms with uncharacteristic humility. He had, she felt, 'a gift for knowing what's what'.

Clive was without originality and had no creative gift. It would be cynical to add that he had thus two of the qualities essential to a critic, but it was a critic that he became. He had taste as well as enthusiasm and he absorbed from Roger and others a set of ideas about art which guided his preferences and formed the basis of the articles for which he soon became well known. He was, in fact, for years the leading publicist for the new movement in art, reaching perhaps a wider, if less knowledgeable, public than Roger ever commanded.

He was, however, not content with the reputation he enjoyed. He felt within him the need to produce some major work that should establish him in the eyes, not only of Bloomsbury but of the intellectual world at large, as a genuine heavyweight. He felt this need for years, but it was not until his long romance with Mary Hutchinson was over that, as it were on the rebound, he began to assemble his ideas. *Civilization*, as he entitled his book with an almost arrogant simplicity, was published by Chatto & Windus in 1928; they issued it in the Phoenix Library four years later, and there were two Penguin editions in 1938 and 1947. It can claim therefore to have had a good publishing life.

The book is a development of his early book *Art* and repeats many of its ideas, which may still have had some freshness. It is not, however, a book which wears well. There is too little straw in his bricks and his 'de haut en bas' manner and heavy humour are not appealing. There is much liveliness in the book and several epigrams. But boisterousness and jocularity do not help aesthetic theorising, and his style, with its constant pointless inversions, is clumsy and inappropriate. What Roger had said in his review of *Art* could as appropriately be applied to *Civilization*. '[Clive] entered' he wrote, 'the holy of holies of culture in knickerbockers with a big walking-stick in his hand.' Leonard described him in his review of *Civilization* as a 'wonderful organiser of intellectual greyhound racing tracks'. Neither comment could have given him much pleasure and Virginia, to whom he dedicated the book, was disappointed in it. She had liked the opening chapters when she saw them in manuscript but 'in the end' she said, 'it turns out that *Civilization* is a lunch party at no. 50 Gordon Square'.

He attempted nothing so ambitious again. There was indeed a book on Proust and one on French Painting, and not least his memoirs, *Old Friends*. But his reputation was made by, and rests upon, ephemeral pieces of art criticism. In these, liveliness gave point to ideas which were often new if not original, and they were not long enough to be irritating. He made one excursion outside his chosen field: his pamphlet *Peace at Once* had the distinction of being destroyed in 1915 by order of the Lord Mayor.

Clive outlived Roger by thirty years. Each had made his own contribution to Bloomsbury and each found in that society comfortable friendships and the indulgence which their faults demanded. Bloomsbury would have been poorer without them.

IX

Wartime Bloomsbury

THE war changed Bloomsbury, not so much by its direct effect upon their lives as by their efforts to avoid its impact altogether. They were all—though not all to start with—opposed to the war, either on pacifist principles, like Bertrand Russell, or because, like Lytton and Clive, they thought it an unnecessary and improper war, or simply because they found violence emotionally repugnant. As intellectuals, without firm political attitudes, their case was put by Lytton in a letter to his brother James. 'I think one must resist if it comes to the push. . . . As for our personal position, it seems to me quite sound and coherent. We're all far too weak physically to be of any use at all. If we weren't we'd still be too intelligent to be thrown away in some really not essential expedition. . . . It's no good pretending one isn't a special case.'

Bertie campaigned heroically against the war, Clive wrote his pacifist pamphlet, and Lytton took part for a while in the anti-conscription movement, but otherwise Bloomsbury's opposition was largely passive. Partly as a result of the expedients to which they were driven, and partly for other reasons, the war permanently altered the pattern of their lives. It was through the war that a number of younger people were drawn into their circle. And it was during the war that London ceased to be the single focus of their lives.

It was not until the introduction of conscription in 1916 that it became necessary to take action to avoid personal involvement. In some cases, no action was required. Maynard had joined the Treasury in 1915 and was, for the time being, immune. Roger, at 50, was left in peace at the Omega Workshop, where he encouraged and sold the work of young craftsmen and artists. James, who was sacked in 1915 by his cousin St Loe, from the staff of the *Spectator* for his pacifist views, joined Lytton in the short-lived campaign against conscription. When that failed, Lytton who would have been a dangerous liability in any army, and was totally unfitted for any work which would have exempted him from military service, had to trust to the force of the arguments he could place before the tribunal. As we have seen, it was the weakness of his body, rather than the strength of his conscientious objections, which saved him. Clive and Adrian took up farmwork which, as long as it was of a kind which could be classified as work of national importance, conferred immunity from military service.

Philip Morrell had spoken out in the House of Commons, a single brave voice, against our entering the war. It was an act both of courage and political suicide. Neither the House nor his constituents wanted any more of him. But at least he could at Garsington provide work on the farm for Ottoline's friends and many, like Clive, took refuge there.

Another who became a farm-labourer was David Garnett. Enthusiastically received into the Bloomsbury circle after his Christmas with Lytton and Duncan at the Lacket, he was to remain the truest of their younger friends, on intimate terms with them all, and to be, in his autobiography and other works, a faithful recorder of their doings and personalities. Meanwhile, in 1915, he was getting his bearings, both for his future career and for his personal life. He turned away from the study of science and for a while, under Duncan's influence, took up painting with enthusiasm, showing sufficient talent for Roger Fry to compare one of his works to a Monet. He had still to make up his mind about the war. With Francis Birrell he joined a Quaker organisation, the 'Friends' War Victim Relief Mission' and went with him to France. Here at least there was positive work to be done. Within a few months he discovered that he was a pacifist. He returned to England but was soon in Paris with Duncan, designing dresses for a production of 'Pelléas et Mélissande' at the Vieux Colombiers. Duncan was almost immediately deported as a 'pacifist anarchist', and David, after a short stay in Paris, rejoined Francis Birrell with the Quakers. He did not stay long. Maynard was urging him to come home and start writing and he felt no longer able to take however a small a part in the war.

His return to England was warmly welcomed by Bloomsbury. There was a marvellous ten-day visit to Asheham with
Virginia and Leonard, Vanessa and Clive, and Duncan. Lytton
and Harry Norton were there for part of the time and Maynard
for a weekend. There was affection, good talk, and for David
and Duncan some boisterous teasing of Vanessa. Later came
his first weekend visit to Garsington, along with a group of
painters—Duncan, Carrington, Barbara Hiles and John Nash.
It at once became evident that Ottoline had an ulterior motive
in her invitation—the 'Monastic Building' in the grounds of
her house was to be painted with scenes from rural life, and she
ordered her guests to work. After a good start on the Saturday,
Sunday dawned fine and the artists went on strike. Ottoline
however insisted that Duncan should not join them in the sun
but carry on with his work. He refused to go on painting, but
stayed indoors. David now left the others to keep Duncan
company and gradually they began again to paint. In the
event all the murals except Duncan's and David's were
obliterated.

David was never really happy at Garsington. He could not
easily or for long tolerate either Philip's uneasiness under
Ottoline's shadow, where his good nature was concealed by
false attitudes, or Ottoline's authoritarianism and the meanness
which ran alongside her acknowledged generosity. He thought
that Philip's pose as a farmer 'exhibited precisely the kind of
humbug which the Victorian novelists, such as Surtees and
Thackery, loved to make the object of their good tempered
fun.'

As for Ottoline, she had a wicked tongue and after David
refused to take part in a 'malicious discussion of Vanessa's
character', he found that he received no more invitations.

Vanessa was a totally different kind of person from Ottoline.
Her love for her friends was deep and genuine. However much
she teased them, it was without malice, and she did not, as
Ottoline did, make use of them. 'She was extremely alive and
gay,' wrote David, 'almost always critical, but full of humour,
and she possessed, when among her friends, the great attraction
of complete unselfconsciousness and spontaneity.' Men loved
her. 'She was the only woman that any of us knew who could

join in the talk of a group of men and allow them to forget
that she was a woman, forgetting it herself.' She was famous
for her deliciously bawdy jokes, and also for her inaccurate
rendering of catch-phrases which sometimes produced memorable absurdities, like those quoted by David in his autobiography: 'In that house you meet a dark horse in every cup-
board.' 'It runs off his back like ducks' water.' 'Ah, that will be
a canker to his worm.'

When in 1916 Duncan rented Wissett Lodge in Suffolk, and,
with David, set up as a fruit farmer, it was Vanessa who took
charge of their domestic arrangements for most of the summer.
It was, it seemed, an ideal and idyllic way of escape from conscription. It was a healthy out-door life and they were never
short of company. Wissett, for that summer, was an outpost of
Bloomsbury: Lytton, accompanied by Harry Norton, spent a
week there in June and was entranced: Oliver Strachey, Saxon
Sydney-Turner, and Barbara Hiles paid visits. Duncan's
father, Major Bartle Grant, who was an expert on orchids, and
thus had some interest in other growing things, liked what he
saw there, and seemed to approve of David, although he never
quite learned his name, and referred to him to Duncan as 'your
friend Garbage'. Ottoline made a single spectacular appearance.
When the maid brought morning tea to her room during her
visit she found her still in bed but in the full panoply of daytime make-up. Was she perhaps hoping for a visit from one of
her hosts? When she left at the end of her stay her appearance
astonished even those who were accustomed to her flamboyance. It was an extraordinary caricature of some half-realised
Dostoevsky character which got into the taxi in high red boots,
a loose blue tunic under a white kaftan with cartridge pouches
and an astrakhan fez. The Portland pearls which she was also
wearing seemed not quite appropriate. Nor perhaps was a
colour-scheme of red, white and blue the most suitable for a
person of well-known pacifist views.

David had now to a good extent replaced James as Lytton's
confidant. It was to him that Lytton confided that he was in
love with Carrington. He was anxious that the fact should be
concealed from Virginia and Ottoline, both of whom could
cause mischief by spreading gossip. It seems clear, however,

that, at this early stage in their relationship, Lytton believed that in Carrington he had found a woman with whom he could have a normal sexual relationship.

The Wissett experiment was not to prove a success for long. The authorities were not satisfied that, as self-employed fruit farmers, Duncan and David were making a contribution to the national war-effort within the meaning of the act. After a series of appeals, in which Maynard as always took charge of the tactics of the campaign, they were allowed exemption from combatant service on condition that they undertook alternative work of national importance. Vanessa once more took charge. Knowing Lewes from her stays at Asheham, she visited the market there and succeeded in finding jobs for them both on a nearby farm. There was an empty house available too. It was called Charleston.

David was required on the farm before it was possible to complete the move to Sussex and on his way to take up his job he collected Carrington and Barbara Hiles hoping that they could all be put up somehow at Asheham. Unfortunately, Virginia and Leonard were not there and the house was shut up. Never deterred by practical difficulties of this kind, David broke in through an upstairs window and let the girls in. Finding only one bed with any blankets they all spent the night in it. If Carrington is to be believed, David attempted to put into practice his theories as a 'libertine'. She wrote to him on her return to London, apologising for having been 'so solidly virtuous' and explaining how difficult she found it to 'make love with someone else in the same bed'.

When, inevitably, Virginia and Leonard learned of this escapade they were greatly incensed, more perhaps by wild rumours from the village and an unsatisfactory letter of explanation from David than by the actual event, though, according to Roger Fry, they were understandably annoyed about that too. The wretched Carrington was summoned to dinner 'to explain about Asheham', and was terrified at the prospect. As always, Vanessa came to the aid of the miscreants and undertook to pacify Virginia. In the end it all blew over.

It was nevertheless an unfortunate prelude to the establishment of Charleston as Vanessa's new home. Virginia had for a long time been urging Vanessa to come to Sussex and had in fact already extolled the merits of Charleston as a possible base. 'It has a W.C. & a bathroom, but the bath only has cold water. . . . It sounds a most attractive place—& 4 miles from us, so you wouldn't be badgered by us,' she wrote. Leonard was not so keen. His concern was to guard the peace which was essential to Virginia's health. He did not associate David and Duncan with peace. He could not forget David's burglarious entry at Asheham and Duncan's jokes could lead to mischief. 'I think the Woolves have a morbid terror of us all—I can't think why' wrote Vanessa to Lytton. She was at least partly right.

By the autumn of 1916 the decision, for better or worse, was taken and Vanessa took up residence at Charleston. The house was to provide accommodation not only for Duncan and David but also for her young family—Julian was 8 and Quentin 6— who were still living in war-time London except when she was able to rent Eleanor, the St. John Hutchinson's home at Chichester. Clive had his own establishment in London but would make frequent visits. From now on Charleston became the Bells' family home. Duncan and David lived there throughout the war and Duncan became a permanent resident. He was to continue to live there even after the deaths of Vanessa and Clive nearly fifty years later. As this book goes to print, he lives there still.

Charleston was a commodious family house, with plenty of bedrooms and with servants' quarters, known as High Holborn, reached by a back staircase from the kitchen. There was a walled garden at the back and a pond in the front. Furniture was at first a problem, solved by large-scale raids on 46 Gordon Square and the purchase of extraordinary items from second-hand shops in Lewes. Duncan and Vanessa painted walls and doors with delightful decorations and landscapes. Later, behind the house, studios and a pottery-kiln were added. Meanwhile a steady stream of guests came to inspect and stay at Charleston. Bloomsbury was in fact colonising a corner of Sussex.

Until the war, Bloomsbury had in fact been the home of the 'Bloomsberries'. Increasingly, however, they had found country life attractive. Leonard and Virginia were at Asheham, Mary and St. John Hutchinson at Chichester. Lytton, after having to leave the Lacket, was searching for another country cottage. Now Vanessa, Duncan and David had joined the exodus. Charleston and Asheham, Eleanor and later Lytton's house at Tidmarsh became the focal centres of Bloomsbury life. The claims of London remained, of course, unique and they constantly found themselves there. Leonard's work as a journalist and later as a publisher required him to be in London a great deal, and Virginia nearly always accompanied him. But they escaped to Asheham as often as possible and particularly when, as so often happened, Virginia's health showed signs of breaking down. Some of their friends, like Saxon Sydney-Turner, who worked at the Treasury, had to remain in London. Clive did so from choice. Maynard, though continuing to live at 46 Gordon Square, which he had bought from Clive and Vanessa, belatedly joined the migration to the country when in 1925 he bought Tilton, a farm which shared a boundary with Charleston. Oliver Strachey and James and his wife Alix still lived in Gordon Square, and both James and Maynard had enough room in their London houses to keep rooms, some on a permanent basis, for their country-dwelling friends as required.

The situation after the war ended therefore was that the London-based members of the circle had Tidmarsh and three or four houses in Sussex in which they could stay as welcome and familiar guests, while those who lived in the country were always sure of a bed in Gordon Square when pleasure or business called them to London.

In 1915, when Virginia was still acutely ill, Leonard had taken a lease of Hogarth House at Richmond and they moved there in March. Virginia gradually recovered and by the end of the year needed no resident nurse. Meanwhile, Leonard at the request of Sydney Webb, was researching into the causes of war and making a detailed study of the feasibility of an international organisation for the preservation of peace; this appeared in book form in 1916. Leonard was, strangely enough, never a conscientious objector. He was ready, if necessary, to serve as a soldier, but on the two occasions when he was called up, he was rejected on medical grounds: he had always had a nervous tremor of the hands, a disability of some gravity in a war still largely conducted with rifles.

Meanwhile, Virginia had since the beginning of 1916 been relatively free of illness and was absorbed in writing *Night and Day*: it was not finished until the spring of 1919. Since her breakdown in 1914, Leonard had understood that he must be her guardian, constantly watchful to protect her from the strains that could bring on another attack of crippling illness. It was for this reason that he had moved house to Richmond, where Virginia would be less accessible socially. 'It was a perpetual struggle,' he wrote, 'to find the precarious balance of health for her among the strains of writing and society.' At the first onset of the headache which was the usual symptom of impending illness she had to be put to bed, where she remained in a state bordering on coma until, if all went well, it abated. At all times, it was necessary to regulate the time she spent working or in company. The excitement of social life was damaging to only a slightly less degree than that of writing. The intense interest she had in people and their doings expressed itself in her passionate devotion to her writing, where in her novels she ceaselessly changed words, sentences and paragraphs in an obsessive determination to get every nuance of character and emotion exactly right and to bring to vivid life by an intensely imaginative use of words the scenes she described. As long as she was well she enjoyed the intensity of the effort involved, but it was always an exhausting activity which had to be rationed. When she was ill, effort became strain and she was in danger.

Every morning was spent writing, seated in a very low, 'disembowelled' armchair, with a large board on her knees. She wrote in quarto notebooks which she covered with gaily-coloured paper. Entirely absorbed in her work, she was impervious to the untidiness, amounting to squalor, of her workroom, the accumulation of what Lytton called 'filth packets' which littered the table, the piles of papers and bottles of ink which stood about on the floor: unconscious too of the comings and goings of those who had to have access to her room.

In the afternoon, she typed what she had written, with

endless revisions, and took walks along the river at Richmond, or in the Sussex lanes when she was at Asheham. Neither walking nor any other activity, however, enabled her to emerge from the world she was engaged in creating. 'The novel' wrote Leonard, 'became part of her and she herself was absorbed into the novel.' The difficulty for him was 'to find any play sufficiently absorbing to take her mind off her work.' It was Leonard's search for an occupation attractive enough to provide Virginia with some relief from the tension of writing that led to the foundation of the Hogarth Press.

In March 1917, they bought a small hand-press, with the object of printing short pieces of merit which might otherwise not find a publisher, and printing them with as much style and taste as they could summon. Virginia was delighted with the idea, seeing in it the ultimate possibility of producing her own work without the agonising necessity of offering it for judgment to publishers' readers first. As a trial run they produced between them, carrying out all the processes themselves from the setting-up of the type to the binding in gay, hand-stitched covers, a little volume containing two short stories, *The Mark on the Wall* by Virginia and *Three Jews* by Leonard, with four woodcuts by Carrington. *Two Stories*, in an edition of 150, was almost entirely sold out, largely to friends. The authors paid themselves no royalties and Leonard records, with characteristic accuracy, that the venture showed a profit of £7. 1s. 0d. It was enough to encourage them to continue with an activity which relaxed Virginia's tensions and whose processes they both found absorbing, though at times physically exhausting. They obtained access to, and eventually bought, a mechanical press. Through their acquaintance with gifted but unpublished writers they had no shortage of material, and Vanessa joined Carrington as an illustrator. They published *Prelude* by Katherine Mansfield, a friend whose writing Virginia admired with just a hint of jealousy. They had got to know and to like T. S. Eliot, whose *Prufrock* had appeared in 1917; he agreed that they should publish his next book of poems. He kept his promise and in 1919 *Poems* appeared, followed in 1923 by *The Waste Land*. It was through Eliot that in 1918 they obtained the manuscript of James Joyce's *Ulysses*, which was much too big an undertaking for them to print, but which they agreed to publish if they could find a printer brave enough to undertake the commission. They failed. Perhaps Virginia was not altogether sorry. Writing to Lytton in 1922 she was utterly scornful. 'Never have I read such tosh' she said. Much of it seemed to her 'merely the scratching of pimples on the body of the bootboy at Claridges.'

Meanwhile, in the last years of the war, the Hogarth Press gradually lengthened its list, and by the time peace came could be regarded as established. Its success defied what were thought to be the facts about publishing. With practically no capital, in absurdly unsuitable premises, and run unassisted by two intellectuals who had to learn the most elementary techniques of the printer as they worked, it could not possibly, the experts agreed, do anything but fail. Its success Leonard put down to two reasons: nothing was published which was not, by Hogarth standards, of high quality, and the overheads, themselves minimal, were subsidised by the proceeds of Leonard's and Virginia's work as journalists.

As a therapeutic device, the Hogarth Press seems also to have been at least a partial success, and to have contributed to the improved state of Virginia's mental health which was to last through the twenties. Leonard was enabled to pursue his increasingly successful career as a left-wing journalist and as an advocate of what was to become the League of Nations. With Oliver Strachey, he founded the 1917 Club, with premises in Gerard Street, which attracted as members not only those with left-wing political sympathies for whom it was mainly intended but the Bloomsbury aesthetes, who liked to take tea there. Ramsay MacDonald was a founder-member. Leonard at this stage was canvassing the idea of starting an international political review with foreign socialists as members of the board. MacDonald, while warmly supporting the project to Leonard's face, worked quietly and successfully behind his back to kill it. Leonard's comment reveals the extraordinary detachment which made him such an acute observer of human character. 'One certainly gets a great deal more pleasure' he wrote, 'from contemplating the psychology of a man like Ramsay than pain from the way in which he treats one.'

Leonard's work as a left-wing journalist was, to the extent that it was concerned with post-war political reconstruction, relevant to the war itself: but it was not devoted either to its prosecution or to attempts to bring it to an end. For him, the war was a disastrous idiocy and he well understood that the voice of reason would not be listened to while the madness lasted. This was the view generally held by Bloomsbury, with two major exceptions: Maynard and Bertrand Russell were both, in different ways, caught up in the war, and their lives were transformed by it.

Maynard, who went from King's to the Treasury in 1915, was from then on directly and fully engaged on war-work. He played an increasingly important part in Britain's economic struggle in which success was essential to victory. Maynard's work as an economist is outside the scope of this book: it is enough to say that his reputation soared in the war-years and that, when the armistice came, he was an inevitable choice as an expert British representative at the ensuing peace conference. As Leonard said, Maynard was 'as brilliant and effective in practice as in theory.' He demonstrated the truth of this opinion when he took charge of the finances of King's College and turned it in a short time from one of the poorest to one of the most prosperous of the Cambridge colleges. Maynard was shocked by the peace terms imposed by the allies on Germany, which seemed to him to make economic nonsense, and, after handing in his resignation, produced, in two months' intensive writing at Charleston, a masterly analysis of their implications for victors and vanquished. *The Economic Consequences of the Peace* immediately established Maynard as an economist of international eminence; he was to become the leading economic theorist of the post-war period.

Maynard had always tended to behave like a pundit; now he had really become one. His tendency to make *ex cathedra* pronouncements, not always as authoritative as they sounded, had alternately irritated and amused his Bloomsbury friends. From now on, when Maynard gave utterance to his views on economic affairs, he had a world-wide audience who listened with hushed reverence, and were right to do so. Bloomsbury, without really understanding, was undoubtedly impressed, and, with reservations, rather proud of him. The reservations arose from their feeling that his ambition had led him astray from the narrow path of ethical pure-mindedness. He had touched pitch. His influence in the exalted circles in which he now moved could, of course, be only good, but their influence on him was less benign. It was no longer possible to trust him to react in the way the rest of Bloomsbury did to the situations, personalities and events which make up life. Clive feared that he now attached more importance to means—power, honours, conventions, money—than to ends—the good states of mind described by Moore in *Principia Ethica*.

He was, thank goodness, still capable of disinterestedness: his devoted efforts in support of Lytton and the others at the National Service tribunals, which could have done him little good in official circles, showed this, particularly since he himself was never convinced of the validity of conscientious objections to war. And his financial acumen could at times be turned to unexceptionable uses. Thus, when in 1917, on the death of Degas, the artist's collection of pictures was put up for sale in Paris, it was Maynard who acquired for the National Gallery a Cézanne still-life, several Degas charcoal drawings, an Ingres and a Delacroix, for a few hundred pounds. 'Nessa and Duncan' wrote David Garnett to him, 'are very proud of you . . . you have been given complete absolution and future crimes also forgiven.'

This was, as it turned out, a rash undertaking, and there was always, in any case, so much to forgive. His table-manners, for example, were appalling: he grabbed whatever he wanted, helping himself without regard to others. His cool assumption of superior knowledge, too, was maddening, particularly when, as sometimes happened, he was quite wrong. If he corrected Cabinet Ministers when they were right and he was wrong—as when he insisted that it was not Scipio Africanus but Fabius Maximus who defeated Hannibal—that was merely amusing. But it was irritating when he treated his friends in the same way. 'Maynard' wrote David Garnett, 'picked up knowledge with lightning rapidity and occasionally got it wrong and would bluff it through if possible.' He was particularly prone to muddling dates and figures. Not even Maynard's brilliance could excuse, in Bloomsbury's eyes, the cavalier treatment of facts which, as incidental manifestations of truth were, of course, sacred. It was a question of values, and there was no doubt that Maynard's sense of values had, in Bloomsbury's eyes, been vitiated by worldly success. The 'phenomenal', to use Moore's term, was increasingly important to him. When, for example, he dined with the Duke of Connaught, his report on this notable event showed delight and self-congratulation: it entirely lacked the irony and amusement of a true Apostle. Perhaps Bloomsbury asked too much. Maynard, by virtue of his eminence, necessarily participated in the life of the great, and played a great part in the shaping of great events. It would perhaps have been impossible, certainly it would have been immensely difficult, for him to have retained at the same time the detached and sceptical attitude characteristic of Bloomsbury. That was an attitude appropriate and comfortable to observers, but inconvenient and indeed perhaps improper to participators.

Maynard remained, however, a member of the inner circle of Bloomsbury, sharing houses in Gordon Square, a familiar guest at Charleston, Eleanor and Tidmarsh, corresponding actively with Lytton and the others. With Vanessa and Duncan he had an especially close intimacy. His qualities as a friend simply outweighed his defects. His brilliance and charm certainly had much to do with it. 'He was the cleverest man I ever met,' wrote Clive. 'Also his cleverness was of a kind, gay, whimsical and civilised, which made his conversation a joy.' At the practical level, where friendship is often best tested, he was always ready to help his friends with money if they needed it: he was a member of the syndicate which enabled Lytton to rent Tidmarsh and he gave Duncan and David Garnett annuities, ensuring their acceptance by explaining to them that unless both of them agreed to take the money, neither would get it. Clive Bell considered that 'his supreme virtue was his deeply affectionate nature', and it was among his Bloomsbury friends that he revealed most freely this aspect of his personality. At a dinner preceding one of the meetings of the Memoir Club,[1]

---

[1] The Memoir Club, like its short-lived predecessor, the Novel Club, was an exclusively Bloomsbury society. One of the purposes of both clubs was to encourage Desmond MacCarthy to write his great novel. Members

Maynard looked round at those present and said 'If everyone at this table, except myself, were to die tonight, I do not think I should care to go on living.' It was a confession of love and no one giggled.

Bloomsbury friendships were deep and lasting: they were hardly ever ruffled except by absurdities. One such led to a permanent coolness between Vanessa and Duncan and Maynard. During the war Maynard had bought 46 Gordon Square from Clive and Vanessa who, with Duncan, continued to have a pied-à-terre there. When in 1925 Maynard married Lydia Lopokova, the Russian ballerina—a step peevishly regarded by Vanessa as a kind of betrayal of their friendship—Duncan and the Bells moved across the square to No. 39. An argument at once arose about the ownership of a painting by Duncan, to which both Vanessa and Maynard laid claim. To prevent its removal, Maynard screwed it to the wall in No. 46. Vanessa concealed her fury at this act of force but planned an effective counter-measure. She invited Maynard to Charleston and while he was on his way slipped up to London with her own screwdriver. She had a key to No. 46 and she had no difficulty in unscrewing the painting and depositing it safely at No. 39. Such childish behaviour on both sides was more damaging than a disagreement on a serious issue, and their relationship was never the same again.

This rift was an accident of peace: meanwhile the war went on. While Bloomsbury as a whole had made a satisfactory accommodation to the situation it created, one of their friends and closest associates had not. Bertrand Russell's pacifism, unlike theirs, was whole-heartedly militant. Lytton, who had at the outset been active in opposition to conscription, gave up the struggle when conscription became law. Maynard, who was also against conscription, had thought of resigning from the Treasury if it were introduced. But he did not do so and,

read papers on whatever they pleased, discussion was completely free, and no records were kept. Two of Maynard's papers were published posthumously as *Two Memoirs*: one of these, *My Early Beliefs*, is a vivid analysis of the influence of G. E. Moore on the Cambridge Apostles. The club met at irregular intervals from its foundation in 1920 for many years, outliving its original membership.

when he received his own call-up papers, blandly informed the
authorities that he was too busy to comply. Later, when this
impertinence, was no longer effective, he formally obtained
exemption. To temporise or compromise like Maynard was
not in Bertie's temperament. Nor, philosopher or not, could
he, as Lytton did, accept the inevitable. He campaigned
vigorously, in and out of season, in lectures and writing, against
the war. He was prepared to suffer for his activities and indeed
drew attention to them in ways which ensured punishment.
Thus he wrote to *The Times* claiming, as the author of a leaflet
held to be subversive, his own right to be prosecuted along
with those who had already been imprisoned for distributing it.
He refused to pay the fine imposed at his subsequent trial and
would have gone to prison had his friends not paid it for him.
In 1918, as the result of an article advocating the acceptance of
a recent German peace offer, and suggesting that American
troops would be used as strike-breakers in Britain, he was sent
to gaol for six months, after a trial, attended by his Bloomsbury
friends, at which he was subjected to every kind of insult and
calumny both by the prosecution and the presiding magistrate.
All of this was predictable and acceptable in the circumstances.
Bertie expected nothing different and was quite content to be
martyred if the process helped the cause by the propaganda
resulting from it. He was, however, shocked and distressed
when, because of his prison sentence, his fellowship at Trinity
was abruptly taken from him. Absolute freedom of thought
and expression is of the essence of a university: it was appalling
to discover that the passions of war were able to blind his own
college to its responsibility as an academic body.

Bertie's heroic stand as a pacifist, no less than Maynard's
ambivalent position as a Treasury official prosecuting the war
with the weapons of finance while at the same time giving aid
and comfort to Bloomsbury's conscientious objectors, exempli-
fies the gap which existed between Russell and Keynes and the
circle to which Lytton and Virginia, Vanessa and Duncan and
their friends belonged. While Bertie and Maynard were
participators by temperament, Bloomsbury stood aside,
observing the human drama, even at its most tragic, with
ironic detachment. While Bertie laboured with great courage

and no hope of success to stop the war, and Maynard lent his gifts to the task of winning it (no doubt at times uncomfortably aware that his career was benefiting in the process), Bloomsbury on the whole was stimulated into activity only by the need to avoid being personally involved. It was a perfectly legitimate reaction to a situation which, in their view, had been created by politicians for whose intellectual capacity and ethical standards they had little respect. A number of them they knew personally and had already rejected as unacceptable in their society. Nationalism and national rivalries were stupid and irrelevant. But it would have been almost as stupid to waste time in a hopeless struggle against forces in which passion drowned the voice of intelligence. They were neither rebels nor reformers, except incidentally in those areas of intellectual activity or personal conduct in which unconventional ideas or behaviour might ultimately have the effect of rebellion or reformation. In the long view, they were certainly right. Bertie's militant pacifism did not stop the war nor even noticeably affect public opinion: the uselessness and horror of war became clear to all without his aid and, although more wars were to come, they came in the face of mounting opposition in all quarters. On the other hand, Lytton's war-effort, the writing of *Eminent Victorians*, made a unique contribution in the moral as well as the literary field. Never again would it be possible for the great figures of any time, past, present or future, to be taken at their own valuation or that of their adulators. They would be subject to close and disenchanted examination, and not only in retrospect. The lead which Lytton gave was followed by others; in our day there are no heroes and no paragons, only the heroic deeds and noble achievements of men of whom not only the feet are of human clay. It would be absurd to exaggerate Lytton's contribution to what is plainly a healthy change in attitude, but it would also be wrong to forget that he was the first to express it effectively. In this sense, *Eminent Victorians* was literally epoch-making.

With all his fastidious distaste for violence and extremism in any form, Lytton as a writer had his own boldness, and it was more effective than the noisier demonstrations of his tougher and less sensitive contemporaries. In his personal life he was bold, too, though he dressed his boldness in quaintly disarming and even appealing costumes. His homosexuality was as genuine and active as that for which others had gone to prison, and, unlike Wilde, he was completely frank about it among those with whom friendship made this possible. His sexual rebellion was only a generation in advance of history, but it was all the same a rebellion.

There is, of course, an inherent absurdity in regarding Lytton as a rebel. It is similarly inappropriate to regard Virginia as a rebel in the literary sphere, although she preceded Joyce in the use of the stream-of-consciousness technique. Clive and Roger Fry, for all their attacks on contemporary artistic taste and their propaganda on behalf of painters whose work infuriated or revolted the art-lovers of the day, did not set out to lead a movement. They observed, judged and made their comment, while Vanessa and Duncan, with as little self-consciousness, painted in the way their eyes and hands led them to paint, without regard for the opinion of others. Leonard Woolf, as a political writer, sought to persuade, but only by the force of the arguments by which he was himself convinced. He was committed to a left-wing position only to the extent that, and for as long as, it seemed to him intellectually sound and he was sceptical enough to know that no political position is ever quite sound. It was partly for this reason that Beatrice and Sydney Webb, whose views he largely shared, and with whom he worked for many worthy causes, found him irritatingly unsatisfactory. He lacked the dynamism which comes from commitment. To remain, as Leonard remained, open to argument, is a drawback in a reformer and a positive disqualification in a rebel.

It is, of course, entirely consistent with Bloomsbury's philosophy that, holding views and pursuing ways of life widely different from those of contemporary society, they should nevertheless not set out to found a movement or even to proselytise. Any such activity would have tended to compromise their integrity since a movement inevitably has to over-simplify or modify its doctrines in order to gain the support of potential followers. Bertie became an extremist: Maynard, however slightly, a trimmer. Both, by these actions, deserted the Bloomsbury fold. Bloomsbury's exclusiveness arose precisely from its instinctive refusal to persuade others. One either accepted the Bloomsbury 'Weltanschauung' and thus qualified as a member of their society, or disagreed and was excluded. There is thus an element of intellectual snobbery, though not of arrogance, in the Bloomsbury attitude. Those who were found wanting by Bloomsbury were considered simply not to measure up to Bloomsbury standards: the implication of intellectual and indeed of moral inferiority, clear though it was, was not generally stated. Bloomsbury was saved from arrogance by its capacity to laugh at itself, by the irony with which it regarded its own activities as well as those of others, and by its joy in absurdity, wherever encountered. If Bloomsbury gave a lead, it never expected that it would be followed and found plenty of reason for thinking that there were few who were ready, either intellectually or emotionally, for the gospel as it had been revealed to the small band of the elect who met each other in Gordon Square or at Charleston.

The 1914-1918 war was probably a unique phenomenon. It was, one hopes, the last of the old-style European wars, that is, wars which arise from treaty commitments undertaken to preserve the balance of power. It was a political war. But because of its huge scale and the power of new weapons, the whole nation was for the first time directly involved in its conduct. The civilian population, and not only the soldiers, came under enemy attack and had to man its own defences. It was something very near to total war and everyone, or almost everyone, was emotionally as well as physically committed to the cause of victory.

Bloomsbury was quite incapable of sharing this sense of commitment. The war to them was not only an irrelevance and an interruption to what was otherwise an orderly and generally tolerable form of existence, but ethically indefensible. Since there was no effective method of getting it called off, it had to be endured, and means found to minimise its effect on their individual lives. They found themselves, not for the first time, in a tiny minority. The fact made so much the more valuable the intimacy and freedom they possessed within their small society. It perhaps confirmed too their well-founded sense of difference from the common run of humanity.

For the first time, when the Armistice came, Bloomsbury found itself in tune with the national mood. They, like everybody else, rejoiced. Those who were not in London converged upon it. Lytton came up from Sussex with Jack and Mary Hutchinson whose guest he was. Carrington came in from Hampstead where she was visiting Barbara Bagenal, the former Barbara Hiles, in hospital with her new baby. Vanessa was immobilised by pregnancy (Angelica, later to be David Garnett's second wife, was born on Christmas Day), but Clive came up. The others were already there. Virginia began the day, inappropriately enough, with a visit to her dentist, but joined Leonard in Trafalgar Square, and from there struggled back through the crowds to Richmond. Everyone else, after celebration lunches, congregated at Monty Shearman's flat in the Adelphi for a party which went on into the small hours. Roger, Maynard, Duncan, David and Ottoline were there with the others. Mark Gertler surprised Carrington by being present. Osbert and Sacheverell Sitwell came, and an exotic note was introduced by the presence of Diaghilev, Massine and Lydia Lopokova. D. H. Lawrence made an appearance with Frieda but was characteristically at odds with everybody. He saw no reason to rejoice since Germany was bound to rise again as a threat to peace. Such prophetic gloom was out of keeping with the general mood of gaiety. Everyone danced, even Lytton, who, as Osbert recorded, jigged about with 'amiable debility', though clearly 'unused to dancing'. Carrington danced energetically for three hours, largely with David Garnett. It was just the kind of party Virginia would have loved. It was a pity she had to miss it.

X

Variations on a Domestic Theme

FOR Lytton, life as the war ended was as complete as possible a contrast from life before 1914. Then he was an unknown reviewer, with one modest little book to his credit. He lived in cramped discomfort in a bed-sittingroom in his mother's house. He had no money to speak of. Now he had his own country cottage with an adoring and adorable young woman to look after him. He was famous, and, though not yet rich, had quite enough money for his needs and the prospect of a good deal more to come. *Eminent Victorians*, appearing six months before the Armistice, had brought him the triumph he had always longed for. After reviews that could hardly have been more enthusiastic, it was reprinted seven times that year. The book was a sensation.

So was its author. London hostesses competed for him. Great men expressed their admiration to his face. Lytton loved it all, and particularly the sensation of being recognised at last as a person of consequence. It was nice to spend an intimate week-end with the Asquiths and to describe it afterwards to Ottoline in a letter full of Christian names. It was nice, at distinguished social occasions in London, to be among the most distinguished. But he found himself too often beset by bores, and then it was even nicer to return to Tidmarsh, to be spoiled and cosseted by Carrington. She herself might have returned there only on the previous day from some visit or other but, with her slightly crazy genius for domesticity, would have contrived for him all the comforts he most liked: there would be bright fires, meals that were unusual but often delicious, wine at the right temperature, and, best of all, her affectionate presence. Instead of the charming, ill-spelt and inconsequent letters with which she showered him when they were apart there was now her even more delightful chatter, full of irreverence and indecency and original, uninhibited comments on their friends and their habits. Afterwards, Lytton would retire gently to his study, to work or rest, and Carrington would sometimes paint but more often work in the garden, with marvellous energy and enthusiasm, obtaining effects which, as she knew little about gardening, were a surprise to her and often a shock to visitors.

She was still seeing Mark as often as she could when she was in London, but her hold on him was now irretrievably weakened. Although he was always susceptible to her attraction, her relationship with Lytton made it impossible for him to return to his old intimacy with her. He was not ready to share her. For Carrington, however, to be shared seemed to be essential. Mark had overcome to a great extent her prudishness and aroused her sensuality. Released and stirred by him, she needed more than Lytton could offer by way of masculine stimulation or consolation. There were plenty of opportunities, not all of them attractive: Augustus John's frank attempts at love-making merely amused her. But she had been happy to take her bed up on to the roof at Garsington with Aldous Huxley when it was too hot to be indoors, and when he stayed with her under her parents' roof at Tatchley, they spent the night together, behind a door insecurely fastened by a watch-chain wound round two nails. To Aldous' intense irritation, she refused to take off her pyjamas, which were thick and tickled. 'Such a nightmare,' she reported to Lytton, with other, more detailed descriptions of the night's activities. Aldous' portrait of her as Mary Bracegirdle in *Crome Yellow*, though physically unmistakable, is unfriendly.

Episodes of this kind were unsatisfactory: Carrington's heart was not in them. They provided little more than amusing material for her letters to Lytton; she gave him, of course, detailed accounts.

There now begins, however, a decade of extraordinary sexual entanglements with Carrington at their centre and Lytton, himself also involved in them on his own account, trying with endless patience and a good deal of wisdom to help her towards a satisfactory accommodation of her physical and emotional needs. It could hardly have been more difficult. Carrington's love-affairs, however passionate, were always subsidiary to her relationship with Lytton: had even, if need arose, to be prolonged beyond their natural life if that seemed the best way to protect her position with him. Her lovers, not under-standing this, were often puzzled and sometimes driven frantic with frustration. Lytton's affairs were less troublesome. Emotionally, or at least romantically, intense, they stood on their own feet (or lay in their own beds) without upsetting anybody. Whatever their physical posture, they did not look over their shoulders. Even when Lytton and Carrington were both in love with the same man, there were no problems on Lytton's side. He was neither possessive nor jealous of Carrington.

For ten years from 1919, two men, in succession and then simultaneously, offered Carrington the kind of love Lytton could not give her. Ralph Partridge and Gerald Brenan were friends: they had met in the war as fellow-officers and were soon on the intimate terms made peculiarly possible by a life lived at close quarters in conditions of squalor and shared danger. They were both good soldiers and, in different ways, enjoyed soldiering. Gerald describes Ralph as 'a magnificent infantry officer with a judgment that could always be relied on in practical matters.' At twenty-three he was a Major com-manding a battalion. Each was awarded the Military Cross for gallantry, and Ralph gained a bar to his medal and the Croce di Guerra as well. Although they were profoundly unlike in temperament, the friendship which began in the trenches endured for the rest of their lives, surviving and perhaps even being strengthened by strains which would have destroyed most similar relationships. For both, Lytton's household became an emotional focus and it was to remain so for Ralph until Lytton's death.

Ralph Partridge (his real name was Reginald, but he had always been known as Rex, until Lytton finally re-christened him Ralph) was physically an enormously impressive figure, 'a good-looking man of powerful build', in Gerald's words, 'with the brightest, bluest eyes I have ever seen.' He was a natural athlete with the vitality and zest which belong characteristically to men of outstanding physical gifts. In manner he was gay, open and warm-hearted. He liked girls, and when on a visit to Amiens with Gerald he was more interested, Gerald records, in finding a tart than in inspecting the cathedral. It would have been easy to dismiss him as a cheerful philistine whose tastes and interests were dominated by the requirements of an extremely healthy body. This would have been quite wrong. He had gone up to Christ Church in 1913 with a classical scholarship from Westminster. Carrington's brother Noel was his contemporary in the same college and became a close friend. He remembers Ralph as one of a brilliant Oxford set, a man of wide reading, who introduced him to Voltaire, Rabelais, Swift, and the lesser Elizabethans. 'He excelled,' says Noel in a private letter, 'in debating clubs and not only by his quick wit and forcefulness but by his unexpected range of knowledge.' Examinations caused him little trouble. He could, Noel records, 'gut a book in half the time anyone else could,' and so was able to concentrate his reading into a brief period before an examination. When he returned to Oxford after the war he obtained, with the minimum of apparent effort, a distinction in his final examination. He had, it was clear to all who knew him, a first-rate brain, and a brilliant career was forecast for him.

This is not the picture which emerges from Gerald's autobiography nor that which Holroyd presents in his Life of Lytton. Gerald, and Holroyd after him, describe a likeable 'hearty' without intellectual interests, though possessing considerable latent ability. Holroyd paints him, on his early visits to Tidmarsh, as a virgin mind awaiting, without necessarily longing for, the fertilisation which Lytton, with his wide culture, was to supply. But it is simply not true to say, as Holroyd does, that under Lytton's tutelage Ralph was changed from a 'bluff and breezy extrovert' to an 'intelligent and cultivated man of letters'. He never ceased to be an extrovert—which does not necessarily imply insensitivity—but he was already both intelligent and highly literate before he came under Lytton's influence. The implication of 'heartiness' is dismissed by Lord David Cecil, who knew him well, after Lytton's death, for nearly thirty years. In a letter to the present author he says 'I cannot believe that Ralph was ever in the least "hearty" in manner or anything else. "Heartiness" is . . . a sort of conventional mask. Ralph . . . wore no mask but was spontaneous, passionate, uninhibited and congenitally unconventional.'

Ralph's later history is comprehensible only if it is understood that he entered Lytton's life as a man of culture with an able and well-furnished mind. Lytton gave it, no doubt, new directions and enriched it with his own unique contribution. But he was never Svengali to Ralph's Trilby.

Whereas Ralph seemed, superficially at least, merely a highly successful version of the standard-pattern, unreflective young Englishman, Gerald was an individualist, an eccentric and a rebel against all the conventions of his class. The son of an undistinguished Irish soldier, he had been dragged about the world as a child from Malta, where he was born, to South Africa and India and back to Ireland until his family settled in the Cotswolds and he was sent off to his public school. He was by now thoroughly unsettled and miserable. At the age of sixteen he came under the influence of John Hope-Johnstone, an odd character, at one time tutor to Augustus John's sons, living by himself in a nearby Cotswold cottage. Hope-Johnstone was a bohemian romantic of artistic tastes, and he introduced Gerald to poetry—Yeats and Blake—to the art of Beardsley and the philosophy of Nietzsche. It was heady stuff for a boy intended as Gerald was for a military career. After dutifully passing the Sandhurst entry examination, he planned and executed with his mentor a trip abroad conceived as a realisation of the dream they both seem to have shared for a vagrant life in the East. Hope-Johnstone already claimed to know Arabic and Romani and took with him a collection of the grammars of other outlandish tongues as well as the works of Alesteir Crowley. They got little further than Italy, where their money ran out. It was in many ways an absurd trip, but the absurdity was supplied by Hope-Johnstone, who always had one foot in the conventional camp. Gerald, as his later life showed, was a true bohemian, totally at odds with bourgeois life.

Gerald's attitude to the war was ambivalent. He admitted that although he was horrified and intellectually repelled by it he was at the same time fascinated and excited. 'Although . . . everything one could see was horrible' he wrote, describing the

scene after a battle, 'I could not help liking it.' He seemed to
have little or no sense of danger—a dubious merit in a soldier—
and lived for some time, happily and alone in a house evacuated
by the French owners because of a large unexploded bomb in
the fireplace. His conduct as an officer had earned him his
decoration; but he was able at the same time to infuriate Ralph[1]
by putting a strong case for pacifism.

If Ralph had been merely the cheerful but brainless philistine
he generally appeared to be there would have been little basis
for the long friendship which began in the trenches. The
admiration which Gerald felt for him as a soldier and a
womaniser would not have been enough, and there were large
areas of experience in which they could not meet. 'I could not
share with him my feelings about poetry or the inner life'
wrote Gerald, 'for he was not . . . one of the elect.' But
Gerald recognised Ralph's latent powers of mind and his total
lack of worldly ambition made a strong bond between them.
Leonard Woolf, at a later period, was also conscious of hidden
qualities in Ralph: he describes him a year or two after the war
as 'very large, very good-looking, enormously strong . . . a
great he-man, a very English Don Juan. But behind this façade
of the calm unemotional public school athlete, there was an
extraordinary emotional vulnerability. . . . He was easily
moved to tears.'

This was the man to whom Carrington was introduced in
the summer of 1918, by her brother Noel. Carrington was
tremendously excited at their first meeting in London. 'I am
so elated and happy' she wrote to Lytton. 'It is so good to find
someone who one can rush on and on with, quickly.' She
found him 'not very attractive to look at. Immensely big. But
full of wit and reckless.' He shared, she found, 'all the best
views of democracy, and social reform, wine and good cheer
and operas.' Either Ralph was setting out to please, or
Carrington was crediting him with interests she wanted him to

---

[1] Before the war ended Ralph had modified his views. Frances Partridge
informs the author that he was by then 'completely disillusioned with war
as a means of settling problems, had decided the only thing to do was to
try to save his men's lives, and from then to his death remained a convinced
pacifist',

have: Ralph as a social reformer is not a convincing figure. However that may be there is no doubt that he had made a sensational hit, and Carrington was eager to have him to Tidmarsh to meet Lytton. Ralph, for his part, responded instinctively to her vivacity and charm, but was puzzled by her eccentric personality and put off by her unconventional views.

Lytton, titillated by Carrington's description of this gay giant who sang Italian songs, gesticulated, and wished, it seemed, after the war, to sail cargoes of wine to Mediterranean islands dressed as a brigand, was all for inviting him to the Mill House, and as soon as possible he duly arrived. The visit, in August 1918, was a calamity. There was an argument about pacifism. Ralph, about to return to the trenches, had at this stage not much sympathy with pacifist views. At last, outnumbered and under strong attack, he hit back with the statement—quite at variance with his real opinions which were civilised and tolerant—that he thought all pacifists should be shot. Lytton retreated into silence. Carrington, to relieve the strain, took Ralph off to the river. He showed no sign of having literary or artistic interests and he confessed to being put off by Lytton's 'billowy beard and alternating basso-falsetto voice', as he later described them to Noel. Writing to Gerald after the visit he described Carrington as 'a painting damsel and a great Bolshevik' and Lytton as 'of a surety meet mirth for Olympus'.

It was on this basis of what seemed to be extreme incompatibility and mutual distaste that a strange and durable intimacy was to be built. After the war, Ralph returned to Oxford to continue reading law. Tidmarsh was only twenty miles away and Carrington was a female attractive enough for Ralph—at first accompanied by Noel—to cycle as far as that to meet her. He began to pay regular visits and soon found himself deeply in love. At Easter, Ralph, Noel and Carrington, with Ralph's sister to make up the party, went on a walking-tour through Spain. Ralph and Carrington became lovers. For Carrington, as always, Lytton held the key to the relationship. No-one unacceptable to him could have been acceptable to her. Luckily, Lytton, like Gerald before him, and Leonard later, saw through

Ralph's ebullience to the intellectual and emotional potentialities concealed beneath his bluff manner. Moreover, his huge virility and marvellous physique dazzled and delighted Lytton, who saw in him the masculine splendour he himself so lamentably lacked. Thoby Stephen, 'the Goth', had affected him in the same way.

Soon enough, he was in love. So the currents began to trend together. The attraction Carrington held for Ralph was balanced and complemented by Lytton's feeling for him. Carrington, typically, shared herself between them. Her female instincts were strongly stirred by Ralph's virile charm, and when fully revealed as he kindly posed naked for her to draw, they moved her so much that she could barely control her pencil. 'I confess I got rather a flux over his thighs and legs,' she wrote to Lytton. Her heart, though, remained with Lytton, and perhaps the best hours they spent together were at night when Lytton read aloud to them, his deep reading voice in striking contrast with his conversational squeak.

It was on a visit to Tidmarsh to see Ralph in the summer of 1919 that Gerald Brenan first remembers meeting Carrington. He did not take to her immediately, for she was said to have made fun of Hope-Johnstone, to whom Gerald was romantically loyal. At this stage, Gerald's contacts with Bloomsbury were remote and second-hand. There was an indirect link with Roger Fry, who had just appointed Hope-Johnstone editor of the *Burlington Magazine*, and he knew Augustus and Dorelia John and had stayed with them in Dorset. But his visit to Tidmarsh was his first contact with Lytton, as well as with 'the blue-eyed, honey-mouthed girl' who, as he later wrote, 'for seven years was to be the leading person in my life.'

Lytton made a confused impact on Gerald. Seeing him for the first time in a deep armchair and a poor light, he had the impression of a 'darkly bearded he-goat, glaring at me from the bottom of a cave.' As he gradually attuned himself to Lytton's appearance and, less successfully, to his voice, his first impression altered and he saw him as 'gravely remote and fantastic, with something of the polished and dilettante air of a sixteenth-century cardinal.' The meeting was to be the beginning of a lifelong friendship. Meanwhile in September,

Gerald left for Spain, where he settled permanently at Yegen, a remote village in mountainous country midway between Granada and Almeria.

Ralph was now beginning his last year at Oxford where he did a minimum of reading and divided his time between constant visits to Tidmarsh and rowing in the Christ Church eight. It is typical of his indolence and contempt for personal glory, as well as of his natural excellence as an athlete, that he was offered and refused an invitation at this stage to row for the University. When the Christ Church boat won the Ladies' Plate at Henley (where Ralph had agreed to row on condition that he did no training) and was invited to represent Great Britain in the Olympic Games, Ralph again declined to be a member of the crew. In the athletic field at least, Ralph showed a contempt for the 'phenomenal' worthy of a Cambridge Apostle.

He had in fact a more interesting plan in view. This was no less than an Easter visit with Lytton and Carrington to Gerald's mountain fastness. Gerald received Ralph's suggestion with enthusiasm, only slightly damped by the fact that he had only ten pounds in the bank and that only two rooms in his house were so far furnished. He decided to sell some War Loan and asked a relative for a loan to tide him over. He then walked fifty-seven miles over the mountains to Almeria to choose furniture. This done, he waited for money to arrive. But his request for a loan was refused and he spent his last pesetas on bread and oranges and walked back to Yegen. When the proceeds of his War Loan eventually arrived, he returned to Almeria (this time by bus), paid for the furniture and put it on a carrier's waggon. Arriving home he found a telegram announcing that his visitors were already at Granada and expected him to meet them there in two days' time. He again had no money, he was recovering from influenza, Granada was seventy-one miles away, and he had little more than twenty-four hours in which to get there. He borrowed twenty-five pesetas from Maria, his servant, and set off, again on foot. Miraculously he reached Granada in time, but fainted from sheer weakness in the tram he had just enough money to pay for, and missed his guests by half an hour. He managed, however, to catch up with them as they were boarding the bus which would take them for the first part of the journey and at the hotel where they spent the night was able to consider the daunting problem of getting Lytton, already in a state of considerable physical and moral debility, to Yegen. The first plan involved fording the Rio Grande with a couple of mules, and Lytton not unexpectedly declined at the last minute to risk this performance. They returned to their hotel. Next day they set off again by a different route, but Lytton was suffering from piles and could not get astride his mule. He had therefore to walk, except when the frequent need to ford a river made it necessary for him to mount. Just before sunset, they reached an inn where they planned to spend the night. The bed offered Lytton so appalled him, however, that he insisted on pressing on. It was now necessary to climb 2,500 feet by a steep path to join the main road above. Carrington and Lytton rode side-saddle on the two mules, while Ralph and Gerald walked. Lytton's sufferings were now intensified by vertigo.

It is not surprising that Lytton was an uncommunicative companion for the next few days. Much more surprising is it that anyone should have thought Lytton capable of such a journey or that he should have succeeded in making it. With time he was able to take gentle walks in the neighbourhood and consented to be photographed side-saddle on a mule, holding an umbrella—an exotic, aristocratic, oriental, incongruous sight, Gerald records.

It was not till the last evening of their stay that Lytton became at all himself and could take pleasure in conversation. In Gerald's opinion the qualities of Lytton's mind were better shown in talk than in writing. (This was also, incidentally, the view of Leonard Woolf.) 'He needed more than most people,' wrote Gerald in one of the most sensitive word-pictures of Lytton's personality, 'an attuned and sympathetic audience, but, given this, he became the most easy of companions, listening as much as he talked, making whimsical or penetrating comments and creating around him a feeling of naturalness and intimacy. One remembered afterwards his doubts and hesitations, his refusals to dogmatise, his flights of fantasy, his high whispering voice fading out in the middle of a sentence, and forgot the very definite and well-ordered mind that lay underneath. . . . One observed a number of discordant features —a feminine sensibility, a delight in the absurd, a taste for exaggeration and melodrama, a very mature judgment, and then some lack of human substance, some hereditary thinness in the blood that at times gave people who met him an odd feeling in the spine. He seemed almost indecently lacking in ordinariness.' In the same passage, Gerald shows how well he had penetrated into the mind of the strange figure who somehow had managed to become his guest in a primitive and inaccessible Spanish village. 'I got the impression' he says, 'that privately he thought of the world with its incomprehensible stupidity as something which it was best to keep at a distance. Unlike Voltaire, whom he admired so greatly, he regarded it as irreformable . . .'.

Lytton, Carrington and Ralph left by car. It had not been an entirely successful visit either for Lytton or for his host, who had the impossible task of making acceptable to his guest 'the ruthless cuisine of Spanish villages, with its emphasis on potato omelette, dried cod and unrefined olive oil.' Later, when Virginia and Leonard were planning a trip to Yegen, Lytton warned them against it. 'It is DEATH,' he wrote.

The situation as they returned to Tidmarsh was beginning to be extremely complex. Lytton was in love with Ralph who was by now devoted to him and was typing the final draft of Queen Victoria for him. Ralph was in love with Carrington who had become his mistress and he was demanding that she should marry him. Carrington, who was fond of Ralph without being in love with him, had been immensely attracted by Gerald and was conducting an enthusiastic and emotional correspondence with him. She did not want to marry Ralph—she was opposed to formal marriage anyway—but feared that a continued refusal might alienate Lytton. Lytton was or pretended to be sublimely unaware of any problems. Not long before he had written to Ralph 'It seems so good when we're all three together that I grudge every minute that keeps us apart.'

By the beginning of 1921, Queen Victoria was ready for publication. When it appeared a few months later, it had a universally rapturous reception. Lytton was almost distressed.

'Can a popular author be a good one?' he asked. 'It's alarming to be welcomed with open arms, by Gosse, Jack Squire and *The Times*.'

Ralph, now down from Oxford, was working at the Hogarth Press, one of the series of bright young men whom Leonard recruited as potential partners. He was to be no more permanent than the others, but he profited by his close contact with Leonard and Virginia to confide in them his problems with Carrington. Leonard was emphatic; he should present her with an ultimatum. Either she should agree to marry him or their association should be terminated. Virginia concurred with Leonard. But whereas Leonard's advice was based on an objective analysis of Carrington's character (she was, he wrote 'the classic female . . . if the male pursued, she ran away; if the male ran away, she pursued'), Virginia's was coloured by her love of mischief and a certain jealousy of Carrington's—to her mind unwarranted—ascendancy at Tidmarsh. She hinted that Lytton was getting tired of Carrington and that in future he planned to spend less time at Tidmarsh. If a showdown led to a break with Carrington, that might be the best answer for Ralph. With an extraordinary lack of tact, only to be explained by the state bordering on nervous collapse to which Carrington's attitude had reduced him, he passed Virginia's remarks on to her. Carrington, horrified, capitulated at once. If marrying Ralph would help to maintain her position with Lytton, a position she well knew she was not by Bloomsbury standards qualified to fill, she would marry Ralph. Within a fortnight they were man and wife.

The day after she had accepted Ralph's ultimatum, Carrington wrote to Lytton who was on a visit to the Berensons at Settignano, to tell him and to explain the feelings that had led her to do so. It was only with Lytton that Carrington ever found it possible to be totally frank. Her letter is long and profoundly moving, with a flow of emotion which partial quotation would destroy.[1] Lytton's reply was full of tender understanding and reassurance. He thought she had made the right decision for Ralph's sake and hoped that it would not

[1] It appears in full in David Garnett's selection of her letters, pp. 175-7 (Cape 1970).

'make much difference to anybody.' 'You and Ralph and our life at Tidmarsh' he said, 'are what I care for most in the world—almost (apart from my work and some few people) the only things I care for.'

On the face of it, then, all was well. The marriage of Ralph and Carrington was necessary and therefore justifiable if the strange Tidmarsh ménage was to survive. Everyone was happy. The honeymoon in Paris and Italy was a success (although on her wedding-day Carrington had characteristically written to Gerald regretting that he could not accompany them) and they went on to meet Lytton in Venice. Nevertheless, the marriage was an expedient forced on Carrington by her need for Lytton, and recognised as such by her. However fond she was of Ralph it seems clear that she felt a carefully hidden resentment that her feelings about marriage had been violated and that she had been tricked by her own deep needs into an almost sordid action. There is perhaps psychological significance in the fact that she lost her wedding-ring during the honeymoon and even more in her request that she should remain 'Carrington' to her friends.

At all events she did not feel in any way restricted by her new status. She continued her emotionally charged correspondence with Gerald, in which archness was relieved by practical tips, possibly unwelcome, to ensure the privacy of their letters. 'If you wish,' she wrote from her honeymoon, 'to write a particularly passionate one, put a red stamp on the outside upside down, then the faithless wife can conceal it before [Ralph] reads it.'

Although Gerald was already attracted by Carrington, he felt a strong conventional—and indeed hardly surprising—loyalty to Ralph at this stage. In England in June, he was shocked when, on a picnic 'à deux' which she contrived on the Berkshire Downs, Carrington embraced and kissed him. It was after all only a month after the wedding. But the next weekend at Tidmarsh broke through Gerald's inner resistance. 'As I sat in an armchair, I saw her move across the window with the evening light behind her, and I knew I was in love.' In August he joined Lytton, James and Alix, Ralph and Carrington on a holiday in the Lakes. While Ralph fished, Gerald and Carrington kissed and cuddled nearby. Once they were almost caught. It is likely that Carrington, with her natural taste for duplicity, was excited by the deception. But Gerald was anguished by it, and in any case, the situation was so dangerous that in the end Carrington sent him away. The letter she wrote to him as soon as he had left is a superb example of her naïve faith in the possibility of having one's cake and eating it. 'Really I love Ralph so much' she wrote, 'that is why I am a little disconcerted that he isn't rather more to me. You mustn't think' she went on, 'I ever do not care as much as you do. Now, we neither of us feel any guilt,' but 'I pour coals of contempt on my head for not taking more risks.'

Ralph suspected nothing. Gerald returned to Spain. Ralph read the letters which again began to flow between his wife and his friend but not the surreptitious postscripts. In the following spring they all met again in the Pyrenees, as guests of Professor Bollard and his wife Clare, a handsome passionate woman with whom Carrington had been at the Slade. She now confided in Clare her feelings for Gerald. At the same time, Gerald seems to have suggested to his hostess that it would be convenient if she tried to occupy Ralph's attention and so allow him to have more privacy with Carrington. She took up the suggestion with such enthusiasm that she and Ralph ended the holiday in bed together.

In May, Gerald was staying in Pangbourne to be near Carrington, and Clare had come to England to enjoy more of Ralph's virile attentions. Ralph made no secret of his affair with Clare, and his openness was as extraordinary as Carrington's secretiveness and in the event much more damaging. The danger of his attitude was not at first apparent. Indeed, Gerald and Carrington seized upon it to become lovers in the full sense. After Gerald had left at the beginning of June, Carrington still sang about the house, lost in retrospective ecstasy. She told Lytton all about her feelings and wished Gerald could have heard her. 'I LOVE GERALD VERY MUCH, AS MUCH as prunes, as roast duck and peas, as Venice, as crown imperials, as tulips, as Devonshire cream and raspberries, as walking on Combe Downs, as Padua, more MORE MORE MORE than all these things, do I love Gerald' she wrote to him.

But catastrophe was only days away. Clare, with the obvious intention of destroying Carrington in Ralph's eyes, gave him a dramatised account of the 'plot' hatched on their holiday, to which she added details of the love-making that had gone on in the Lake District, and, incredibly, information that she had acquired from Mark Gertler, also an old Slade friend, about his earlier relations with Carrington. Ralph, whose sexual attitudes were crudely, even brutally, instinctive, behaved like a stag one of whose hinds has succumbed to a rival. He proposed to kill Gerald, but settled for a confrontation, at which Gerald, for Carrington's sake, denied having slept with her. He also agreed to return to Spain and to cease all communication. All this he explained to Carrington at a last meeting at Tidmarsh. Within a week he had returned to Yegen.

The crisis was over. But it came close to destroying the Tidmarsh household, which was now as important to Lytton as it was to Carrington. If Ralph had possessed the Bloomsbury attitude to life, in which sexual jealousy had no place, there would have been no crisis. But he had never really been entirely comfortable among these strange aesthetes and perhaps only his affection for Lytton, which was deep and life-long, held him within the circle.

Somehow Lytton had kept his head through it all. His love for Ralph and Carrington enabled him to understand the feelings of both, and he strove nervously to reduce the temperature of the situation. He counselled Carrington to patience. His own natural incapacity for action of any kind, and more especially, his revulsion from violent action, provided not for the first time, the right treatment. He was sure, though perhaps not always quite sure, that it would blow over. Gerald, after all, had the Bloomsbury temperament: as he wrote to Carrington, it was part of his philosophy 'that love is free and unrestricted and is increased by being divided.' It was lucky that Ralph never saw that letter.

After Gerald had gone, Lytton wrote to him. 'Never forget' the letter ended, 'that, whatever happens, and in spite of all estrangements, you are loved by those you love best.'

Ralph's affair with Clare was made more painful for Carrington by the fact that she too was more than a little in love with her. It would be heartless to suggest that it was all rather like a theatrical bedroom-farce, but there were, emotion aside, strong farcical elements in the cat's cradle of relationships which Lytton patiently set about disentangling. He tried everything. He went to Venice, in the hope that in his absence Ralph and Carrington might come to terms, at the same time installing Barbara Bagenal at Tidmarsh as a protection for Carrington in case of need. Later in the year he tried to persuade Leonard and Virginia to give Ralph more congenial work at the Hogarth Press: they could not see how to do so and Ralph left and Lytton took him on as a secretary and general assistant: he bought a car, which Ralph alone was qualified to drive. With Ralph as chauffeur, he took them both on a tour of Devon and Wales: but they argued continuously. Clare meanwhile had found a new lover in Mark Gertler, and Lytton's patient and loving efforts at last began to bear fruit.

By the autumn some kind of peace was patched up, and it held through the winter. But Lytton was taking no chances; for the new year he planned for them, and carried out, a programme of travel—North Africa for two months in the spring, and France in the summer—interspersed with an almost unbroken stream of interesting visitors to Tidmarsh. It was a successful policy: Ralph and Carrington stopped quarrelling and began to sleep together again. As if to demonstrate that the past was over, in December the two of them decided to go —it seemed the natural thing to do—to Yegen to stay with Gerald.

The past, however, was never over for Carrington. Her letters to Gerald at this time—she had never of course kept her side of the bargain not to communicate—are as intimate as ever and always have coy sexual undertones and secret references which Gerald would at once understand. All the same, Ralph was able to tell Lytton in a letter from Yegen that he felt 'no jealousy at all now seeing them together.' What he did not tell Lytton was that his own attentions were now directed away from Carrington. He was already in love with David Garnett's sister-in-law, Frances Marshall, a beautiful, cultivated and intelligent girl, whom he had met as an assistant at the bookshop which David and Francis Birrell were then running.

His love, he had reason to believe, was returned, although no intimacy had so far been allowed him.

In these circumstances, the visit to Yegen was bound to be a success. Carrington, writing to Lytton, could say of Ralph 'I don't think . . . I ever realised before quite how unselfish, and charming he could be until this journey.' He was unselfish enough, when Gerald came to England in the spring, to allow him to spend weekends alone in London with Carrington, though he still asked to see the letters she received from him, some of which revealed Gerald's feelings too clearly for Ralph's liking.

Carrington's letters to Gerald constantly protested her love, perhaps too much. She had new preoccupations. The first was a domestic one. Tidmarsh had proved to be too damp in the winter for Lytton's delicate health—he was almost always ill there, as he was this winter—and in January 1924 he bought Ham Spray, a house near Hungerford which Carrington had again discovered for him. A long, low farmhouse with Regency additions, it was bigger than Tidmarsh and more ambitious, with its imposing tree-lined drive, and its long verandah looking towards the downs. Lytton's bedroom could at last have its own fireplace—a symbol to him of wealth—and there was plenty of accommodation for visitors. It lacked a modern drainage system and had no electricity, and while these were being installed Lytton lay at Tidmarsh battling with influenza and lumbago. Carrington nursed him but spent every possible moment working on the new house, decorating it throughout in her own strongly individual style and getting Vanessa, Duncan and Harry Lamb to contribute paintings and drawings. She herself painted whimsical designs—legs of mutton and cats playing fiddles—on the crockery.

One of the helpers whose aid she enlisted was Henrietta Bingham who, at a different level, absorbed as much of Carrington's interest at this time as Ham Spray. Henrietta was the very beautiful young daughter of the American ambassador. She was, with Carrington at least, silent and unforthcoming, repaying affection 'negatively'. But the feelings she aroused in Carrington were strong and were to become more dominant as Carrington passed out of youth into the maturer years that come after thirty. She dreamt of Henrietta six nights a week, she told Alix 'dreams that even my intelligence is appalled by': the seventh night was, of course, allotted to Gerald. He could not fail to see signs of the division in Carrington's make-up and was made miserable by it. In a letter to him she tries to explain. She tells him again of her resentment at being a female though with all a female's enjoyment of sex with a man. With Henrietta she had more ecstasy 'and no feelings of shame afterwards'. 'It's not true' she asserts, 'to say I don't care for [sex] with you. . . . But at moments these other feelings come over me, and I dread facing that side of my character. (It's *not* a dread against you, but against myself, against my own femaleness.) Somehow it is always easier if I am treated negatively, a little as if I was *not* a female, then my day-dream character of not being a female is somehow pacified. . . . I have never completely told R this, or anyone. It is a confidence I make only to you. Merely thinking of this makes me so agitated I feel I can hardly bear any relations with anyone again. In the past I think everything I believe went wrong for this reason. Always this struggle with two insides, which makes one disjointed, unreliable and secretive. . . .' After this frank exposé of her emotional structure, she adds, characteristically 'I don't see how I can ever give you up.'

Perhaps not. But their relationship was beginning to disintegrate. One cannot easily imagine Gerald enjoying lovemaking with a woman who could say that 'afterwards a sort of rage fills me because of that very pleasure.' Lytton's brilliantly attractive niece, Julia, had now replaced Henrietta in Carrington's affections. She still wrote assiduously to Gerald, and they occasionally met and made love, but her letters are increasingly concerned with impersonal matters—meetings with friends, horse-rides on the downs, breakdowns in the hot-water system at Ham Spray—and by the end of 1926 she wrote 'I am sorry that you are no longer I.L. . . . with Miss Moffat [i.e. in love with me] this I take to be the import of your last letter.' If she was right—and she may not have been entirely right, so strong a hold she had on him—it was not surprising. The complications and deviations of her character and behaviour had reduced Gerald at one stage to a nervous condition bordering on mental imbalance. There was irony in the fact that it was Carrington's literal interpretation of his own doctrine that 'love . . . is increased by being divided' that was the main source of his agonies. She was the very embodiment of his view that 'love is free and unrestricted.' *She* was capable of being in love with a woman on weekdays and a man on Sundays: *she* was quite content for Ralph and Gerald to share her bed alternately. It was she, not Gerald, who 'did not understand the possessive instinct and did not share it.' The more she let him see into her heart, the less he liked what he saw, until, when the pain had subsided, there was little left for him but resentful memories of a relationship which had gone wrong. It all ended on an absurd note which has the true Bloomsbury timbre. In an access of goodwill, knowing his poverty and having an almost neurotic hatred of waste, she sent him a parcel of Lytton's unwanted ties. For Gerald it was a ridiculously vivid illumination of the place he held, and had always held, in her life. There was one final scene, which cannot have been a particularly dignified one. In the following year, 1930, Gerald married.

Meanwhile, Lytton's peace had been threatened once more. Ralph and Frances had gone to Spain for a month in 1925, had become lovers and decided that their lives belonged together.

Direct and open as always, Ralph explained the situation to Carrington. He denied any wish to distress her or Lytton, but his love for Frances had to be his main consideration. He went over the ground again, this time to Lytton and Carrington together. Frances could hardly join the Ham Spray household: there were, after all, limits which even Bloomsbury had to recognise. So Carrington was again faced with the prospect that, Ralph having left Ham Spray to live elsewhere with Frances, Lytton would find her an inadequate sole companion and so her life would collapse about her. By now Ralph's presence was as important to Lytton as it had been when he was in love with him. He provided the down-to-earth practical element necessary to any household, as well as understanding and good humour. Without him the future of Ham Spray was likely to be dim and short. And what then would happen to Carrington?

All this Lytton discussed next day with Frances in a private talk at his club. She was marvellously reasonable. She understood the problem fully and had no wish to exacerbate it. She, too, was fond of Lytton and Carrington, and, if she could not be included in the household would like to be with them regularly. If she and Ralph set up house together, she would want him to spend a lot of time at Ham Spray and sometimes accompany him.

And so an arrangement, hard to imagine except in a Bloomsbury context, was arrived at.[1] Frances and Ralph took rooms at 41 Gordon Square, the house of James and Alix. Ralph would spend as far as possible a day and a night with Carrington each week at Ham Spray, Frances joining them the next day.

Lytton heaved a sigh of relief at this potentially happy compromise. Carrington, at first outside herself with delight that such a jolly solution had been found, one that enabled her to share herself as comfortably as she wished, found eventually that it was far from perfect. After the arrangement had been running for a few weeks she wrote to Ralph that 'although everything is for the best in the best of all possible worlds for you and F, if you chose to live one day in Lytton's life or mine you would realise the difference . . .'.

Lytton was perhaps slower to appreciate the importance of the change that had come over the life of Ham Spray. He had more to occupy his mind than Carrington. *Elizabeth and Essex*, for which he had a contract with Chatto & Windus, went very slowly. It was on his conscience rather more than it was on his work-desk. And there were new and exciting friendships. Later he felt impelled to write to Ralph, with the utmost diffidence and modesty, to suggest that Frances should not always accompany Ralph on his visits. Not that either he or Carrington disliked Frances—she was charming and indeed

[1] The letters exchanged between Carrington and Frances before this solution was arrived at, written under great emotional stress, do them both honour, showing how they were striving to solve an appalling problem with the minimum of hurt to the four people involved. The letters are given in full in *Carrington: Letters and Extracts from her Diaries*, pp 332-335. (Cape, 1970.)

aroused strong sapphic emotions in Carrington. It was simply that there was no way in which she could be fitted into the Ham Spray pattern. Her presence acted like grit in the workings of a delicate mechanism.

It is not strange that this was so. It was of the essence of the Ham Spray household that its focal point should be Lytton. Love flowed to and from him. The presence of Frances interrupted the emotional circuits, and this was a matter almost as serious for Lytton as for Carrington. Both had, in fact, underestimated Ralph's feeling for Frances: neither was ready to understand that his love for her was deep enough to make their old triangular relationship impossible for the future.

Ralph saw the point and did what he could to improve matters. But nothing effective could really be done. When Gerald departed from the scene, Carrington was increasingly desolated. She was well aware that without Ralph's presence she could not hope to supply Lytton with a fully satisfactory domestic background. Now only her female lovers, who usually belonged to someone else, could give her the emotional thrills which were beyond Lytton's range. The diary which she began to keep reveals despair as well as tedium.

Nothing, in the three years that remained at Ham Spray, would happen to mend the situation. It was a sad ending to the strange adventure which had begun with such gay promise at Tidmarsh twelve years ago.

XI

Virginia and Leonard

BY the time the war ended, the pattern of life for Virginia and Leonard had settled into what was to be essentially its final form. They had and would always have two bases, one in Sussex, one in or near London. Virginia, with her second novel *Night and Day* ready for publication, could be regarded as a professional novelist. She was now in permanently fragile health. Almost every winter she fell ill and recovered only slowly. As each new novel reached the point of publication she came dangerously near to mental breakdown, or actually broke down. She took part as often as she could, and with great zest, in the hectic life of the London season, at the price of an exhausted reaction which Leonard foresaw but could not prevent. Sometimes she collapsed suddenly and was ill for months as at Charleston in the summer of 1925, and again in 1930 at Rodmell, after 'a very violent summer'. Once she had a momentary, terrible glimpse of her old madness, when she went one night to meet Leonard at the railway station and he was not on the expected train. She felt, she wrote in her diary, that 'now the old devil has once more got his spine through the waves', using, to describe what she felt, that symbol for madness which in her writing more commonly took the form of an emerging black triangular fin like that of a shark. Travel abroad, particularly after Leonard acquired his first car in 1927, was the best kind of relief: she loved it, and it produced in her, writes Leonard, a 'strange state of passive alertness' which she never experienced in England.

In 1919 they had to move house. The owner of Asheham gave them six months' notice in March and the spring was devoted to house-hunting. Virginia's contribution to this process, which always gave her pleasure, was eccentric. First she took three adjacent Cornish cottages near Zennor, previously occupied by D. H. Lawrence: they never lived there.

Then, in irrelevant reaction to a quarrel with Vanessa, she bought a former windmill in Lewes. It was totally unsuitable and had to be re-sold. Leonard remained patient throughout and some weeks later they found on the outskirts of Rodmell, a village a few miles south of Lewes, the house which was to be their permanent home. Monk's House, though some three hundred years older than Asheham, was not so beautiful or romantic. It did not stand, as Asheham did, in a sea of green and there were no great elms to form a framework. Nor was it reputed to be haunted. It was little more than a pleasant cottage of brick and flint, weather-boarded on one side, standing in a wild garden, with an orchard. The rooms were small, the stairs narrow, the floors downstairs of brick. Like most of the houses of its type in the country at this time, including Asheham, it had no bath, no W.C., no hot water. But it made an appeal which they could not resist. They bought it and, after a last sad month at Asheham, moved in at the beginning of September.

Houses meant almost more to Leonard than to Virginia. He enjoyed solving the practical problems they set—the opening-up of the ground floor at Monk's House to give fewer but larger rooms for example. He loved gardening and loved it more as he grew older.

At this stage, however, he had little time to spare for the enjoyment of the new house. *Night and Day* was published in October and Virginia needed his watchful care. They were both ill that winter, and it was not till the following summer that they were able to spend more than a few days at a time at Rodmell.

Leonard was immensely busy. Money was short and the income he obtained from journalism, together with Virginia's fees as a reviewer, did not go far. Writing did not pay, or paid very little. Leonard, always a meticulous accountant, records that up to 1921 Virginia's income from this source amounted to only £205. His own two novels—*The Village in the Jungle* based on his life in Ceylon, and *Wise Virgins*—brought in only £62. It was of this period that Virginia could later say 'For years I never had a pound extra; a comfortable bed, or a chair that did not want stuffing.' Without her private income of rather less than £400 a year they could hardly have carried on.

The Hogarth Press, conducted always as a part-time activity, was slowly turning into a viable commercial publishing house, though profits were small. By 1923, 32 titles had been published, including *Jacob's Room* and numerous lesser productions by Bloomsbury friends, often adorned by Vanessa or Carrington. T. S. Eliot's *Poems* and *The Waste Land* were in the list and their author had become a close friend. Middleton Murry, Katherine Mansfield, Logan Pearsall-Smith, and Vita Sackville-West each had a book with the Hogarth imprint. There were also in this period, eight translations from the Russian— Gorky's *Reminiscences of Tolstoy* and works by Dostoevsky. These translations were done by Koteliansky, one of the most extraordinary inhabitants of the literary world at this time. A Ukrainian Jew whose family had been wiped out in the Revolution, he had come to London before the war and now made a precarious living as a translator. In appearance and manner he was impressive—a 'major Hebrew prophet' Leonard called him—with a powerful physique and a penetrating gaze. Of 'iron integrity and intensity' he judged his friends with devastating clarity and insight. Few passed muster—D. H. Lawrence, Katherine Mansfield, Virginia were rated 'real persons', others were shatteringly condemned. His translations suffered from his eccentric grasp of English, and Leonard and Virginia had to re-translate his version. Leonard even started to learn Russian to help the work on.

A volume of translations from Freud also appeared in this period and marked the beginning of the special role of the Hogarth Press as the publishers of psycho-analytical literature. The translation was by James Strachey, assisted by his wife Alix. James, after following Lytton to Trinity, had been private secretary to his cousin St. Loe the owner and editor of *The Spectator*, but was sacked early in the war, as we have seen, for his pacifist views. He then decided on a medical career but abandoned it almost at once and became for a while dramatic critic of Middleton Murry's *Athenaeum*. Alix, one of the younger members of Bloomsbury whose meeting-place was the 1917 Club and who were collectively and rather unattractively referred to by Virginia as 'Cropheads', had been the first, and briefest, assistant taken on by Leonard at the Press. She lasted less than a day, finding the work entirely uninteresting. In 1919 she and James, with whom she had long been in love, were living together at 41 Gordon Square, where they remained after their marriage and which was to provide lodgings for Bloomsbury for many years. In 1920 they went to Vienna to study psycho-analysis under Freud. It was natural that the translations which James began almost at once should be offered to the Hogarth Press and proper that they should be accepted. Twenty-five years later he embarked on the official translation of the complete psychological works of Freud: it was a daunting task, which occupied him for twenty years and produced twenty-three volumes published by the Hogarth Press. (It is interesting that, although Adrian and Karin were psycho-analysts as well as James and Alix, no attempt appears to have been made to get Virginia to undergo analysis. Perhaps it was understood that she would certainly have refused or, additionally, that her condition, though it had Freudian aspects, was unlikely to be susceptible to analytical techniques and might well have been made worse by their use.)

Apart from his work at the Press, Leonard was immensely busy as a political writer and journalist. In 1919 he had completed *Empire and Commerce in Africa* and was engaged on *Socialism and Co-operation*. In 1920 he became the editor of the *International Review* and in 1923, when Maynard became chairman of the amalgamated *Nation and Athenaeum* he became its literary editor, after T. S. Eliot had refused the appointment because of its insecurity. It was secure enough to provide Leonard with a job and an income until in 1930 he resigned in order to start the *Political Quarterly*, of which he was part-founder and joint editor. In the midst of this and other journalistic work, he found time to stand unsuccessfully for Parliament, to be the permanent secretary of two Labour Party committees and to attend to the affairs of his 1917 Club.

It is hard to believe that under the pressure of all this work and the growing demands of the Hogarth Press, Leonard's first preoccupation, and the responsibility which took absolute priority in his mind, was Virginia's health. But it was so. After her appalling breakdown in 1913 from which she might so easily have failed to recover, he knew that their life had to be patterned against a background of danger. The interval between Virginia, gay and creative, composing at the Press, entertaining their friends at Rodmell, and Virginia tortured with headaches and battling with madness was so brief, the barrier appallingly thin. Leonard had to learn more than the doctors knew of the treatment most likely to fend off attacks. He was restlessly vigilant, judging every activity of their lives in terms of its possible impact on his wife's health. He was not, could not be, always successful; but to the extent that Virginia was able to live and work normally for the rest of her life she owed it to Leonard. It was not only, on his part, love: he was eternally conscious of his role as the guardian of a strange, unique talent which he, the soberest of judges, rightly identified as genius.

Virginia's novels are so much an expression of her personality, so literally an extension of it, that it is not possible to examine her life without at the same time examining her writing. It is even right to say that she was never so completely herself as when she was writing. It must be said at once, however, that for Virginia writing meant writing novels: her other literary work—reviewing, writing her diary—was a relaxation. Leonard claimed that he could tell by the depth of the flush on her cheeks whether she had been working on a novel or a review. Aware as she always was of her own incompleteness as a person, never for long free from the subconscious influence of the traumas of her childhood and adolescence, she sought to create an alternative world of fiction from which were excluded, not all the problems of the world of fact, but the unsatisfactory, untidy, painful or distressing elements of that life which was sometimes too much for her to bear. Writing to Madge Vaughan, her cousin by marriage to whom she had sent some of her first attempts at fiction, she said 'My present feeling is that this vague & dream-like world, without love, or heart, or passion, or sex, is the world I really care about, & really find interesting. For, though they are dreams to you, & I can't express them at all adequately, these things are perfectly real to me.' It was a statement which remained true throughout her life as a novelist. At the same time it already indicated the nature of the problems she would have to solve as a writer. The novel, as it had hitherto been understood, was essentially a story, a tale in which events were as important as the characters who took part in them. Indeed in most of the great novels characters were delineated and brought to life by their behaviour in relation to events rather than by any direct description. A novel too had a beginning and an end: it progressed, it was essentially dynamic. And perhaps, most important of all, the story it told had to be credible in terms of a recognisably real world.

On these terms Virginia had neither the desire to be a novelist nor the temperamental qualifications needed. She could indeed tell a story: but if she did so, as in *Orlando*, it would be a fantasy. *Night and Day* was, in its way, a novel of fact. But her heart was not in work of this kind. She needed a different medium in which to construct the world of her dream-life. Prose itself was hardly adequate. In her third novel, *Jacob's Room*, she found the form she needed. In it she broke out of the bonds that she found intolerably restrictive—she rejected the necessity to link event to event in a logically consecutive narrative, she rid herself of the encumbrance of a plot, she dispensed with an ending. She described in her diary the form she meant to use, with 'no scaffolding; scarcely a brick to be seen; all crepuscular, but the heart, the passion, humour, everything as bright as fire in the mist.' The 'stream of consciousness' technique enabled her to create the 'vague and dream-like world' about which she had written fifteen years earlier to Madge Vaughan. She was at the same time free to turn prose to poetry, the language of dream. Narration, in the usual sense, was not required. Lastly, and of this advantage she was perhaps not consciously aware, she was now exempt from the difficult requirement of creating solidly three-dimensional flesh-and-blood characters engaged in the unseemly activities of everyday life. She was able to exclude those elements of human life from which she herself shuddered away: of these sex and the lust which is part of love were the most important.

A novelist who is not interested in narrative and who is repelled by the instinctive drives which largely move mankind requires unusual sources of independent power. These Virginia had. She had a painter's urge to depict, his imperative need to record accurately, his eye for a scene, his sense of composition. She was a passionate observer with a unique gift, by the use of the unlikely but marvellously right word, of almost *trompe l'œil* description. Every paragraph is packed with detail, irrelevant to narrative, but of brilliant importance in a picture. The characters who people her novels are portraits on a canvas: they live but do not move. Over all her work there plays a fancy and an ironic humour sharpening at times into savage satire, which give, on the one hand, extraordinary charm and on the other a keen edge to what she wrote. She could be Hogarth as well as Gainsborough. She was poet, too, as well as painter, with the poet's love of words and eye for resemblances: almost every aspect of every scene evokes a simile, fanciful as a rule, but often wonderfully illuminating.

At times she felt the desire—perhaps she felt it almost her duty as a novelist—to write what she called 'a novel of fact', a narrative of the usual kind. Most compellingly she felt this urge in the autumn after the appearance of *The Waves*, in which her natural genius as poet and painter had had perhaps its freest expression. An entry in her diary, towards the end of 1932, records what she had in mind. She would write a story which would 'take in everything, sex, education, life, etc.: and come, with the most powerful and agile leaps, like a chamois, across precipices from 1880 to here and now.' The notion excited her tremendously. She was in 'a haze and dream and intoxication, declaiming phrases, seeing scenes . . .'. Phrases and scenes—these were what excited her imagination. But there had also to be a story, a progression of event and fact, characters developed in action of some sort, a plot of however slight a kind, even preferably a dénouement.

Before the year was over she had written over 60,000 words of the novel which was eventually called *The Years*. She had never been more excited over a book, and the excitement lasted for much of the following year. But slowly she found herself coming to a halt. She put her manuscript aside and came back to it only unwillingly. At times it went well again, but once more she would be baulked by a transition in the story which she did not know how to make.

All through 1934 she wrestled with it—'grinding' was the word she mostly used to describe her efforts to find her way through. Then in September, Roger Fry died. It was an almost unbearable loss. After Lytton, who had died nearly three years earlier, Roger had been the closest of her men-friends, much the most understanding, the warmest-hearted and the most admired. And as Vanessa's old lover, he had a special place in her affections. He had hoped she would one day write his biography and now she agreed, against the misgivings of Leonard and some of her friends, to do so. She found it a relief to turn to it when *The Years* refused to make headway.

A month after Roger's death, Wyndham Lewis published a book of criticism in which she was swept aside as a writer of no account, and other negative criticism followed. Neurotically sensitive as she was to adverse opinions which shook and could shatter her always unstable self-confidence, she found it often impossible to go on with a novel which was in any case proving increasingly intractable. The first draft was admittedly done, but it had to be re-written, it was too long, it was not right. She became ill. For the whole of 1935 writing was a torture. She wished for death. Her brain was 'almost extinct, like a charwoman's duster.' She was constantly aware of the danger that lurked just beyond the despair she experienced almost daily. And when, in the spring, it had all at last gone to the printer, 'now will come the season of depression, after congestion, suffocation.' The worst of all was that she sensed that Leonard was disappointed. And so he was. So too was she. She was convinced that the book was a failure. Leonard, reading the corrected proofs, looked anxiously for merit enough to give her the reassurance which she desperately needed. Of course he found it. How could any work of Virginia's to which she had devoted four increasingly anguished years be without merit? He gave his verdict: he thought the book 'extraordinarily good'. His opinion, given against his true judgment, may well have saved her from suicide. It was a 'wonderful revelation'. 'Now,' she wrote in her diary, 'I wake from death —or non-being—to life.'

But *The Years* was not the book she had intended it to be. It did not 'take in everything', it did not move 'with powerful

and agile leaps, like a chamois'. It was indeed something like a
triumph in terms of its reception by the reviews and her
readers. But she had tried to be what she was not—a story-
teller moulding everyday material into a convincing narrative-
form. She remained what she was, an observer, a painter of
portraits and scenes, a composer using words for notes, an
ironic commentator on character. It is significant that each of
the eleven episodes of the book begins with a description of the
weather: it is as though a painter were beginning with the sky
as the background for a canvas. The scenes she paints are vivid
enough, but they remain scenes. The book had first revealed
itself to her in phrases and scenes. It never moved beyond them.
There were leaps, but they were not 'powerful and agile'. Her
characters, bright and alive as they seemed, refused to move
forward. And then somehow they had to be removed from the
stage. *Mrs Dalloway* had ended with Clarissa's party, where the
characters circled in a stately saraband, making no progress,
stopping where they had started. She used the same device in
The Years, with the difference that here, in the effort to create
mobility, she employed a kind of syncopation, jerking her
characters about as if to force them into movement. It was
largely a vain effort and they remained puppets, lifelike,
beautifully made, brightly painted, but only mobile when a
string was pulled. They had no vitality of their own.

Only Leonard knew the cost of it all. He was almost as much
involved as she was. 'We had a terrifying time with *The Years*
in 1936,' he wrote. For six months of this year her diary was
blank. It was, said Leonard, an 'unending nightmare'.

It was in a way strange that after *To the Lighthouse* and *The
Waves* had seemed to show that Virginia had found the path
that suited her she should turn aside and follow what turned
out to be a dead end. 'It is as though' writes Quentin Bell, 'one
saw Virginia run gaily and swiftly out upon a quicksand.'
Perhaps in *The Waves* she had gone as far as she could towards
her objective as a novelist—to produce a book from which all
that was external, adventitious, 'phenomenal', factual, had been
distilled and what remained was the essence of life itself, free
of all impurities and irrelevancies. She had set out consciously,
years before, to make bricks without straw, and now perhaps

she needed to regain touch with the less exacting familiarities of everyday existence, to think once more in terms of ordinary human values.

Or perhaps she simply wanted to tell a story. She had already done this once. *Orlando*, written at a great pace and with great delight, had appeared in 1928 and, although her friends were dubious about it, it had been a huge publishing success. *To the Lighthouse*, published in the previous year, had firmly established Virginia in the minds of the review-reading public as an essential figure of the contemporary literary scene. One could not be regarded as a person of culture unless one had read one's Virginia Woolf. But it was such difficult, uphill work. Of course, there were great beauties both of style and description, there was emotion and insight, but the events which give movement to a novel just did not happen. The characters, too, were generally so bloodless that an event of any magnitude would probably have collapsed them utterly. *Orlando* was so different. Here, within a fantasy, was drama, event, pace, passion and catastrophe. Now it was easy to be genuinely enthusiastic. And *Orlando* made Virginia a best-seller.

An explanation for this change of literary mood must exist. Why, after *Mrs Dalloway* and *To the Lighthouse*, interrupting that series of novels so characteristic of their author that literary historians could gleefully for ever after point out similarities, demonstrate consistency and generally feast on the material provided for them—why suddenly this gay, picaresque, absurd biography of the life of a man-woman?

Perhaps the first thing to say, by way of explanation, is that Virginia, as long as she was well, was a gay, fantastic, fun-loving person. This was the main impression she made on those who knew her even quite well. In the middle of a sober down-to-earth conversation she would take off, burn into orbit with an incandescent blaze of imagination that left her listeners breathless with astonishment and delight. She would take a tiny shred of fact, twist it, whisk it out of its context and use it as the basis for a whole fabrication of nonsense, fragile, frivolous and marvellously funny. Leonard regarded this faculty as an aspect of genius. (Others, given absurd and unflattering roles in one of Virginia's fantasies, took a less objective view. And her accounts of conversations and events sometimes owed too much to her 'creative imagination'. Mischief was frequently caused and was indeed not always unintended.) Clive expressed a less analytical view than Leonard when he wrote that 'She was about the gayest human being I have ever known.' Children, for whom fantasy is the best part of everyday life and not separate from it, found her the perfect companion, as her nephew Quentin recalls. Adults, like Clive, were 'made to feel that the temperature of life was several degrees higher than we had supposed.' Even in the black years leading to the Second World War, 'at Monk's House and at 52 Tavistock Square' writes Quentin Bell, 'the prevailing sound was still one of laughter.'

This is not the Virginia for whom writing led to despair: who re-wrote *The Voyage Out* five times, on Leonard's estimate, in the morbid conviction that each new version was valueless: who, after completing *The Years* said to her diary 'I'm going to be beaten, I'm going to be laughed at, I'm going to be held up to scorn and ridicule.' But it was the Virginia of *Orlando*.

Something had happened, some element existed in her life, some force was present which enabled her to forget the sick anxieties which harassed her writing at other times and which permitted her natural gaiety to express itself without impediment. She describes how she began. There was a book of literary criticism which she had in mind and which Leonard was keen to have. But it would not start. 'I couldn't screw a word from me; and at last dropped my head in my hands; dipped my pen in the ink, and wrote these words, as if automatically on a new sheet: Orlando: A Biography. No sooner had I done this than my body was filled with rapture and my brain with ideas. I wrote rapidly till 12.' She went on writing rapidly for six months and the book was published almost exactly a year after she had written its title on that new sheet.

It was to Vita Sackville-West that she wrote describing how she began *Orlando*. And Orlando, himself and herself, was Vita Sackville-West. It is never safe with anyone, and certainly not safe with so complex and secret a person as Virginia, to identify a single cause as the fount and origin of a particular effect. It is, however, permissible in some cases that are clearer than others to recognise and acknowledge the influence mainly responsible. And in this case there can be little doubt that it was Virginia's relationship with Vita which was the mainspring of *Orlando*.

Virginia met Vita first, with her husband Harold Nicolson, at Clive's dinner-table in 1922. Vita was beautiful, charming and aristocratic. Virginia was perhaps attracted, but characteristically critical. 'Not much to my severer taste' she notes in her diary '. . . could I ever know her?' She did not think highly of Vita's gifts as a writer. She was also well aware of her frank lesbianism. But they met with increasing frequency and Vita's admiration, which existed from the outset, was matched as time went on by feelings in Virginia which had all, or almost all, the qualities of romantic love. Vita made no bones about it: she was in love with Virginia, wooed her and presumably set out to win her as a lover. Although one must assume that she failed in this objective—she called her 'inviolable'—there is no doubt that, at the emotional level at least, there was a love-affair between them.

Vita's open admiration for Virginia, with its instinctive and unrepressed sexual overtones, could hardly have failed to give pleasure. 'Her being "in love" (it must be comma'd thus) with me, excites and flatters and interests'. Nothing could be more natural. Vita had all the glamour of a beautiful, high-born inhabitant of the world of international diplomacy. She might have been cast as the heroine of a Ruritanian romance. The great ancestral house at Knole—her childhood home—was as glamorous as Vita herself, and as beautiful, with its glorious brick and stone, its superb gardens and above all, its associations. As for Vita, 'she shines . . . with a candle lit radiance, stalking on legs like beech trees, pink glowing, grape clustered, petal hung.' This could be the language of love, even of infatuation.

But Virginia was not infatuated. She observed herself, as always, critically and with sardonic amusement. She distinguished between her sense of glamour, her enjoyment of admiration, and her feeling for the whole Vita. Her emotions were always held in check by her mind. Vita might be, indeed was, a 'real woman', a successful mother, hostess, writer, with charm, poise and beauty. But she had not the sensitive insight of Vanessa, and when she wrote, however competently, it was with a 'pen of brass'. Moreover, her amorousness was alternately amusing and rather alarming. From the days of Madge Vaughan and Violet Dickinson, and in her maturity, with Katherine Mansfield, Virginia had always been capable of being emotionally stirred by another woman. But it would not do and she did not want it to do. Her life was with Leonard and she wished it so. Thus, when she went alone with Vita to France for a week on the eve of the publication of *Orlando* she warned Vita in advance not to expect too much. 'I would not have married Leonard had I not preferred living with him to saying goodbye to him.' She wrote to Harold Nicolson thanking him for having married Vita; she telegraphed anxiously to Leonard after not hearing from him for three days. She was clearly aware of danger and insuring against it.

What was safe and great fun at the same time was to translate it all into fiction. Here she could give full rein to romantic emotions which in real life she recognised for what they were and kept in check. In Orlando himself, who was always a man even when he was a woman, she could symbolise and romanticise the masculine attributes of a woman like Vita, and at the same time leave the reader in no doubt that it was all nonsense. Because the story was a fantasy, she could use the gifts which were normally seen only in her conversation. She was conscious as she wrote that she was giving herself a 'treat': it was an absurd, but highly satisfying spree. And it was also a tribute to Vita, an act of recognition for the delight which she gave Virginia. Not only the character of Orlando, but the setting and the events within the setting are drawn directly from Vita and their life together.

The book has always irritated the critics. It does not fit in with the otherwise acceptable development of Virginia as a novelist. It is not difficult enough to call for commentaries. It does not provide material for questions in examination papers. Above all it is not serious. The damned book is entertaining and is entitled therefore to be damned. But when, with the passage of time, the language and mood and form of Virginia's other novels have become too difficult and strange for any but the literary specialist to enjoy, if that time ever comes, *Orlando* will remain available to all as a marvellous tale with which to beguile a winter's night. It will keep its place along with all the other joyous tales. Just for a moment, Virginia finds herself in the company of Boccaccio and Lesage.

The relationship between Virginia and Vita continued to be a source of excitement and delight to them both after *Orlando* had appeared and through the writing of *The Waves*. Only as she fought her dark way through *The Years* did Virginia discover that the sheen and glamour had faded. Warm friendship remained till the end. In 1940 there was a pound of butter from Vita's farm, which in those days of severe food-rationing was a gift of unbelievable splendour. Virginia wrote a letter of ecstatic thanks. Her emotion was no doubt as genuine as those she had recorded in her diary fifteen years before, even if passion this time was absent.

The tendency for Bloomsbury's emotional affairs to be flawed by some fatal absurdity, some grotesque element which reduced them, if only momentarily, to farce, has already been mentioned. Now Virginia, at the beginning of the thirties, became enmeshed in a relationship in which the grotesque predominated. Early in 1930 she met Ethel Smyth, the composer, then 71. Virginia was 47. Ethel was a boisterous, clumsy, knockabout figure, with huge vitality and courage, a big heart and very little consideration for, or even awareness of, the feelings of other people. She fell, or rather plunged headlong, into love with Virginia. Virginia admired her as a character, for her masculine qualities of energy and indomitability and was moved by the admiration with which Ethel showered and even assaulted her. But to find that the extraordinary old creature was in love with her was too much. 'It is like being caught by a giant crab,' she wrote. And her techniques as a lover were defective. Conversation, and even correspondence—at one stage she was writing to Virginia twice a day—were from the start catechisms to which Virginia had not the time to give the responses—she was deeply engaged in writing *The Waves*—even when she knew what they should be. It was one thing to be told that getting to know her was like hearing the music of Brahms for the first time. That was very touching and, from a musician, extremely flattering. It was quite another thing, when one was ill with exhaustion and near collapse from the strain of writing *The Waves* to be told that one was simply liverish and to receive a postcard decorated with a picture of a sick monkey. And on top of it all her table manners were worse than Maynard's. The 'vigorous charm' which Virginia was sensitive to was always there, but accompanied by so much that was unattractive, by so many unanswerable demands that an end had to be made. After numerous abortive attempts by Virginia to do so, the affair finally lost its heat. Ethel had to recognise that her passion—for this, in spite of her years, is the right word—was not returned. On these terms friendship was possible and indeed continued to the end.

There were so many friendships. Two of Leonard's recruits at the Hogarth Press became particular intimates. George Rylands, known always as Dadie, was at the Press only for six months in 1924. As a brilliant undergraduate he had begun to move in Bloomsbury circles a year or two before. Now, while writing his Fellowship thesis, he wanted to learn something of the production of books. At the same time, Leonard was looking for someone to share the burden of management. He offered Dadie a partnership with one third of the profits if he would give half his time to the Press. The arrangement never worked and came to nothing. Dadie soon found that Leonard's conception of half-time work did not coincide with his, and in any case he got his Fellowship at King's at the end of the year. Although as an example of business partnership the six months at the Press was a failure, they laid the basis for a long and close friendship between Dadie and Virginia. Leonard and Dadie too remained on good terms. For Virginia what began as a gay and teasing comradeship in the basement at Tavistock Square grew into a warm and much-valued relationship, in which Dadie's judgments on her writing, always encouraging, were sweetened by affection. If, she told him, he had thought *The Waves* 'a barren and frigid experiment' she would 'have probably taken a vow of silence for ever.' But his encouragement was 'a draught of champagne in the desert'. Their meetings at Cambridge, the last within weeks of her death, were a delight.

It was Dadie who in 1930 introduced Leonard and Virginia to the work of John Lehmann, a young poet just down from Cambridge where he and Julian Bell had become friends. Leonard and Virginia were attracted by the poet as much as by the poetry. They wanted the author as well as his work. Not only did they agree to publish his verse but Leonard persuaded Lehmann to join the Press where, after learning the ropes, he would continue as manager. Once more, the arrangement broke down and in little over a year he resigned, though not before he and Virginia had found common ground. John understood and admired her work: Virginia knew that he understood and trusted his judgment.

Leonard's inability to find a partner, or even the right kind of assistant, at the Hogarth Press is interesting enough to deserve examination. The Press was now a thriving commercial publishing house, demanding an increasing amount of the time and energy which Leonard would have preferred to devote to political journalism and Virginia to more worthwhile activities than reading unsuitable manuscripts and, often enough, helping in the preparation of book-parcels. On the face of it, the sensible course was to recruit a young man of ability to learn the business from Leonard and, in due course, to share with him the responsibility of running the Press. It was not difficult to find such a person. The contacts which Leonard and Virginia had at Cambridge and elsewhere brought them into touch with any number of young intellectuals of literary leanings. They had an attractive offer to make: to join, with the prospect of a partnership, a publishing-house with the reputation acquired by the Hogarth Press for publishing only what was good, to become the colleague of one of the leading novelists of the day and of a distinguished political writer, to be introduced by them into the select society of the authors, artists and thinkers who were their friends—what could be more excitingly attractive?

The young men Leonard appointed, and in whose appointment Virginia no doubt had a large hand, all seemed to have the qualities that were needed, and they all failed. Why? The combination of brilliance and inexperience has catastrophic potentialities in a commercial undertaking. Was it perhaps unfair to put men like Dadie Rylands and John Lehmann, and Angus Davidson who survived for three years at the Press, into a position where these potentialities were ever-present dangers? It might have been. But Leonard was wise and cautious, and, if John Lehmann, writing much later, may be believed, a kind and patient master.

The problem was different. Part of it was inherent in the daily work of printing and publishing. Repetitive and mechanical tasks had to be performed and unless they were carried out promptly and efficiently all the more intellectually satisfying work would go for naught. It was important that a future partner in the Press should learn these hard realities at first hand. The packing of books, the invoicing of consignments, the oiling of machinery and the cleaning of type were processes that it was right that he should learn.

It was less right that he should be given routine responsibility for such work; but there was never enough staff and the work had to be done. Leonard and Virginia each took a heroic share in it at times of special pressure, as when 10,000 copies of Maynard's pamphlet *The Economic Consequences of Mr. Churchill* had to be rushed out to clamorous customers. Until 1925 there was no traveller, and it was therefore understandable that Dadie should be sent out as a salesman. Equally understandably, he hated it. He was not made to be a drummer.

There is no doubt that an unfortunate streak of parsimony in Leonard's make-up contributed to the difficulties. Not only was the Press under-staffed and the embryo partners badly underpaid, but economies were pursued to absurd lengths. The expenditure of sixpence on toilet-paper would be questioned (Quentin Bell seems to recall that galley-proofs served this purpose at Monk's House). Sheets and, where possible, half sheets of old letters were used for file copies of correspondence. Punctuality was another of Leonard's neurotic preoccupations leading on one occasion to a ridiculous scene with Angus Davidson over his alleged lateness for work. They were only prevented from going out to check their watches with a public clock by Virginia's sudden appearance—with a request to know the time!

Leonard, in fact, was a pernickerty boss. But he was also

supremely intelligent and fair-minded, with qualities that far outweighed his defects, defects which in any case were risible as often as they were irritating. There must have been deeper reasons for the incompatibility that quickly and invariably arose between Leonard and his young men. John Lehmann, who returned to the Press in 1938 and shepherded it through the war-years, says that Leonard had an emotional attitude to the Press 'as if it were the child they had never had'. If this is perhaps an over-statement, it is certainly true that his feelings were extremely possessive. From 1927 on he was conscious that the burden of running the Press was increasingly intolerable and that Virginia, too, found it so. They talked of giving it up, and by 1930 seem to have agreed to close it down at least as a commercial concern. But for once Leonard was unable to take a step which Virginia's health called for. The Press was not given up. Nor were any of Leonard's brilliant young recruits allowed a responsible share in its running. When policy-issues were to be decided, they always found themselves outnumbered two to one. The fact was that Leonard did not want a partner and when John Lehmann during his second period with the Press (this time as an actual partner, having bought out Virginia) tried to exercise his proper function as joint-owner it was the start of an acrimonious wrangle that went on growing in intensity until in 1946 the association was dissolved. Leonard was by then 66, Virginia was dead and he was tired. Through Alice Ritchie, the first official traveller for the Press, who had died in 1941, he had got to know and trust Ian Parsons, a director of Chatto and Windus, whose wife was Alice's sister. They became close friends and it was soon clear that they had an identical attitude towards publishing. When John Lehmann decided to dissolve his partnership, Leonard asked Chatto and Windus to take over the Press. The negotiations proceeded without a shadow of disagreement and by mid-1946 were complete. Only now, when age and loneliness had come, was he able to give up the Press which he had started, nearly thirty years before, largely for Virginia's sake. They had built it up together and used love as well as labour in the process. It had been the one field in which they could work together, meeting as author and publisher, each as deeply involved, though in different ways, as the other. While Leonard dealt with customers or correspondence, Virginia spent happy hours setting type, a process she found relaxing. Each book as it was published was the product of a close partnership at every stage of the process. It is perhaps not strange that Leonard could never share such a deeply personal thing as the Press with anyone else.

For Virginia, Dadie's short and John Lehmann's longer association with the Press were of immense value. She felt able to go to them as colleagues for the criticism and advice which, when it came from uncommitted outsiders, reviewers and the like, terrified and damaged her. She confided her hopes and aims to them in a way which she could not perhaps do to Leonard. His judgment she immensely respected and depended on totally: nothing she wrote would appear without his stamp of approval. But he was no poet. Her cast of mind and his were worlds apart. It was the finished product which he could judge. The processes which went before—the first dim vision, clarified gradually into an aim, the management of words and images, the communication of feeling and the creation of mood, the slow careful building of a structure of imagination which a wrong phrase could topple—these he was not equipped to appreciate. He could only, as she wrote and re-wrote, pro-ducing version after version of whatever novel she was engaged on, support her by his faith in her genius and by his endless patience and solicitude enable her to work. Without him she was lost.

But it was not to Leonard but to John Lehmann that she exposed, with a freedom which demonstrates a kind of joyous confidence in his understanding, her purpose in writing *The Waves*. 'I wanted,' she wrote, 'to eliminate all detail; all fact; & analysis; and myself; & yet not be frigid and rhetorical; & not monotonous (which I am) & to keep the swiftness of prose & yet strike one or two sparks, & not write poetical, but pure-bred prose, & keep the elements of character; & yet that there should be many characters and only one; & also an infinity, a background behind—well, I admit I was biting off too much.'

It was to John Lehmann too, that she sent, a week before her death, the manuscript of *Between the Acts*, about which she was deeply troubled. Leonard had read it and given his view that it was the best thing she had ever written. But she wanted John to decide between them. He had no doubts as to its merits and telegraphed his certainty that it should be published. Her reply rejecting the idea of publication and undertaking to revise reached him only after her death.

XII

Friends of Lytton

LYTTON at Cambridge had already shown a genius for friendship. It was a genius which consisted of a rather less than infinite capacity for friendliness. Lytton was not in the accepted sense a friendly man. He was often bored or disgusted by the people he met, however distinguished their reputation, and always critical. He was also shy, and painfully aware of his own inadequate physical appearance. But where he found a kindred spirit he was different. Inhibitions disappeared and his extraordinary charm transformed his personality. Charm, that much underrated quality, was for Lytton an expression of love. It was revealed to his friends and to those whose friendship he wished to kindle. To others it was as likely as not to be replaced by a grim impenetrable silence.

Lytton never lacked friends. Those Apostles who became his intimates at Trinity—and some, like Bertie Russell, did not—remained on close terms with him all his life. Maynard, Leonard Woolf, Desmond MacCarthy, Charles Sanger, Saxon Sydney-Turner, Morgan Forster, all took a larger or smaller part in his life to the end. Clive and Duncan were lifelong friends from Cambridge days. As Lytton grew older, however, contemporaries meant steadily less to him. His emotions did not age with his body, and his last great love was for a man over twenty years his junior.

More than most men, perhaps, Lytton was the kind of person who stood in need of the support of a wife. He needed domestic comfort and security. He was absurdly impractical, and firmly shut his eyes to the dull essentials of living: he demanded, quietly but consistently, that all such things should be looked after for him. He even filtered through an agent—usually Carrington—the simplest requirements, like a pot of tea, that would involve some humble domestic action by a servant. He hated and feared loneliness. And he needed the experience of passion to give to life the brilliance it sadly lacked.

His deep-seated homosexuality barred him from the relationship of marriage which might have met all those needs. But the needs remained. They had to be met by devices, almost never totally satisfactory, designed to provide piecemeal what marriage, had it been possible, might have given him in a single whole experience.

Carrington could, and marvellously did, in due course solve his domestic problems. She did more for him than most wives do for their husbands, without any prospect of formal recognition or status, without the ultimately consoling intimacies and with the ever-present consciousness that there were key areas of his emotional and intellectual life where she had no place, and which he would always have to share with others. She found his houses for him and made them into homes. She catered, without complaint or jealousy, for the steady flow of friends for whom Lytton was the attraction. She loved him, quite simply, and he returned her love as well as he might, with solicitude, tenderness and gratitude. The embarrassment he felt in expressing his feelings towards her, to which he frequently refers in his letters to her, and which did not noticeably affect his relations with his other loves, arose, simply and certainly, from the fact that his feelings were not those of a lover, as he knew she wished them to be.

They were both passionate. But whereas Carrington could go to bed with her lovers or with her female loves happily enjoy a sentimental intimacy which seemed to content her, Lytton, for a number of reasons, found life less simple. In a society which had dealt as it did with Oscar Wilde, a society which labelled Lytton's emotions as criminal in intent, there were obvious difficulties. Moreover, because sexual inversion is the condition of a minority, there were rebuffs and misunderstandings. Most of all, perhaps, Lytton's emotional needs were complex and sophisticated and no single man was ever able to meet them all or even to meet a part of them for very long.

At the purely aesthetic level Lytton was always enthralled by male beauty and the glory of masculinity itself. The aura cast

by Thoby Stephen's maleness shining through his splendid
body, or George Mallory's marvellous beauty, filled him with
ecstasy. 'Mon dieu' he had written to Clive and Vanessa,
'George Mallory! When that's been written, what more need
be said? My hand trembles, my heart palpitates, my whole
being swoons away . . . he's six foot high, with the body of an
athlete by Praxiteles, and a face—oh incredible—the mystery
of Botticelli, the refinement and delicacy of a Chinese print,
the youth and piquancy of an unimaginable English boy. I
rave. . . . The sheer beauty of it all is what transports me . . .
desire was lost in wonder. . . . For the rest . . . his intelligence is
not remarkable.' This incoherent outburst not only expresses
Lytton's delight in Mallory's physical attributes but indicates
his limitations as an intimate: in that capacity intelligence was
essential. And then Mallory grew fat.

Lytton's meeting with Mallory took place a year after the
ending of his affair with Duncan Grant had plunged him into
desolation and a year before Henry Lamb entered his life to
bring new delight and new despairs. The thrill that Mallory
provided was not love although it clearly had a strong sexual
element. Lytton was always happy to enjoy the sensations
which physical beauty gave him, and at times ready to pursue
them to passionate extremes. But he differentiated. 'Passion
without affection . . .' he wrote, '. . . doesn't count.' What did
count is more difficult to say. The years between going down
from Cambridge and the outbreak of war were dominated for
Lytton by two major love-affairs, each as shattering in their
moments of bliss as in their periods of black hopelessness.

It is curious, and no doubt, significant, that both Duncan and
Henry Lamb were artists. Facile interpretations, as that Lytton
identified himself—also, he hoped, an artist—with the objects
of his love, both quite undeniably artists, are unlikely to be
wholly reliable. Lytton's heart was a complex organ. And love,
like the Holy Spirit, bloweth where it listeth. No doubt the
talents which Duncan and Henry both so obviously possessed
and could demonstrate so convincingly on canvas symbolised
to Lytton the possibility of achievements of his own in some
misty future and in his own literary sphere. Painting never
stirred him as an art in the way that music did. An hour at an

exhibition, enough to write a few enthusiastic or critical notes to Duncan, was also enough to satisfy his visual appetites for the day. At Roger Fry's Post-Impressionist Exhibitions the behaviour of the public interested him more than the pictures. In the National Gallery his attention was liable to wander, as on one celebrated occasion when he hopefully followed a beautiful fair-headed youth from room to room only to discover with horror that his quarry was the Prince of Wales.

If therefore Lytton could announce to Maynard that Duncan was a genius, and to James that Henry was one too, the statements do not represent the view of an art-critic, but reflect the enthusiasm of a lover. Both Duncan and Henry were magnetic characters and each possessed an unselfconscious wholeness which was as attractive to Lytton by its contrast with his own tremulous incompleteness as Mallory's physical magnificence was in contrast with his own meagre frame. If only they could respond to his passion some of their divine ichor might flow into his veins. Through kisses and in bed some such magical transfusion might occur. And so, one after the other, he wooed them. But with both of them the intensity of his emotional need, expressed in a bombardment of letters in language which at times rose to wild heights of lyrical incoherence, led to embarrassment or irritation. They were both fond of him, and Duncan at least loved him and told him so. But neither could respond in the way that Lytton needed. Kisses and caresses did not after all bring the result he desired.

For three years he agonised over Duncan whose absences and silences filled him with despair and whose attitude when they were together alternately charmed and chilled him. He hardly ever felt sure of Duncan's love, and when he did it was almost worse to contemplate his idol's feet of clay. If Duncan could love such a feeble creature as Lytton felt himself to be, what virtue could there be in him? A year after their affair began, Duncan announced that he had fallen in love with Edgar Duckworth, the most brilliant and charming of the new Apostles, and that his love was returned. At the same time he assured Lytton, who was shattered by the information, that their friendship need not be affected. Nothing could demonstrate more clearly the different values each set on their relationship.

The end came two years later when Duncan, who had recovered from his tender passion for Duckworth, fell much more seriously in love with Maynard, and Maynard with him.

This development strikes the true Bloomsbury note of absurd irony. From the beginning of Lytton's affair with Duncan, Maynard had been the recipient of his most reckless, most lyrical confidences. It was Lytton who had insisted that Maynard and Duncan should meet and had gone to considerable lengths to ensure that they did. It was Lytton who had advertised Duncan's qualities, who had been determined that Maynard should admire him. He had not meant to succeed so well. It is not difficult to see that the event was a horrible shock. To understand its catastrophic effect on Lytton however one must try—and this *is* difficult—to appreciate his extraordinary emotional hypersensitivity. He was literally at this time in his life, and not for the first or last time, the victim of his feelings. His misery and despair were literally beyond his control. It would have helped if he could have hated or even disliked one or both of them. But he could not. When his anguish was at its deepest he sent Maynard a gift of finely-bound books for his rooms at King's, where he was shortly to take up a lectureship. At the same time he paid for a course of lessons in art for Duncan. They were both moved to tears by Lytton's marvellously generous reaction to what he might so easily have regarded as betrayal. Holroyd[1] interprets Lytton's attitude at this stage as a calculated counterthrust to the wound he had received, designed to demonstrate his own vast magnanimity and a true Bloomsbury rejection of jealousy as an uncivilised emotion. The present author finds it difficult to accept this view. Lytton's distress seems so all-pervading as to leave no room for conscious devices of this kind, and nothing in his history suggests that he was vengeful by instinct. The constant theme of his letters to Maynard and Duncan at this period is his undying friendship for both of them. Short of crediting Lytton with a degree of duplicity he never again revealed, it is not possible to think, with Holroyd, that Lytton now detested Maynard 'more than at any other moment in his life.' When in the following spring, Maynard gained his

[1] *Lytton Strachey: A Critical Biography*, Vol. I, pp. 339-41. (Heinemann, 1967)

Fellowship at King's, Lytton wrote to him, '. . . you must always think of me as your friend. I shall think of you in the same way.' Holroyd's sceptical gloss on this letter is once more hard to accept. The later history of all three is one of close friendship, though naturally the element of passionate intimacy is lost for ever.

But calm was slow to come to Lytton. To the overtures which both Maynard and Duncan frequently made he was unable to respond naturally. He was often silent, as if tongue-tied by confused emotions, wishing only to be free of the feelings they aroused in him. The extent of his disorientation is shown by his proposal of marriage to Virginia which occurred at this time. Within a few weeks of this strange event, which was a momentary denial of his own nature, he was to meet George Mallory, describing his feelings in the letter already quoted. His health was wretched and he twice undertook cures at a Swedish sanatorium which were restorative but very dull. Even duller was domestic life in the Strachey household.

Lytton's needs at this critical period in his life were twofold. He needed on the one hand independence from his family in order to develop the gifts he felt almost sure he possessed: another, and perhaps a deeper side of his nature, yearned for the dependence which only being in love could give him.

He had met Henry Lamb and been interested in him before the affair with Duncan. Now they met again at Ottoline's parties in Bedford Square and Lytton's emotions were increasingly stirred. Henry was not only strikingly handsome, with slanting eyes which hinted at fascinating depths of wickedness, but he was gifted and charming. Ottoline found him so too. There now began for Lytton a relationship as painful as that with Duncan and rather less rewarding. Between Ottoline and Lytton, Henry found himself doubly the object of affection and desire. He could not return either at this stage with the required intensity, and he was restless and irritable under their unremitting siege. He was fond enough of Lytton to accompany him on ill-starred journeys to uncomfortable parts of Scotland and Ulster, but not fond enough for affection to outweigh the physical hardship which they both had to endure. He sulked or was bad-tempered. Lytton did his best to please, to the extent, as we have seen, of adopting a Bohemian style of dress. He wore his hair 'very long, like Augustus John' Ottoline recorded. 'He discarded collars,' she adds 'and wore only a rich purple scarf round his neck, fastened with an intaglio pin.' The famous beard followed. But it was not in Lytton's power to build the stable kind of relationship he wanted: Henry always had the whip-hand. His moods were unpredictable and ranged from charming solicitude to outbreaks of sharp and painful animosity. A key expression used by Lytton in connection with their friendship is 'if only'. 'I tremble to think of what an "idyll" it might be, if only' he wrote to James, leaving the condition unspecified. Writing to Ottoline in 1931 long after the affair was over, he could not help surmising 'that if H.L. had been a *little* different—things would have been *very* different'. If only Henry had been a little less exclusively heterosexual, if only he could have sympathised even slightly with Lytton's passionate tenderness! But that, he recognised, was impossible. All he could beg for was understanding of a less exacting kind: short even of that he would accept pity. 'Perhaps you don't realise how horribly I've suffered during the last 6 or 7 years from loneliness' he wrote to him.

When nothing would do to soften Henry's heart and the yearning was more than he could bear he fell into an unattractive vein of masochistic infantilism. 'Won't you take me back under your charge again and cure me with the severest of your régimes?' He felt like a naughty child who had been 'flogged hard for some mysterious naughtiness he hasn't understood, and then been shut up in a dark room to repent. . . . Won't my papa come and open the door, and take me into his arms again?' He had sometimes had similar feelings in Duncan's day: 'I want to go back to childhood, to be two years old' he wrote to him on one occasion.

It is for the psychologists to put a diagnostic label on Lytton's nostalgia for the time when in his mother's warm embrace he felt safe perhaps from life itself. It is for them to say too to what extent her passionate maternal care which moulded his life until he went up to Cambridge was responsible for his homosexuality. These are technical matters. It is however of general interest, and of importance to an understanding of Lytton's personality, that the past, his youth if not his childhood, exercised an irresistibly magnetic pull upon him. Youth in this context means Cambridge, to which he constantly returned, staying for a weekend, or a week or even a term, long after most men would have found it uncomfortable or irrelevant to do so. Physical and nervous debility had robbed Lytton of the experience of exuberant well-being characteristic of youth. Subconsciously perhaps he hoped, by exposing himself again and again to the atmosphere of the university, to catch a reviving whiff of that bracing ozone. The thought of growing old and the consciousness that he was doing so, dogged him from his earliest graduate years. The onset of age could perhaps be held off or at least temporarily forgotten in the company of those still young. The young, some of them anyway, were so delicious too. There were embryo Apostles to get to know and assess by feeling as well as judgment. In 1920 Maynard introduced him to Sebastian Sprott, a psychologist studying at Clare, with whom he was later to enjoy trips to Venice and the Dolomites and who later still undertook the massive task of reducing to order Lytton's hoard of old correspondence. Sebastian was invariably charming and temperamentally the opposite of Henry. He was not, however, to use Lytton's own word, 'sentimental' towards the older man.

Lytton's 'sentimental' needs were met at this time by his love for Ralph Partridge, which has already been mentioned. After the marriage of Ralph and Carrington, that strange triangle was held together more by mutual fondness and dependence than by passion, and Lytton was free once more to fall in love. Then there was suddenly an 'embarras de richesse'. In 1923 at Garsington Lytton met Philip Ritchie, an Oxford undergraduate of great charm, considerable intellectual ability and attractive ugliness. Philip's closest friend was Roger Senhouse, an Etonian undergraduate at Magdalen, a handsome, volatile, elusive, unpredictable charmer. Lytton soon found himself involved in another triangular relationship. He fell in love, one after another, with both the friends, and for two years he wavered between them. By 1926 his heart was fixed, and Roger, now working in London, had to tell Philip that they were in love with each other. It was to be Lytton's last serious affair, and with all its drawbacks perhaps the most satisfactory, certainly the most romantic. There was tenderness and excitement as there had been with Duncan. But there was also a community of tastes: Roger shared to the full Lytton's love of literature and music. And he was an intellectual which Duncan had never claimed to be. But whereas Lytton and Duncan were almost contemporaries, there was a gap of over twenty years between Lytton and Roger. It was perhaps partly because of this disparity in age, raising its own barriers to a natural relationship, that Lytton introduced into the affair a whole fabric of fantasy, in which he and Roger adopted roles from literature or history. Roger became Nero and Lytton his slave, or they returned to school where Lytton became Roger's fag. The imagined relationships always included the element of subordination which Lytton's nature required, as did his playful offer to become Roger's manservant. Roger enjoyed the fun until he began to fear that it was more than fun to Lytton; that Lytton wanted to replace reality by fantasy. That way madness lay. Gently and tactfully he let Lytton know that he could no longer accompany him on such excursions. Lytton was thrown into despair, imagining that Roger no longer loved him. It was not so. In 1927 Philip Ritchie suddenly died and the shock and sorrow that overwhelmed them both drew them together. Tensions were somehow relaxed and there was left a tenderness which sustained Lytton over the few remaining years of his life.

It is of interest and significance that Lytton's romance with Roger coincided in time and mood with the writing of *Elizabeth and Essex*, which occupied him from the end of 1925 to the summer of 1928. The book had begun as one item in a collection of love-stories he envisaged making. Very quickly, however, the hectic romantic relationship between the elderly monarch and the brilliant young courtier absorbed his whole imagination. Since at that very moment he himself, an ageing dowager as he often felt himself to be, was falling in love with a handsome and charming young man, it was inevitable that the parallel should strike him. It would be amusing to slip in a secret reference which Roger would understand: '. . . in the evening there was more talk, and laughter, and then there was music, until, at last, the rooms at Whitehall were empty, and they were left, the two, playing cards together.' This may be an imaginative reconstruction of the domestic intimacy of Elizabeth and Essex, but it is also an exact description of Lytton's and Roger's favourite way of spending an evening. Whether it was the glamour and high romance of the Elizabethan age that spilt over into Lytton's actual life and led him into the fantasies which so worried Roger, or whether his own romantic passion led him to treat the story of Elizabeth and Essex in a manner almost entirely lacking the surgical ruthlessness of *Eminent Victorians* or even the acerb irony of *Queen Victoria*, is a matter for speculation. What does seem clear is that at least on this occasion, life and literature had for Lytton something in common, and that the same mood would do for both.

It is perhaps a general truth that life consists largely of relationships. It is at least a statement that can be defended. Little or no defence is needed in Lytton's case. When he emerged from the solitude of his study, he sought at once the company of friends and lovers. When they were away he wrote to them unceasingly. It was as if the core of his being was so fluid and unstable that he needed the help of others to prevent it from breaking down or seeping feebly away until there was nothing left. Without their support his whole personality could barely avoid collapse, and indeed when at times the support failed he did in fact collapse. Even his frequent periods of sickness that defied diagnosis and of lassitude that nothing would lift, though they certainly had physical causes, can plausibly also be related to unfulfilled emotional needs. His huge consumption of Sanatogen could represent, more than symbolically, his appetite for love. The suggestion should not be pressed to the point of absurdity. It is enough to stress that Lytton was the least self-sufficient of men. A perhaps farfetched analogy would be that of an atom of which his friends were the motive particles, spinning round a nucleus which, though central to the structure, had no life independent of the energy they contributed. No analogy, however, can illuminate fully the complexity of a human being, and Lytton was more complex than most, particularly in the range of his social propensities.

At one end of the gamut of relationships which made up his life are his coy exciting excursions into London society, where he was alternately flattered and bored to speechlessness. At the other were the pretty ploughboys, gondoliers or blatant tarts who at least gave him more pleasure in the short run than the pious frauds he sometimes met at the Asquiths' or the humourless pedants who infested the University.

But neither peeresses nor peasants provided the comfort and support essential to him. For these he needed trusty uncensorious confidants. Lytton's need to confide was integral to his character. He *had* to communicate his experiences and the feelings they aroused in him. Neither were completely satisfactory unless he could do so. And the more intimate the experience, the more thrilling the emotion, the more urgent it was to tell someone about it. He was quite conscious that his love-affairs were a breach of the contemporary moral code and that he himself by his essential make-up was an incurable delinquent. He had no feelings of guilt on this account—he was made as he was made—but he did perhaps feel a certain shame, as he felt shame for his physical ugliness and debility, and he could purge this feeling only by confession. 'Brother Confessor' was the name he used for his Apostolic confidants, and it was a confessor that he always needed. From Cambridge days there was always someone to play this role in his life—Leonard Woolf, Maynard until his relationship with Duncan disqualified him, David Garnett and then for years his brother James. Dadie too, though so much younger and unfortunately not sympathetic to Lytton's extremes of romantic emotionalism, was understanding and kind.

As he grew older he found that women were more receptive to his confidences, and also seemed to enjoy it when he indulged the taste for indecency which was a deeply-ingrained part of his make-up. He had discovered this consoling fact years before. Once, when they were all in their twenties, he had been alone with Virginia and Vanessa when he noticed a stain on Vanessa's dress. 'Semen?' he inquired. 'With that one word' writes Virginia, 'all barriers of reticence and reserve went down.

A flood of this sacred fluid seemed to overwhelm us. Sex permeated our conversation.' He showed some of his most indecent poems to Vanessa who delightedly got them by heart and distributed copies to friends. so at least Maynard reported to Duncan. Lytton's correspondence with Virginia with its recurrent use of the contemporary equivalent of four-letter words, confirms the enjoyment they shared in improprieties. It was with Lytton that she could most freely indulge in naughty, intimate references to sperm and similar phenomena. (Bawdy talk was of course characteristic of Bloomsbury and it is entertaining to think that the practice may have originated with that one startling word of Lytton's.)

Virginia was never Lytton's confidante, though always his friend. However uninhibited their correspondence and conversation seemed to be, and indeed often were, there was a point, short of intimacy, beyond which neither was willing to go. On Virginia's side there was a certain jealousy for a more obviously successful competitor in her own field: Lytton, for his part, knew that she could not be trusted with confidences, which she had a way of circulating, with improvements of her own, among their friends. Carrington, sharing his life as she did, was much more and much less than a confidante. On the one hand there were intimacies which only she shared with him: on the other there were compartments of his emotional life into which he could not expect and never asked her to enter. With Ottoline, as we have seen, he could give free rein to romantic notions which Bloomsbury would have laughed at and he did not have to conceal from her his emotional entanglements. But he could not expect much help here either.

It was in his cousin Mary Hutchinson that he found the ideal confidante. Roughly contemporaries, they shared the Strachey family background. Much therefore never had to be explained because it was part of their inheritance or of their own experience. When she married St. John Hutchinson, a leading barrister, and became a London hostess, Lytton was her frequent guest. Eleanor, her house near Chichester, became one of his favourite weekend retreats. Clive's love-affair with her created another link. Without being a member of Bloomsbury, she was known to them all and greatly liked. Only with Virginia had there ever been any trouble and this arose partly because Virginia mistrusted London hostesses as a category and partly because of her own vaguely proprietorial feelings towards Clive. It was Mary's transparent sincerity and simplicity which restored confidence between them.

Since before Tidmarsh days, Lytton had written to her regularly, describing his life and his feelings about life. They were frequently in each other's company. She was one of the party at Asheham which was Carrington's introduction both to Lytton and the Bloomsbury circle. It was after one of her parties that Mark Gertler, a friend and protégé of hers, had assaulted Lytton. Lytton was recovering from shingles at the house she and her husband then had near Robertsbridge in Sussex when the Armistice was declared, and all three went up to London that day and attended Monty Shearman's party at the Adelphi. When in the immediate post-war years there were two young children in the house, confidential sessions with Mary at Eleanor were difficult, but time solved that problem and Lytton continued to make frequent visits.

Mary always understood and never censured him. She was, he once said, 'the only sympathetic person in London'. Time sent Lytton's old confessors on voyages that took them far apart: Leonard was immersed in political journalism and preoccupied with Virginia's health; Maynard had become grand and distinguished; James was invisible beneath the mountainous works of Freud; David Garnett was a successful writer and parent leading his own full life. But Mary was always there with time and love for him. He knew she would giggle when he told her that the lake-bridge at Blenheim (where he was the guest of the Marlboroughs) 'positively gives one an erection'. But she would not giggle when he told her of the 'exquisite paradise' in which he found himself when Roger Senhouse responded to his passionate overtures. He kept her 'au courant' with the affair as it proceeded, sharing with her his ecstasies, irritations, despairs and perplexities as they succeeded each other pell-mell in accordance with Roger's unpredictable attitudes. He could use with her the same language of febrile excitement and tremulous emotionalism as he had used with

Maynard about Duncan. And he could trust her a great deal more.

Sometimes, when there were no fresh developments in his love-life to report, he simply thought aloud. From Amsterdam, where with Carrington, Ralph and Sebastian Sprott, he had been visiting picture-galleries and admiring Dutch domestic architecture, he wrote to Mary 'I wish I could write poetry; but the mould seems to be lacking into which to pour the curious fluid—melted silver? porridge? gilded sealing-wax?—of my emotions. I have found no solution in these antique masterpieces—another world! another world! With them everything is fixed and definite and remote; but with me there is nothing but hazard, intensity, and interrogation.'

The irony of his words was not meant to conceal the essential truth of the thought they expressed. The progression of mood in his major literary works, from the merciless non-involvement of *Eminent Victorians* through *Queen Victoria* to the warm, exclamatory lyricism of *Elizabeth and Essex* may indeed represent a search for a subject or even, tentatively, a 'mould' (which might under James's guidance have a Freudian form) into which he could pour the whole of his multiplex personality. He never found it. From the summer of 1928, assisted by Ralph Partridge and Frances Marshall, he was preparing the first complete edition of the Greville Memoirs. While Ralph and Frances transcribed the manuscript at the British Museum, Lytton annotated and collated. It was pleasant and, he felt sure, valuable work, but it held little to excite him and nothing to involve his emotions. He contributed a few essays to Desmond MacCarthy's *Life and Letters* and they were re-published, with others, in his last book, *Portraits in Miniature and other Essays*, which appeared in the spring of 1931. It was all fairly satisfactory without being at all satisfying.

The fact is that his demands on life, and his hope that at least some of them might be met, were lessening. He was increasingly tired. A visit to Rome with Dadie in the spring of 1930 was charming, but sight-seeing and social demands made it a 'rigorous vigorous life' and he longed instead 'to linger among the cypresses of Tivoli'. By the end of the year he was ill and he continued to be ill for almost the whole of the following year. Recovering somewhat in the later summer, he wanted Roger Senhouse to go to France for a fortnight with him; but, not for the first time, Roger had a preferable alternative which did not include Lytton. He was not, he discovered, any longer perturbed. 'I am really calm' he could write. 'I hope it means that my feelings are at least more rational.' Uncharacteristically he went off alone, visiting Paris, Rheims, Nancy and Strasbourg, enjoying solitude and the freedom that accompanied it. Both his reaction to Roger's defection and the pleasure he took in being entirely alone and free of the restraints imposed by friends, however dear, were in fact marks of declining vitality. The 'intensity' of which he had written to Mary was an essential—perhaps the essential—part of his emotional character when he was well. Its disappearance was as sure a mark of sickness as any physical symptom. And indeed the disease which the doctors could never diagnose—and could not have cured— was tightening its grip. A few months after his return from France, he was dead.

XIII

Endings

'IF this is dying, then I don't think much of it.' Lytton's comment as he lay at the very verge of death is as characteristic as the better-known remarks of Voltaire and other famous men in a similar situation, and a good deal more sensible. His sense of proportion and detachment never left him and his ironic sense of humour remained. He was surrounded as he lay dying by relations and friends, though they were largely kept from his bedside and he could not have known they were there. If he had known he would have thought it all an unnecessary fuss. He was, after all, behaving in a perfectly conventional way and dying in accordance with the normal human arrangement. He could not recommend the process but he did not complain.

With Lytton's death the meaning of Carrington's life disappeared. She made an unsuccessful attempt at suicide a few hours before he died and a successful one seven weeks later. It was a totally relevant, appropriate act. For sixteen years Lytton had been the source of all her happiness. Lovers came and went, providing an extra zest and excitement. But they were little more than an entertainment, and telling Lytton about them, laughing with him about their absurdities, was a major part of the fun. The very absence of physical intimacy with him gave their relationship a freedom and lack of tension which might otherwise not have existed. Tenderly and without censure he accepted her as a person and her love as a total offering. 'He was,' she wrote in her diary, 'and this is why he was everything to me, the only person to whom I never needed to lie, because he never expected me to be anything different to what I was.' This was indeed the heart of the matter. The evasions and duplicities which she found necessary in all other relationships were not needed with Lytton. With him, and only with him, she could be the simple, open person which, to a great extent she was. Between his death and her own the only peace she found was among the relics of their former life. She sat for hours in the library whose books bore the bookplate she had designed for him and read the diary he had kept on his last visit to France and the letters she had written to him. She made a bonfire of his spectacles and other personal items. She gave some of his ties to Stephen Tomlin and Sebastian Sprott. Ralph, who knew too well that suicide was not far from her mind, tried to arrange that she would be alone as little as possible and persuaded her, against her wish, to go for a week to stay with Dorelia John at Fryern. But loneliness, and loneliness at Ham Spray, was all she now wanted. She planted snowdrops and daffodils in the little grove of yews where she hoped her ashes and Lytton's would ultimately lie. She read by herself the poetry which Lytton used to read to her. Everything she did or wanted to do related to him and to her impossible yearning for him. 'I must and cannot' she wrote in her diary, 'go backwards to his grave.' Her life had for all essential purposes ended with Lytton's. Fifty days later she took the only remaining step necessary to complete her identification with him.

There are few stranger love-stories than theirs and few more moving. With none of the trappings of romance there was passionate devotion on one side and endless tenderness, affection and sympathy on the other. On his deathbed, two days before he died, Lytton said that he had always wanted to marry her. It was not true, but it reflected his genuine measure of their relationship, which was in all significant senses but one a marriage. The absence of a formal tie was an important factor. Not only were they both opposed to marriage as a legal contract, but, as things were, the question of unfaithfulness as each found other lovers did not arise. The notion of an ageing pervert and an adoring young woman living together not quite as man and wife struck many people, including some of their friends, as absurd and vaguely indecent: and indeed the absurd aspect of their relationship is integral to it—they were both in notable ways absurd people. Indecency, too, they both enjoyed. The fact that they were both at heart artists is of immense importance. Although Carrington allowed her remarkable talent to be submerged in her preferred role as Lytton's companion (and it is perhaps hard to forgive Lytton for allowing this to happen), she remained essentially an artist and it is possible to regard her relationship with Lytton as a work of art—her masterpiece in fact. Certainly it needed all the skill, intelligence and emotional insight of an artist to create, in the face of what would seem fatal impediments, the kind of life she made with him at Tidmarsh and Ham Spray. Lytton was able to understand, as a less sensitive man might not have done, that to serve him as she did, to cherish and cosset him, was to her the highest satisfaction and he accepted it all with gratitude and grace. In return he offered her an unique share of his own strange life and an affection which sexual intimacy, had it been possible, would not necessarily have deepened.

Lytton was the first of the original, long-standing Bloomsbury group to die. The group itself could no longer be said to exist. Inevitably the thirteen friends rather solemnly listed by Leonard Woolf as foundation-members had long gone their separate ways, and had constructed lives based otherwise than on close and constant contact with each other. Friendship remained, but with a difference. Virginia, pausing in the middle of writing *The Waves* to cast a glance round at her own personal horizons, wrote in her diary in the autumn of 1930, 'I seldom see Lytton; that is true. The reason is that we don't fit in, I imagine, to his parties, nor he to ours; but that if we can meet in solitude all goes as usual. Yet what do one's friends mean to one, if one only sees them 8 times a year? Morgan I keep up with in our chronically spasmodic way . . . Adrian I never see. I keep constant with Maynard. I never see Saxon.' The Memoir Club, its original purpose long forgotten, continued to meet irregularly at Rodmell, Charleston or Tilton. Morgan Forster attended assiduously.

Bloomsbury itself was hardly any longer a focus, although Gordon Square still had some of its old occupants. Maynard was at 46, and Lytton had towards the end a flat at 51, now the Strachey family home run by his sister Pippa. Adrian and Karin were at 50 and James and Alix at 41. In both houses, however, the preoccupation was psycho-analysis: Adrian and Karin were practitioners and James was for years immersed in his Freud translations. Ralph Partridge and Frances Marshall, who married after Carrington's death, lived together as James's tenants for a few years and Clive had rooms at 50. But these were now addresses rather than centres of hospitality. Only in Sussex at Charleston and Rodmell did something like the old life continue. But the resemblance was faint. Vanessa was preoccupied with her children: Julian and Quentin were in their early twenties at the time of Lytton's death, but Angelica, Duncan's daughter, was only thirteen: to all, three she was deeply devoted. Maynard, involved internationally in high matters of finance, came to Tilton only when he was able to. Virginia and Leonard spent much of their time at the Hogarth Press. They all met when they could and with as much pleasure and ease as ever. But it would have been wrong to think of them as a group and almost nobody any longer did so.

Nor is it sensible, as some have done, to attempt to perpetuate the notion of a Bloomsbury circle by nominating certain representatives of the younger generation as members. It is perfectly true that Dadie Rylands, Raymond Mortimer, Kenneth (now Lord) Clark and others share to a great extent the aesthetic attitudes and the general *Weltanschauung* of Bloomsbury and were on terms of friendship or intimacy with some of its original members. But they themselves formed no group with the lifelong ties which bound their seniors together. In their case the label Bloomsbury, which is sometimes attached to them, is misused.

After Lytton's death the question of a biography naturally arose, but the difficulties were too forbidding and no serious project was entertained. It would have been impossible to write an honest life of Lytton without an account of his love-affairs, and impossible to give such an account at this time—even if any publisher had been brave enough to accept the manuscript—without arousing indignant shock on the one hand and prurient curiosity on the other.

Roger Fry's death in 1934 caused problems of a rather similar kind. He had been Vanessa's lover and had, up to the time of his death, been living with Helen Anrep as his wife in a happy relationship unhallowed by religious or legal sanctions. He was survived by five sisters and a daughter who were naturally sensitive on Roger's behalf and if a biography were to be written their wishes would demand respect. Virginia, when she consented to write a life of Roger, was aware of the problems. Both Vanessa and Helen agreed that their part in his life should be honestly recorded and Helen indeed insisted that this should be so. Virginia acknowledged Helen's right to make this stipulation, but in the end made no mention of Vanessa. She was still to that extent the child of an eminent Victorian family. She began to write in 1938 and found the work increasingly difficult. Not only was she inhibited on the one hand by the awareness that Roger's family were invisibly looking over her shoulder as she wrote and on the other by Helen's anxiety to help which, to a solitary artist like Virginia, was not always helpful, but the management of facts and events which had their own existence and could not be transmuted or re-arranged by an imaginative process was a skill which she had never mastered. Nor was she an art-historian. Virginia was incapable of writing a bad book, but the biography which appeared in 1940 was not one of her successes: it was neither characteristic of its author nor truly representative of its subject.

Meanwhile there had been other deaths. In 1937 Stephen Tomlin died of pneumonia in his middle thirties. 'Tommy' as he was called, had been a close friend of Bloomsbury since David Garnett had introduced him to the circle some fifteen years before. A man of varied gifts, a classical scholar of New College (where he refused to stay more than a few terms), a musician and poet, he had devoted himself to sculpture, and produced remarkable busts of Lytton, Duncan Grant and Virginia. For years he had been a frequent welcome visitor at Ham Spray where he found Lytton an amiable alternative to his own forbidding parent, a senior Judge. Carrington was especially fond of him and he became for a while her lover after her parting with Gerald Brenan. In 1927 he married Julia Strachey, Lytton's niece and also a favourite of Carrington's. So the circle of friendship remained unbroken, and it was to Stephen that Ralph turned on Lytton's death, in the hope that his influence could prevent Carrington killing herself. But he was himself so much in need of comfort that he could help little. He had never in any case, because of his own sense of inadequacy, been someone to lean on. What had attracted

Bloomsbury to him, apart from his charm and artistic gifts, were his deep, human insight, his uncensorious understanding of others—these and his delightful conversation. Virginia was particularly distressed by his death. She regretted that she had been such an unsatisfactory sitter when he was modelling her head. Not only had she found his constitutional unpunctuality irritating, but she had always hated being looked at. To submit herself to close, concentrated inspection for an hour at a time was too much for her, and she refused, after three sittings, to go on. The bust remained unfinished but is nevertheless thought by Quentin Bell to have captured her essential appearance with remarkable truth. Now he was dead too young and Virginia wished she could have been more patient.

It was a tragic year. In the summer, Julian, Vanessa's eldest son, went to Spain to support the republicans in the civil war. Both Virginia and Vanessa were sure that if he went he would never come back and they had tried in vain to deflect him from his purpose. A few weeks after arriving in Spain, he was indeed killed. His loss was almost unbearable for Vanessa and only less so for Virginia. For weeks Vanessa was prostrate and Virginia devoted herself to her sister. Julian had shown promise as a writer and poet: he was a man of great personality and charm. More than this, for Virginia he was, with his great stature and physical beauty, almost a reincarnation of Thoby. She could hardly think of one without remembering the other, and that meant remembering his death. Now, with Julian dead too, the fatal resemblance was intolerably complete.

In the following year Ottoline died and Virginia wrote her obituary for *The Times*. One by one the figures who had made her youth colourful were disappearing and she was left to record their passing. She was not given to feeling sentimental, still less did she live in the past. In fact she found Roger's biography a burden and an impediment to the writing of *Between the Acts*, the novel which now absorbed her imagination. The biography was ready for the printers in the spring of 1940 and, although Leonard had for the first time been severely critical of one of her works, it had given pleasure to Vanessa and Roger's sister, Margery, and Virginia was content with their approval.

The war was now beginning to reveal its true horror. The overrunning of Holland and Belgium was followed by the collapse of France and the air-attack on Britain. In August, the Woolfs' London home in Tavistock Square was destroyed and in the following month the Hogarth Press was severely damaged in the bombing of Mecklenburgh Square. One of the results of these two events, catastrophic in some ways, commonplace in others, was to simplify life for Virginia and Leonard. There were no more trips to London. They stayed at Rodmell, with no petrol for travel and no need for it. 'How free, how peaceful we are,' wrote Virginia in her diary. 'No one coming. No servants. Dine when we like. Living near the bone.' It was not that she was indifferent to the horror of war. Indeed, as the wife of a Jew, she was only too conscious of personal vulnerability as well as universal tragedy. Adrian had supplied a lethal dose of morphia for them both to use if necessary. But there was no drug for the larger calamity. Nor was there any action which Virginia felt to be directly relevant. She was, says John Lehmann, 'one of those writers who felt that the only thing that made sense was to devote oneself to one's work, to the inner world of order, as the outer world collapsed in disorder'. She had felt the same during the First World War, and she could neither understand nor sympathise with Julian's determination to join the war in Spain. 'The moment force is used,' she wrote in her memoir of him, 'it becomes meaningless and unreal to me.'

So through the autumn of 1940 Virginia wrote her novel, in a state of calm happiness which external events seemed almost to intensify. By the end of November it was finished and she was pleased with it. 'I am a little triumphant about the book' she wrote in her diary. 'I've enjoyed writing almost every page.' But her euphoric mood did not last. There was a sudden prolonged attack of acute depression at the end of January. In February she was well enough to revise *Between the Acts* and to take pleasure in doing so, but towards the end of the month she records 'rather a churn in my mind. And some blank spaces . . .'. There are only two more entries in her diary. 'Oh dear yes, I shall conquer this mood' she wrote on March 8th. The entry for March 24th is incoherent.

In the middle of March she and Leonard had lunched with John Lehmann in London; he noticed that she 'seemed in a state of unusual nervous tension, her hand shaking slightly now and then.' She talked agitatedly about her novel which she felt to be totally unsuitable for publication. Leonard disagreed strongly and a few days later Virginia sent the typescript to John Lehmann for his casting vote. The typing and spelling, he found, were more eccentric than usual and there were endless corrections. He received, as he read it 'an extraordinary impression, as if a high-voltage electric current had been running through her fingers.' She was, he felt, 'pushing prose to the extreme limit of the communicable.' The book was 'filled with a poetry more disturbing than anything she had written before.' He wired at once to say 'publish'.

By now Virginia was seriously ill and in the care of Octavia Wilberforce, a Brighton doctor and a friend. She resisted as always the suggestion that she was sick, but perhaps now with more firmness than on earlier occasions. It was almost as if she knew that only she had the key to her trouble, that no treatment prescribed by a doctor would any longer help. She wanted to be left alone to fight what she now felt was the last battle. One day she returned from a walk soaking wet. She had fallen into a ditch, she said. But had she in fact given the key a turn, not skilfully enough to be effective? A few days later she did not return from her walk and her drowned body was not recovered for several weeks. It was the step she knew she had to take.

She left letters for Leonard and Vanessa. To both she explained that she was sure that she would not this time recover from the madness whose grip she could feel tightening upon her. To Vanessa she said 'I feel that I have gone too far this time to come back again . . . I have fought against it but I can't any longer.' To Leonard 'Everything has gone from me but the certainty of your goodness. I can't go on spoiling your life any longer.'

XIV

Retrospect

BLOOMSBURY was an almost unique phenomenon in our cultural history and has been grossly misunderstood. Efforts will no doubt continue to be made to force it into one or other familiar category—as a movement or a salon or a school. It was none of these things. It was simply a group of lifelong, like-minded friends who happened to differ in outlook from their contemporaries. The very word Bloomsbury in this sense conceals as much as it reveals. The essential characteristic of the group of people to whom the name is applied was mutual sympathy and understanding: it was almost—but not quite—the only shared characteristic. The other quality they had in common was the habit of applying reason to all aspects of life, including those in which emotion or sensibility are dominant, and the intellectual insight which enabled them to do so. They did not accept, because they did not find it reasonable to do so, that there were large areas of life in which convention had the force of law. They broke the rules when they thought them stupid.

When this has been said the basic similarity between members of the circle has been stated. Other similarities are superficial. The famous Bloomsbury voice was simply the strangely infectious Strachey intonation which spread among them as a highly appropriate vehicle for the conveyance of ideas which seemed to call for an unusual form of expression. Not all the group were aesthetes, though the leading members were. But there were no Bunthornes among them, and only the hangers-on had to make do with preciosity in default of true sensibility. Bloomsbury was neither a mutual admiration society nor a bitchy group of artists in jealous competition with each other: both views are commonly, and often simultaneously, held. It is necessary only to study the lives and the work of members of the circle to recognise the absurdity of such judgments and

indeed the irrelevance or inaccuracy of much of the rest of the
Bloomsbury legend.

It is, for example, commonly said that Bloomsbury were
snobs. They were no more snobs in the vulgar sense than
anyone else. If Lytton had a passing weakness for duchesses
and Virginia enjoyed, in small doses, fashionable London
parties, they laughed at themselves at the same time for being
rather silly. Clive's name-dropping was regarded with scorn.
Maynard's necessary association with the mighty was generally
felt in Bloomsbury to have harmed his character. Intellectual
snobbery, on the other hand, is a charge which it is more
difficult to dismiss out of hand. Far from suffering fools gladly,
Bloomsbury did not see why it should suffer them at all. One
of the unspoken functions of the group was to keep out the
unintelligent or insensitive. There is nothing wrong in excluding from a difficult environment those who cannot thrive
there. There is, however, something wrong in treating such
unfortunates with contempt. On the whole Bloomsbury
reserved its scorn for the pretentious and for those who,
considering their role as politicians, writers or leaders of
opinion, were more stupid than they ought to have been.
Sometimes, however, they leaped to conclusions and were
unfair in their condemnations, and occasionally they were
venomously critical. They should have been kinder. They
ought to have shown more humility. Saints are humble,
creative artists and original thinkers rarely are. Bloomsbury,
it can be admitted, had faults which would have disqualified
them as saints. In them the sin of pride, which is a wrong thing,
arose from a sense of pride in their abilities and achievements,
which is a perfectly right thing.

In its own day Bloomsbury was regarded as an immoral as
well as an infuriatingly exclusive set. It is interesting that we no
longer, on the whole, feel this. In its attitude to homosexuality,
marriage and love-affairs generally, Bloomsbury was only a
short distance ahead of its time. Bloomsbury can almost be said
to have invented permissiveness, without falling into pro-
miscuity. It is perhaps in this field that Bloomsbury's habit of
applying rational processes to emotional questions has been of
particular importance in shaping present-day society.

It is too early to tell whether Bloomsbury's influence, already clear in the field of literature, will be a lasting one. The current upsurge of interest in this odd group of intellectuals, artists and individualists is, however, curious and perhaps significant.

We live in an age of protest. There is a clamorous and widespread demand for change of all kinds from mild reform to outright revolution. Youth in particular is rebellious. So too, in its own way, was Bloomsbury. But its rebellion was a quiet one. Bloomsbury did not campaign or march against the barricades: its only demonstration was that which showed the possibility of living rationally and happily in peaceful defiance of convention. Bloomsbury first applied rigorous thought to the structure of society and then designed its own, different life in accordance with conclusions drawn from rational imperatives. The result was a kind of rebellion which omitted the step of revolution with all its unpredictable and often malign side-effects.

The present tendency is to reach the conclusions first without the painful process of relentless analysis which Moore insisted upon with the Bloomsbury Apostles. Simple, high emotive concepts—as that war is evil, that skin-pigment is irrelevant, that capitalism is a faulty system, that nuclear weapons are too dangerous, and other uncomplicated and largely uncontroversial ideas—arc taken as guides to action rather than thought. Instead of a study being made of the complex causes of social evil and workable solutions sought to problems which so far have none, protest-marches and demonstrations are held in the naïve hope that they may provide a short cut to the answer. Not all the marchers any longer believe that the technique has much chance of success. It is also a boring, primitive and often physically exhausting procedure. It makes no demand on, or use of, the mind. It thus represents a highly unsatisfactory activity for an intelligent person. In the long hours of a university sit-in and in the intervals between the shouting of semi-articulate slogans there is plenty of time to consider whether there are not better ways of presenting an argument or indeed whether the arguments themselves are flawless. It is not surprising that scepticism and discontent sometimes creep in. It is not surprising either that a footsore and frustrated intellectual, resting between demonstrations, should look towards Blooms-bury with something not far short of yearning. Here were other intellectuals, with consciences as tender and convictions as strong as his own, whose understanding of the human paradox included the awareness that Rome was not built in a day and that most members of the Italic tribes, invited to give an opinion, would have been opposed to its construction anyway. Bloomsbury was ruefully content to be in a minority, there being, it seemed to them, no alternative. Bloomsbury stuck to its guns but did not fire them. Was this not, in retrospect, a more effective protest than the waving of banners and the shouting and the marching? It was certainly more civilised and less offensive to those who secretly shared Bloomsbury's views and would later help to give them currency and effect. More-over, by recognising the futility of striving for large-scale, overnight conversion to more enlightened attitudes, Blooms-bury could get on with its own work and make the con-tribution that gifted persons are qualified and perhaps even called upon to give.

Perhaps Voltaire was right. 'Cela est bien dit,' said Candide, 'mais il faut cultiver notre jardin.'

Select Bibliography

Beerbohm, Sir Max: *Lytton Strachey* (The Rede Lecture) (Cambridge University Press) 1943

Bell, Clive: *Civilization* (Chatto and Windus) 1928

Bell, Clive: *Old Friends: Personal Recollections* (Chatto and Windus) 1956

Bell, Quentin: *Bloomsbury* (Weidenfeld and Nicolson) 1968

Bell, Quentin: *Virginia Woolf: A Biography*, 2 vols. (Hogarth Press) 1972

Bowra, Sir Maurice: *Memories* (Weidenfeld and Nicolson) 1966

Brenan, Gerald: *South From Granada* (Hamish Hamilton) 1957

Brenan, Gerald: *A Life of One's Own* (Hamish Hamilton) 1962

Carrington: *Letters and Extracts from her Diaries*, chosen and with an introduction by David Garnett (Jonathan Cape) 1970

Connolly, Cyril: *Enemies of Promise* Revised Edition (Andre Deutsch) 1973

Fry, Roger: *Letters of Roger Fry* edited by Denys Sutton (Chatto and Windus) 1972

Fry, Roger: *Vision and Design* (Chatto and Windus) 1920

Garnett, David: *The White/Garnett Letters* edited by David Garnett (Jonathan Cape) 1968

Garnett, David: *The Flowers of the Forest* (Chatto and Windus) 1955

Garnett, David: *The Familiar Faces* (Chatto and Windus) 1962

Gertler, Mark: *Selected Letters* edited by Noel Carrington and with an introduction by Quentin Bell (Hart-Davis) 1965

Harrod, Sir Roy: *The Life of John Maynard Keynes* (Macmillan) 1951

Holroyd, Michael: *Lytton Strachey: A Critical Biography*, 2 vols. (Heinemann) 1967-8

John, Augustus: *Chiaroscuro: Fragments of Autobiography* (Jonathan Cape) 1952

Keynes, J. Maynard: *Two Memoirs*, with an introduction by David Garnett (Hart-Davis) 1949

Lehmann, John: *The Whispering Gallery* (Longmans) 1955

Lehmann, John: *I am my Brother* (Longmans) 1960

Lehmann, John: *A Nest of Tigers* (Macmillan) 1968

MacCarthy, Sir Desmond: *Memories* (MacGibbon and Kee) 1953

Morrell, Lady Ottoline: *Ottoline: The Early Memoirs of Lady Ottoline Morrell 1873-1915* edited and with an introduction by Robert Gathorne Hardy (Faber) 1963

'Olivia' (Dorothy Bussy): *Olivia* (Hogarth Press) 1949

Parker, Robert Allerton: *A Family of Friends* (Museum Press) 1959

Russell, Bertrand: *Portraits from Memory* (Allen and Unwin) 1956

Russell, Bertrand: *The Autobiography of Bertrand Russell 1872-1913* (Allen and Unwin) 1967

Santayana, George: *My Host the World* (Cresset Press) 1953

Sitwell, Sir Osbert: *Laughter in the Next Room* (Macmillan) 1949

Stevens, Michael: *V Sackville-West: A Critical Biography* (Michael Joseph) 1973

Strachey, Lytton: *Lytton Strachey by Himself: A Self-Portrait* edited and with an introduction by Michael Holroyd (Macmillan) 1971

Woolf, Leonard: *Autobiography I Sowing* (Hogarth Press) 1960

Woolf, Leonard: *Autobiography II Growing* (Hogarth Press) 1961

Woolf, Leonard: *Autobiography III Beginning Again* (Hogarth Press) 1964

Woolf, Leonard: *Autobiography IV Downhill All the Way* (Hogarth Press) 1967

Woolf, Leonard: *Autobiography V The Journey not the Arrival Matters* (Hogarth Press) 1969

Woolf, Virginia: *Roger Fry: A Biography* (Hogarth Press) 1940

Woolf, Virginia: *Recollections of Virginia Woolf by her Contemporaries* edited by J. R. Noble (Peter Owen) 1972

Woolf, Virginia and Strachey, Lytton: *Virginia Woolf and Lytton Strachey: Letters* edited by Leonard Woolf and James Strachey (Hogarth Press/Chatto and Windus) 1956

Index

Abbotsholme School, 9, 12

Anrep, Boris, 108

Anrep, Helen, 108, 192-3

Apostles, the (Cambridge Conversazione Society), 17-18, 21-2, 25-6, 99, 127n

Asheham House, 47, 49, 84, 116, 118, 119, 120, 154

Asquith, H. H. (Earl of Oxford and Asquith), 6, 65

Athenaeum, The, 100, 157

Bagenal, Barbara (*née* Hiles), 57, 85, 86, 90, 91, 92, 116, 117, 118, 132, 148

Bagenal, Nicholas, 85, 86

Balliol College, 11-12

Barkway, Lumsden (Bishop of St Andrews), 11

Bedford Square, No. 44; 32, 57, 62, 65

Bell, Angelica, 132, 192

Bell, Clive, member of Bloomsbury, 2-3, 110-11; Midnight Society, 14, 98; Character, 16, 110-11; rejected as Apostle, 18; in love with Vanessa, 32; and marries her, 33; Virginia's literary critic, 51, 111; flirts with Virginia, 50-1; meets Roger Fry, 52, 98; relationship with Vanessa, 53-4; in Paris, 97-8; 'significant form', 102, 107; at Post-Impressionist Exhibition, 105; *Art*, 107; as theorist on art, 111-13, 130; *Civilization*, 112, *Peace at Once*, 114; farmwork at Garsington, 115; opinion of Maynard, 126; love-affair with Mary Hutchinson, 112, 185

Bell, Julian, 50, 109, 119, 169, 192, 194

Bell, Quentin, 50, 53, 119, 162, 164, 170, 192, 194

Bell, Vanessa (*née* Stephen), family, 2; childhood and youth, 28-9; death of father, 31; at 46 Gordon Square, 32; marries Clive Bell, 33; motherhood, 50, 192; hurt by Clive's flirtation with Virginia, 51-2; meets Roger Fry, 52; love-affair with Roger Fry, 53-4, 105; relationship with Clive, 53-4; and with Duncan Grant, 53-4, 117, 119; appearance, 60; character, 29, 60-1, 116-17; at Charleston, 118-19; at 39 Gordon Square, 127; quarrel with Maynard over picture, 127; and biography of Roger Fry, 193; prostrate at death of Julian, 194.

Belsize Park Gardens, No. 6; 33, 57

Bennett, Arnold, 57, 76

Bentinck, Lord Henry, 57

Berenson, Bernard, 69, 100, 144

Berenson, Mary, 69

Bingham, Henrietta, 149-50

Birrell, Francis, 59, 62, 115, 148

'Bloomsberries', 20

Bloomsbury, background and composition, 2-3, 20, 45-6, 57; characteristics and attitudes, 4-5, 6-7, 45, 101-2, 197-8; relations with society, 4-6; achievements, 7; 'Bloomsberries', 20; influence of G. E. Moore, 23-5; voice, 35-6, 197; parties, 57-8, 132; and D. H. Lawrence, 62-3; and Lady Ottoline Morrell, 66, 74, 78; and Carrington, 82-3, 110; Clive Bell's place in, 110-11; and the war, 114, 128-9, 131-2; David Garnett recorder of, 115; Wissett Lodge, outpost of, 117; country houses,